IMPOSSIBLE BODIES

"An outstanding collection of essays. *Impossible Bodies* displays a consistently light touch, is impressively researched and covers an astonishing range of fields. The quality of argument is outstanding; the writing is scholarly, yet witty and passionate. Holmlund always resists easy shots, pointing the reader to the more complex questions that lie beneath. This is certain to be an invaluable book."

Yvonne Tasker, *University of East Anglia*

Impossible Bodies investigates issues of ethnicity, gender and sexuality at the margins of contemporary Hollywood. Examining stars from Arnold Schwarzenegger and Clint Eastwood to Whoopi Goldberg and Jennifer Lopez, Chris Holmlund focuses on actors whose physique or appearance marks them as unusual or exceptional, and yet who occupy key or revealing positions in today's mainstream cinema.

Exploring a range of genres and considering both stars and their side-kicks, Holmlund examines ways in which Hollywood accommodates – or doesn't – a variety of "impossible" bodies, from the "outrageous" physiques of Dolph Lundgren and Dolly Parton, to the almost-invisible bodies of Asian Americans, Latinas, and older actors. From the *Pumping Iron* documentaries to *The Quick and the Dead* and *Boys on the Side*, Holmlund traces the broad shifts and startling disjunctures in what counts as desirable images of masculinity and femininity in mainstream cinema.

From lesbian killers to Swedes who never play Swedes, *Impossible Bodies* considers how representations of ethnicity and race, gender and sexuality are played out in contemporary Hollywood films, and shows how popular cinema reflects and communicates contemporary values for audiences.

Chris Holmlund is Associate Professor in Cinema Studies, Women's Studies and French at The University of Tennessee, Knoxville. She is the co-editor of *Between the Sheets, in the Streets: Queer, Lesbian, Gay Documentary* (1997).

COMEDIA
Series editor: David Morley

IMPOSSIBLE BODIES

Femininity and masculinity
at the movies

Chris Holmlund

London and New York

First published 2002
by Routledge
11 New Fetter Lane, London EC4P 4EE

Simultaneously published in the USA and Canada
by Routledge
29 West 35th Street, New York, NY 10001

Routledge is an imprint of the Taylor & Francis Group

Typeset in Garamond by
Florence Production, Stoodleigh, Devon
Printed and bound in Great Britain by
Biddles Ltd, Guildford and King's Lynn

British Library Cataloguing in Publication Data
A catalogue record for this book is available from
the British Library

Library of Congress Cataloging in Publication Data
Holmlund, Chris.
Impossible bodies: femininity and masculinity at the movies/
Chris Holmlund.
p. cm.
Includes bibliographical references and index.
1. Body, Human, in motion pictures. 2. Sex role in motion
pictures. 3. Minorities in motion pictures. I. Title.
PN1995.9.B62 H65 2002
791.43'653–dc21   2001044193

ISBN 0–415–18575–0 (hbk)
ISBN 0–415–18576–9 (pbk)

FOR MY DEAREST DAD

CONTENTS

FIGURES

ACKNOWLEDGEMENTS

Many people have contributed to this book: family, colleagues, editors, students, and friends have all been great. Charles Maland and Justin Wyatt have helped immeasurably, suggesting directions for research, commenting on drafts, discussing films, and more. Thanks to Charlotte Brunsdon for helping concoct the idea in Scotland after watching *Falling Down* (not discussed here, rather acted out then, girl-style, wandering through Glasgow shopping districts).

Heartfelt thanks to everyone who has read and commented on individual chapters and/or generally helped with research, often by generously sharing your own: I single out Dennis Bingham, Christy Bottoms, Chris Cagle, Odile Cazenave, Linda Dittmar, Cindy Fuchs, Krin Gabbard, Stan Garner, Gloria Gibson-Hudson, Sumiko Higashi, Mark Hulsether, George Hutchinson, Diana King, Janet King, Peter Lehman, Kathleen McHugh, Tara McPherson, Kenny Mostern, Hilde Nelson, Jim Nelson, Chon Noriega, Alexander Parks, Mark Reid, Laurie Schulze, Tarsha Stanley, Chris Straayer, Diane Waldman, and Dale Watermulder. Your expertise and enthusiasm have made this book stronger; as importantly, they've made writing it intriguing and fun. Sincere thanks to David Morley for unfailing support and on-target editing. At Routledge, Rebecca Barden has been fabulous and Alistair Daniel invaluable: thanks Rebecca for your keen sense of humor and steadfast guidance; thanks Alistair for facilitating the final stages and for securing such fine photographic "proof" that "impossible" bodies do indeed exist.

At the University of Tennessee, many faculties, students, and staff have provided encouragement. Among them, Nancy Goslee, Karen Levy, John Romeiser, and Flora Shrode deserve *special* thanks. Hugs to past and present "Association of Women Faculty" folks, too – I truly appreciate your presence! The students are the best: I owe you a lot, not only for watching so many of these movies with me (as we know, some were great, some mediocre, some real *dogs*), but also for so openly sharing *your* ideas, information, and insights with me and with each other. Without you there would be no Dolly, and other chapters would be the poorer, too. Thanks, too, to students, staff, and colleagues at the University of Stockholm for *your* perspectives on genres, sidekicks, and stars, and to the Wenner-Gren Foundation for helping make this exchange possible. Without you there would be no Dolph and no Nils, either. To Lucy Fischer, Tom Gunning, and Judith Mayne profound gratitude for assists with things both professional and personal.

Diane Waldman, Vicki Elkins, Kris Hafner, Kathleen McHugh, Sieglinde Lug, Lee Chambers, Michelle Legault, and Carla Kaplan have regularly helped me frame arguments and adjust attitudes at high altitudes: there's nothing like sitting on top of a mountain and talking about life and movies! Hugs and thanks to Kay Stirling, Miss Daniela, Justin Wyatt, and Dale Watermulder for your assistance with so much at lower altitudes, and to Aaron Holmlund and Melanie Zucker-Holmlund (the next generation) for having the good sense to love movies and to live in or near places I regularly go for research.

Lastly and most importantly, "tack så enormt mycket!" to the big male Swedes in my life, my father (Chester/Gösta) and my brother (Steve), for watching so many films with me and, bottom line, for being there and being *you*. You, and mom, have given me so much.

Over the years, this project has benefited also from several University of Tennessee research, travel, and publication grants. Research for the "Latinas in La-La Land" and "Nouveaux westerns" chapters was facilitated by a Faculty Research Grant and the Lindsey Young Library Fund; the SARIF Exhibition and Performance Fund helped provide illustrations.

All photographs are courtesy of Kobal. "Visible difference and flex appeal: The body, sex, sexuality and race in the *Pumping Iron* films," was first published in *Cinema Journal*, vol. 28, no. 4 (Summer 1989), pp. 38–51; a longer version of "Cruisin' for a bruisin': Hollywood's deadly (lesbian) dolls" first appeared in *Cinema Journal*, vol. 34, no. 1 (Fall 1994), pp. 31–51. Both appear here by permission of the University of Texas Press. A longer version of "When is a lesbian not a lesbian?: The lesbian continuum and the mainstream femme film" was first published in *Camera Obscura*, nos. 25–6 (January–May 1991), pp. 145–80. It appears here by permission of Duke University Press.

INTRODUCTION

Impossible bodies, compromised positions

Figure I.1   Arnold Schwarzenegger in *Pumping Iron* (White Mountain Productions, 1976). Courtesy of the Kobal Collection.

Through established and emerging markets – in theaters; on video, laser disc, and DVDs; via network, cable and satellite broadcasts; on the web – Hollywood films shape and express how we see – or don't see – our bodies, our selves.[1] In the last two decades, dramatic changes have occurred. Vertical and horizontal integration have increased substantially as "global companies . . . respond[ed] to the demands of segments of the market . . . 'search[ing] for opportunities to sell to similar segments throughout the globe to achieve the scale economies that keep their costs competitive.'"[2] Transnational corporations have acquired U.S. studios. Media and telecommunications corporations have merged.[3] Production may be farmed out to smaller companies, but "independent" films, too, are marketed through international distribution and exhibition networks.[4] All sizes of films address niche as well as general and cross-over audiences. As before, star power and genre trends propel production cycles, but today directors and dialog matter less to box office take, while bodily spectacle and blasting sound matter more.[5]

On an obvious level, the film bodies we watch are and always have been "impossible": they are, quite simply, not real, but made up of images and sounds and constructed through narratives. Despite – or because of – this fact, the impact that unusual Hollywood bodies have at home and abroad is demonstrable, if debated. An exchange with a short, gawky, 14-year-old boy on a bus in Costa Rica in 1990 was, for me, telling. Making small talk in Spanish on the four hour trip from San José to the Pacific coast, I asked my seat mate which movies he liked best. "*Rambo* and *Rocky*," he unhesitatingly replied. "Why?" I asked. "Because Stallone's everything I'm not," he answered. Images of Sly flashed in my mind and connections between body and power loomed large: Sly = muscular, white, grown-up, gun-wielding, fist-flinging, red-blooded, North American . . .

Ten years later, I find a more devastating example in Bahman Ghobadi's French–Iranian co-production *A Time for Drunken Horses* (2000). Living on the Iran/Iraq border, a family of Kurdish orphans struggles to find the money for an operation that their crippled brother, Madi (Madi Ekhtiar-dini), needs to stay alive. It is winter, and wartime conditions are so terrible

3

Figure I.2 Sylvester Stallone as John Rambo in *Rambo: First Blood Part Two* (Tri-Star, 1985). Courtesy of the Kobal Collection.

that even the pack horses must be dosed with liquor to work. One day the oldest brother (Ayoub Ahmadi) brings home a poster of a pumped-up, beweaponed Schwarzenegger and places it over his sick brother's bed. In the firelight, tiny, misshapen Madi gazes lovingly up at Arnold, happy for a moment in spite of constant pain.

Today, other bellicose stars might replace Sly or Arnold, but male action figures who move a lot and say little continue to entertain audiences everywhere, *because* they are what we are not. The nine case studies in this book squarely target *U.S.* films and *U.S.* reception. Mirroring sentiments shared by most Americans, the majority of the 100 plus films studied here are more overtly preoccupied with domestic issues than with foreign policy concerns: the U.S. has always been self-absorbed, and the relative peace and prosperity of the last two decades have furthered this tendency.[6] Since the majority of Hollywood movies foreground gender (with entire genres structured around male and female characters, played by beloved stars, supported by familiar sidekicks, addressed to male or female audiences), moreover, engagement with "domestic" issues becomes virtually *de rigueur*.

A central tenet of *Impossible Bodies* is that for 1980s and 1990s U.S. audiences, directors, screenwriters, producers, and promoters, some domestic shapes appeared to be more "proper," more "natural," more "common" than others. Other bodies were – and often still are – "impossible" because they exceed the parameters within which we think of "ideal" or even "normal" physiques. My interest is in how popular films function as markers and transmitters of contemporary values; I therefore look primarily at work that is readily available on video, laser disc, and/or DVD and frequently programmed on American television. The emphasis is squarely, though not exclusively, on feature length fiction films produced during the last two decades.

Three basic kinds of "impossible" bodies are explored in these chapters. A first set is outrageous. Arnold Schwarzenegger is known for his muscles, Dolly Parton for her breasts, Rosie Perez for her "mouth," Jennifer Lopez for her "caboose," Sharon Stone for her "ice pick." A second cluster of figures is constrained. Whoopi Goldberg's involvements with white men, in life as on film, are closely watched and highly controversial. Lesbians may frolic together on screen, providing they don't look too "butch"; killing, however, is sometimes OK. Big male Swedish actors have, for six decades, never played Hollywood leads who are Swedes, but rather Asians, Anglo-Americans, Russians or Eastern Europeans. A third group of bodies remains largely invisible. Even in 1990s "nouveaux westerns" (including action and science fiction films), certain bodies are still missing: Asians and Asian Americans, children, and workers. Of the few Latina actresses who get roles, most continue to play maids, mamas and/or spitfires in bit or supporting parts.[7] And, statistically surprising if psychologically understandable, old age goes unexplored, ignored, except when reassuringly tackled by virile septuagenarians like Clint or supportively embodied by loveable old ladies like Jessica Tandy.

Of course, most of us don't possess ideal, perhaps even "normal," bodies, so far from rejecting the impossibly busty, bewigged or "built" bodies that Hollywood proposes to us, we may embrace them, trying on shapes, mimicking poses, and practicing attitudes not routinely accorded us. We may reject heroes, wholly, in part, or in passing, and opt for "the bad guys."[8] We may side with sidekicks. We may fantasize still other options. Because visibility frequently translates to social acceptance and correlates with political clout, "deviant" looks and bodies – though by no means solely queer looks and bodies – are definitely, often defiantly, present.[9] Resistance and reformulation may be fueled by any number of factors, from familiarity with literary sources to knowledge of extra-textual gestural codes to cognizance of performance traditions. The positions we as individuals take up *vis-à-vis* screen and real bodies are always compromised, however, both because we are constrained by broader social and economic factors, and because Hollywood films typically make vague promises to as many people as possible.

Social network, cinematic grid

To sketch the range – and the limits – of the representations and recep-
tions given "impossible" screen bodies, the chapters that follow are fastened
onto a three-dimensional grid. A first part, "Gesturing toward Genres,"
explores 1980s and 1990s documentaries, romances, and westerns. As the
subtitle indicates, the genre "hooks" of these films are not firmly fixed, but
rather mixed. Essays examine, in historical sequence, different tropes of
impossibility. Documentaries about bodybuilding, for example, are rare.
The two *Pumping Iron* films (from the late 1970s and early 1980s respectively) are additionally unusual in that both trouble the status of documentary as "truth" by rigging their investigative "reporting."[10] This chapter
is placed first because the lively debates that occurred, first during the
contests, later around the films, underscore the extent of our investments
in the (naked or near naked) body as "Truth."[11] The next two chapters, on
lesbian romances ("femme films") and "nouveaux westerns" respectively,
tackle "impossible" bodies by investigating subgenres addressed to emerging
and/or previously overlooked audiences: lesbians, Latinos, African Americans,
working women.[12] Both chapters bring out how genre conventions guide
the ways these groups are portrayed on screen, promoted by marketers,
and/or perceived by audiences.[13]

Engagement with social and demographic shifts underpins all the analyses
in the second part, "Siding with Sidekicks." Order is guided by connections: the first essay, on "deadly doll" films, arcs backwards to the chapter
on "femme films" in the first section; the last, on Latina actresses, looks
forward to the star analyses of the third section. Surveying films from the
1920s to the present, these three essays together argue that how sidekicks
are seen, not seen, or differently seen reveals cultural obsessions and blind
spots. As bit or supporting players, African American servants, older white
associates, Swedish homesteaders, and Latina maids and mamas are rarely
the focus of general audience attention.[14] Nonetheless "minority" audiences
are often concerned with what Judith Mayne terms the "space between visibility and invisibility" – i.e. "knowing that others will be oblivious to what
is usually obvious to you."[15] Semi- and invisibility at times extends to
second and third tier stars (Nils Asther, Dolph Lundgren in "Swede as
'Other'," Cicely Tyson, Jessica Tandy in "Cruisin' for a bruisin'") and "indie"
ingenues (Rosie Perez in "Latinas in La-La Land") as well. Only Jennifer
Lopez bursts forward to star(let)dom by sticking her "impossible" derriere
up front, center frame.

The third part, "Staring at Stars," fixes stars who are so popular, so familiar, they are "family," known to audiences by their first names alone.
Whoopi and Dolly are, admittedly, less well known than Clint as film
stars: Whoopi neither directs nor produces and increasingly works in television; Dolly is better known as a singer, though among other business ventures

(Dollywood!) is her own film production company. Significantly, however, all three are working-class heroes who are respected, even revered, for their refusal to mask bodily differences and alterations.[16] Folks love that Dolly is proud of her roots and frank about her cosmetic operations; that Whoopi is militant about her blackness and adamant in her refusal of surgery; that Clint is upfront, if terse, about his aging.[17] Again, the devil is in the details: some "folks" receive and read cues and clues from the films and about the stars, others do not.

Gender fix, sexual dilemma, racial divide

Across and beyond these organizing divisions of genres, sidekicks, and stars, comparisons among chapters reveal broad shifts, striking continuities, and stark disjunctures in how "impossible" screen bodies have been shown and seen in the last two decades.[18] For rough outlines of what counted as desirable femininity and masculinity in the 1980s and 1990s, just juxtapose Dolly, Whoopi, and Clint (even add other contemporary "first name" favorites like Madonna, Arnold, and Sly) with earlier stars like Bogie, the Duke, and Marilyn. For today's female stars, vulnerable voluptuousness is less important than openness and brash independence; men, even "The aging Clint," continue to be associated with power and virility.

Already in 1977, in *Pumping Iron* (Butler and Flore), Arnold Schwarzenegger wins because he is biggest, most articulate, most "manly."[19] Subsequently, of course, he has built on his "build" to achieve stardom, willfully embodying a brand of transcendent "whiteness" common to other contemporary action heroes, among them Dolph Lundgren.[20] In contrast, faced with two extremes in *Pumping Iron II: The Women* (Butler, 1984) – the sleek, flirtatious (American) Rachel McLish and the muscle-bound, outspoken (Australian) Bev Francis – the judges "compromise" by turning to an (African *American*) contestant, Carla Dunlap. Carla is more "independent" (no boyfriend is seen) than either Rachel or Bev and equally outspoken. She is "bigger" than Rachel; she is more "feminine" than Bev. The judges find Rachel neither exciting nor honest enough to win; Bev is scary: she looks "butch" even though she has a boyfriend.[21]

Pumping Iron II's solution is multi-pronged: a binary racial division (of "black" and "white") solves a gender "fix" (i.e. problem); a gender "fix" (i.e. solution) assimilates racial division and masks sexual dilemmas. With variations, Hollywood repeats the same formula – gender "fix," sexual dilemma, racial divide – like a mantra, cross-genre.

Assertive, toned, and muscled women are thus ubiquitous in contemporary fiction films.[22] Nevertheless, as Yvonne Tasker notes, there are decided limits on "musculinity," even for 1980s action heroines.[23] Svelte has certainly been the rule for lesbian characters, beginning with the lesbian romances of the 1980s. And the invocation and evacuation of lesbian sexuality promoted in these "smaller" films continues with a vengeance in bigger 1990s productions. At opposite ends of the genre spectrum, both *Fried Green Tomatoes* (Jon Avnet, 1992) and *Basic Instinct* (Paul Verhoeven, 1992) similarly duck race, doctor homosexuality, and dodge age. As with the mid-1980s "femme films," audiences and reviewers fixated on active, attractive, female characters some saw as lesbian and some did not.[24] Almost everyone ignored the black and older supporting characters who hold the keys to the central murder mysteries.[25]

Nonetheless – undoubtedly to the horror of the Far Right and New Right; quite differently, to the consternation of certain lesbian spectators – the increase of lovely, if sometimes lethal, "lesbian" characters in 1990s neo-noirs, action films, thrillers, and romances in some ways indicates wider public acceptance of gays. By 1999, in fact, a (slim, white) woman's "right to choose" had merged with (white) queer rights, witness the box office success and Academy Award for *Boys Don't Cry* (Kimberly Pierce), an independent film based on the true story of Brandon Teena (Hilary Swank), a transgendered Nebraska teen who was brutally beaten, raped, then murdered, for daring to live as a boy and love small-town beauty Lana (Chloë Sevigny).

Figure I.3   Hilary Swank as Brandon Teena in *Boys Don't Cry*
(Fox Searchlight, 1999). Courtesy of the Kobal Collection.

8

Sadly if predictably, the black man who was killed at the same time as Brandon was written out of the screenplay.

The emphases above on "slim," "svelte," and young are important: for women, especially, fear of fat and distaste for aging have changed much less than restrictions on muscularity in the last 20 years, and these aversions transcend – however unequally – race and region, too. *Fried Green Tomatoes'* bulgy New South housewife, Evelyn (Kathy Bates), happily takes back seat to thinner, prettier, even older white women characters. "Big" Latina actresses like Lupe Ontiveros are triply doomed to stock and bit parts, including in Latino-directed epics and melodramas. (Ontiveros has a supporting role for the first time in 2000, in Miguel Arteta's independent *Chuck and Buck*.) The younger, slimmer Rosie Perez and Jennifer Lopez garner supporting and lead roles, even though they stand out via accent and/or shape because so shockingly few Latinos or Latin Americans are visible in La-La Land.

Clearly aging and spreading, superstar Whoopi Goldberg today plays second fiddle to younger, trimmer, African American actresses. As star she was usually involved, often romantically, with white men and women. Yet so little overt sexuality appears in these mid-1980s to 1990s films that it is obvious Hollywood still regards interracial relationships with suspicion as well as fascination. In partial contrast, though many black viewers also criticize Whoopi's participation in white relationships, they do so for different reasons, and they applaud facets of Whoopi's "sister acts" many whites miss, relishing her send-ups of white attitudes and appreciating her homages to black actors and acting traditions.

The epitome of welcoming whiteness, Dolly Parton's "impossible" body juts out equally chastely at the other end of the color spectrum. A diva for the "safe-sex decade" now in her fifties, Dolly looks much younger thanks to all those plastic surgeries. While these are widely publicized, potentially volatile subjects like her down-home feminism and, especially, her queer connections, are managed, even transcended, thanks to cross-media touting of religion, home, and family. As ever, her Appalachian background and "cracker" accent add zing and zest, spice and spunk.[26]

Meanwhile (regionally unmarked) white men constitute the majority of heroes, and the bulk of the villains too, in action films and western offshoots. Together Clint and compadres boldly promote associations of power and virility as their particular gender "fix" to contemporary sexual dilemmas and racial divides. Sometimes they are helped and/or trained by smaller (expendable) Latin Americans, Latinos, Africans, African Americans, Asians, Asian Americans, and women of all colors; more infrequently these heroes themselves are Latino, African American and/or female. Many fight and win thanks both to bigger-than-ever guns and to superior martial arts skills.[27] Some films register concerns with international standing, defense, and trade, in the late 1980s and early 1990s, for example, replacing white Soviet and South African villains with Japanese and Latin Americans.

These racial and ethnic alterations intriguingly affect the sizes of 1990s male screen bodies. Fully as spectacular, male heroes today are often not all that big: just look at all the young Clint clones, including, most recently, Hugh Jackman as Wolverine in *X-Men* (Bryan Singer, 2000). Clint himself is lean and lanky – hence his versatility, durability? – while Dolph Lundgren's 1990s films often go straight to video and even Arnold has done (doubly – he plays his clone) badly in *The 6th Day* (Roger Spottiswoode, 2000) at the Christmas box office.

But Arnold's accent at least ensures he is perceived as "foreign" – perhaps a plus in a country where, for the first time since 1930, one in ten people is now foreign born. For most whites today, including both Arnold and Dolly fans, distinctive accents thus constitute nostalgic reminders of times when ethnicity was not primarily symbolic, trotted out and toasted only at holiday celebrations. Instead, "casting oneself as an outsider" has become so cool that, Werner Sollors posits, it may even "be a dominant cultural trait. . . . Every American is now considered a potential ethnic."[28]

Of course when white "ethnicity" rules, assimilation of difference and denial of inequality become not only possible but desirable. Nonetheless although "cool" cultural traits are certainly homogenizing, they are not necessarily hegemonic. Could one argue, tongue in cheek and by analogy, that playing "Clint" in *The Quick and the Dead* (Sam Raimi, 1995) Sharon Stone is both every man's ideal and *the* ideal man?

Coda from my millennial *"Matrix"*

After all, in most Hollywood films gender "fixes" mask racial divisions and route sexual dilemmas. More interesting and important is *how* and *why* they do so, in specific films, through groups of films, for individual spectators and for sets of viewers. I agree with Stuart Hall that examinations of popular culture, like "the study of labor history and its institutions, . . . yiel[d] most when . . . seen in relation to a more general, a wider history."[29] These chapters therefore look not only at films as "texts," they also plumb "official" and "subcultural" histories. Readers will find references to recent work on aging, plastic surgery, obesity, violence, fundamentalist religion, interracial relationships, regional stereotypes, immigration law, demographic profiles, foreign policy shifts, star biographies and autobiographies, studio publicity materials, mainstream and alternative reviews, industry statistics, and more.

Bottom line, although trends – of short or *longue durée* – in desirable and undesirable, "possible" and "impossible" screen bodies are identifiable, their outlines are generally fuzzy, both because Hollywood likes to dabble, furthering and following earlier successes, and always thinking "sales," and because U.S. audiences are not "indivisible"; we do not equally enjoy "liberty and justice for all."

In the final analysis, of course, as William Connolly succinctly says, "every revealing conceals."[30] Many "impossible" bodies are missing from *Impossible Bodies*. Much as Neo (Keanu Reeves) and Trinity (Carrie-Anne Moss) find themselves caught within the *Matrix* (Andy and Larry Wachowski, 1999), an organization that controls everyone regardless of whether they consciously agree with game plans or goals, my choices of which bodies appear and whose opinions are tapped are inevitably marked by my own passions and compromised positions.

Given my interest in social and demographic backdrops, I signal three areas in particular as crucial in the near future:

1 The roles – and lack thereof – accorded Asians and Asian Americans cross genres during the 1980s and 1990s, a key topic both because immigration from Asian countries has risen dramatically and because Asian economies are essential to both U.S. foreign policy and the global market. In 2001, we are surely poised for a sea change in both the quantity and the quality of Asian and Asian American screen representations, witness the unexpected success of Ang Lee's *Crouching Tiger, Hidden Dragon* (2000).

Figure I.4   Keanu Reaves as Neo and Carrie-Anne Moss as Trinity in *The Matrix* (Warner Bros, 1999). Courtesy of the Kobal Collection.

2   Unusual children and teenagers, in particular the queer kids who, for the first time ever, are visible in 1990s romances and comedies and who are occasionally present in science fiction and horror, too. They are, and under Bush-*fils* surely will be, pawns in debates around education, child-rearing, abortion, adoption, teen suicide, and substance abuse.

3   The effacement of all regional markings save "Southern" in favor of more easily generalizable (a.k.a. marketable) urban, suburban, and rural divisions. This is perhaps understandable since the South is now the most populous region in the U.S. (providing Texas is included); since rural population has declined to one in four; and since suburban population has risen to more than one in two. But why do we more frequently see the "Old South" than the "New"?

This last issue looms important for me because I have written much of this book in the shadow of Dollywood, in Knoxville, Tennessee. Dolly's full figure – on billboards, in ads – and her baby voice – on radio and TV – remind me constantly how important (how *diversely* important) "impossible" bodies can be. How could I not put her last when her "body" offers such a prime site for investigation of tensions between globalism and localism? Beloved from Appalachia to Zimbabwe, epitome of a timeless "South" yet oddly "world," thoroughly "retro" and quintessentially "pomo," with a nostalgic appeal that easily tippy toes over into camp, Dolly's screen success makes it perfectly clear ("perfectly queer"?) that, as Stephen Prince insists of more overtly political films, "Hollywood cinema is not ideologically univocal."[31]

And – move over Dolly! – other "impossible" bodies will appear, including other singer-stars. I fantasize a new bus trip in Costa Rica, circa 2005 and the (admittedly less likely) possibility of an interview with a young Tica girl traveling alone. If I asked which movies *she* likes best, might she, just possibly, answer *Selena* (Gregory Nava, 1997), *Out of Sight* (Steven Soderbergh, 1998) or *The Cell* (Tarsem Singh, 2000)?

Part I

GESTURING TOWARD GENRES

1

VISIBLE DIFFERENCE AND
FLEX APPEAL

The body, sex, sexuality and race in the
Pumping Iron films

Figure 1.1   Carla Dunlap in *Pumping Iron II: The Women* (Pumping Iron/White
Mountain, 1985). Courtesy of the Kobal Collection.

*P*umping Iron (Butler and Flore, 1977) and *Pumping Iron II: The Women* (Butler, 1984), two documentaries about bodybuilding contests, provide an ideal opportunity to look at the relationships operating between body, desire, and power in the United States today.[1] Taken as a pair, these films are a veritable melting pot of sex, sexuality, race, and sales. Intentionally and unintentionally, they reveal how the visible differences of sex (to have or have not) and race (to be or not to be) mesh with ideology and economy in contemporary American society, and within film fictions. In both films sexuality is adroitly linked with sex and race at the expense of any reference to history or class. The body is marketed as a commodity in its own right, not just as the silent support for the sale of other commodities.

An analysis of the way popular film reflects and shapes the categories of body, sex, sexuality, and race remains an urgent project for film theory. Despite the incorporation of critiques made by the women's, black, and gay movements of the 1960s, 1970s, and 1980s – indeed, in some ways because of these critiques – we continue to see and speak about the body as the last bastion of nature. While the sexual and civil rights movements make it clear that inequalities predicated on sex, race or sexual preference are socially established and maintained, the strategies they employ are nonetheless often based on an idea of the body as unified and unique.[2] Difference is either flaunted (black power and cultural feminism, black and women's separatism) or elided (the "we're just like you" policy of the National Gay Task Force since 1973), but the body remains the silent support of and rationale for political praxis. Even within theoretical discourses the biological status of the body lingers on, masking and motivating a series of power relations. (One has only to think of the multitude of feminist critiques of Lacan's penis/phallus confusion.)

Everyone has difficulty acknowledging the extent to which the body is a social construction and an ideological support because, to invoke Freud, the body (our own and the Other's) is the object and the origin of our earliest fears and desires. The associations established between the body and power are particularly hard to acknowledge when, as is often the case, several kinds

17

of visible difference or its correlates are intermingled: when sex is added to race, or when gender is conflated with sexuality. The original ambivalent attitudes we hold towards the body are then multiplied many times over.

The rush to ignore and deny sexual, racial, and gender differences – initiated and/or encouraged by the Reagan government and other right-wing forces – further obscures the roles assigned to the body today. More than in the 1960s and 1970s, we forget that the ways we look at and speak about the body are historically variable. Knowledge and power of and over the body function within what Foucault calls an "apparatus." Since we live in and create this apparatus, it is hard for us to realize that it is "a formation which has as its major function at a given historical moment that of responding to an urgent need."[3]

The reliance of Western society on images of the body to sell products and promote fictions compounds our confusion. Mass media and advertising see to it that we consume visible difference daily. Foucault notes that starting in the 1960s, "industrial societies could content themselves with a much looser form of power over the body."[4] The joint success of the civil rights and sexual liberation movements, in perverse combination with the post-World War II advertising and mass media boom, has affected "the kind of body the current society needs."[5]

The question for media analysts is to define *what* kind of body this is, or what kind of bod*ies* are needed and/or tolerated by current societies, and to describe how the apparatus of body and power functions in popular culture today. The *Pumping Iron* films furnish a wealth of raw material for such an analysis. Since they deal with bodybuilding, it would seem apparent from the very start that the bodies we see are *not* natural. After all, they are clearly the products of individual obsession, created with great effort in the gym, through dieting and even drugs. Moreover, the contestants clearly try to "sell" their bodies, first to the contest judges, then to a burgeoning group of bodybuilding entrepreneurs who promote a vast array of products. Yet though the contestants' bodies are obviously and necessarily constructions, up for comparison and sale, there is an overwhelming need on the part of the judges, the audiences, and even many of the contestants to see bodies as representative of "Body" with a capital B, a natural and God-given essence, segregated and defined, as the films and contests themselves are, according to sex and gender roles.[6]

Body, capital B, participates in myth, not history. References to the mythical status of these extra-muscular bodies appear throughout both films, reinforcing our perception of bodies as "Body." Both men and women are associated with heroes and heroines, gods and goddesses. The contestants compete for the titles of Mr and Miss Olympia, respectively. The theme song of *Pumping Iron* tells us, "Everybody [every body?] wants to be a hero / Everybody wants to live forever." *Pumping Iron II* opens with shots of mountains and power lines, then shows Bev Francis, the 180 pound

Australian power lifter turned bodybuilder, seated next to and looking up at statues of muscular goddesses. Similar shots of other women recur later, though then the emphasis is on femininity via statues of Venus.

A sense of history is not absent from these films, however. On the contrary, because they are documentaries (albeit staged documentaries), the spectator knows that the contests have taken place, and that the characters are real people. Moreover, because these characters are social actors, the spectator also assumes that the issues they discuss in *Pumping Iron II* (and ignore in *Pumping Iron*) are of contemporary concern. Paradoxically, though, the historical references inherent in the form of documentary hide the fact that the *Pumping Iron* films are films, with narrative and visual strategies. Like the bodies they chronicle, they too become part of nature.[7]

In order to separate myth from history in these films, and in order to evaluate the representation of men and women bodybuilders in the broader context of the societal organization of body and power today, it is necessary to separate artificially the terms they entangle. Therefore, in what follows, I look in turn at how sex/gender, sexuality, and race are perceived and constructed as visible, physical differences, in the film narratives and images. The conclusion recombines the three categories and discusses how history is obfuscated by representation and sales: within the competitions, within the films, and within society at large.

Because women are the subjects of *Pumping Iron II*, the fact of visible difference based on sex is inescapable. It displaces the competition as the central topic of the film narrative. In order to define which woman has the best and most well-defined body, the judges feel compelled to define "body" in relation to "woman." The contestants, too, wonder about the relationship between gender (femininity or masculinity), sex (female or male bodies), and bodybuilding. The film makes their questions its own, marshaling images and sounds to ask: Is a woman still a woman if she looks like a man? Where is the vanishing point?

In contrast, *Pumping Iron* simply chronicles the 1976 Mr Olympia contest. The reason why is obvious in retrospect: because men are the norm in patriarchal society, visible difference cannot be an issue. The association of muscularity with men poses no conflict between sex and gender: muscular men are seen as "natural."[8] As Richard Dyer says of male pin-ups: "Muscularity is a key term in appraising men's bodies. . . . Muscularity is the *sign* of power – natural, achieved, phallic."[9] What then could be more natural, more familiar, more right than men pumping iron?

Images of muscular women, on the other hand, are disconcerting, even threatening. They disrupt the equation of men with strength and women with weakness that underpins gender roles and power relations, and that has by now come to seem familiar and comforting (though perhaps in differing ways) to both women and men. Because of this threat to established values, *Pumping Iron II* has an edge of excitement and danger missing from

19

Pumping Iron. Yet *Pumping Iron II* is not wholeheartedly in favor of muscular women; on the contrary, it is both ambiguous and ambivalent. Contradictions abound within the narrative and between the narrative and the images.

On the surface of the narrative, *Pumping Iron II* seems to promote strong women and to treat women in the same way as men. As the sequel to *Pumping Iron*, it has the same narrative structure: both films begin with interviews of the top contenders, intercut with training scenes; both climax with the bodybuilding contest.

On a deeper level, however, *Pumping Iron II* treats women very differently than *Pumping Iron* treats men. *Pumping Iron* does not need to ask "What is man?" while *Pumping Iron II* cannot do anything else. When the question "What is woman?" is asked about women bodybuilders, it seems topical, even liberal. In actuality, however, it is centuries old, and standard Hollywood practice. Steve Neale could be describing the basic plots of the *Pumping Iron* films when he writes: "While mainstream cinema, in its assumption of a male norm, perspective, and look, can constantly take women and the female image as the object of investigation, it has rarely investigated men and the male image in the same kind of way: women are a problem, a source of anxiety, of obsessive inquiry; men are not. Where women are investigated, men are tested."[10]

Of course, there are individual moments within the narrative which contradict both the deep and surface levels of the film. At these times the majority of spectators in the contest audiences and the film theater are aligned with the more muscular and articulate women. Although the conventionally prettier and sexier Rachel McLish has her ardent supporters, on the whole, Bev Francis and Carla Dunlap appear more intelligent and more likeable. Throughout the film, Bev and Carla come across as outspoken and independent, good sports and good sportswomen, while time and again Rachel is characterized as a whining, cheating, Bible-belting brat.

Similarly, the film does not encourage spectators to adopt the positions articulated by the universally white male International Federation of Bodybuilders (IFBB) officials: on the contrary, they look ridiculous. In a key pre-contest sequence, Ben Weider, chairman of the IFBB, intones: "What we're looking for is something that's right down the middle. A woman who has a certain amount of aesthetic femininity, but yet has that muscle tone to show that she is an athlete." The retort of one of the younger male judges seems far more logical and far less patronizing: "That's like being told there is a certain point beyond which women can't go in this sport. What does that mean exactly? It's as though the U.S. Ski Federation told women skiers that they can only ski so fast." In the final contest scenes the officials' competence as officials is thrown into question: even with the help of a calculator, they are unable to total the women's scores.

Moments such as these, where the audience is encouraged to identify with strong women and to reject "dolls" and patriarchs, are certainly victories for feminism. But they must be evaluated in the context of the entire film and especially in the context of the film images. The images of *Pumping Iron II* are more ambiguous than the narrative because society defines how we look at women's bodies very narrowly indeed.

When bodybuilding is understood just as a sport, the analogy between bodybuilding and skiing made by the young judge and endorsed by a certain part of the film narrative is absolutely valid. The problem is that, unlike skiing, bodybuilding for women entails confronting and judging the near-naked female body. One has only to turn to Freud to appreciate why, for the male spectator especially, the female body is fraught with both danger and delight.

In Freud's analysis, men see women not just as different, but also as castrated, as not men. The male subject simultaneously recognizes and denies difference: the woman is different, *unheimlich* even,[11] yet she is also the same, just missing a part. At one and the same time he desires and dreads the woman's visible difference: it evokes his fears of the loss and/or inadequacy of the penis, while simultaneously establishing male superiority based on possession of the penis.[12] In the essay entitled "Fetishism," Freud maintains men negotiate castration anxiety caused by "the terrifying shock of . . . the sight of the female genitals" in three different ways: "Some become homosexual in consequence of this experience, others ward it off by creating a fetish, and the great majority overcome it" and choose women as their love objects.[13]

In *Pumping Iron II* in particular, the problems posed by the images of female bodies provoke responses involving all three of Freud's strategies: homosexuality, fetishism, and heterosexuality. Male ambivalence towards women's bodies is omnipresent. A fear of visible difference and a fear of the abolition of visible difference paradoxically coexist, so tightly are body and power interconnected here.

The images of the more muscular women inflame male anxiety because they threaten the abolition of visible difference. In an article on a made-for-TV movie about women bodybuilders, Laurie Schulze comments: "The danger to male heterosexuality lurks in the implication that any male sexual interest in the muscular female is not heterosexual at all, but homosexual: not only is *she* 'unnatural,' but the female bodybuilder possesses the power to invert normal *male* sexuality."[14] Since Bev Francis looks and moves "like a man," homophobic patriarchal ideology whispers that men who find her attractive must be gay, and, further, that women who find her attractive must be lesbians. Bev's muscles, dress, heavy facial features, and "unfeminine" body language evoke the stereotype of what a lesbian looks like: the butch, the lesbian who is immediately recognizable as such, visibly different. Women who find Bev attractive would, as a result, be defined as femmes, lesbians who, in Joan Nestle's words, are "known by . . . their choices" while butches are "known by their appearances."[15] In each case, the stereotypes of what kind of bodies gay men and lesbians find attractive are constructed around the phallus and constrained by binary conceptions of masculinity and femininity: gay men are assumed to be wimps who worship "he-men," while lesbians are assumed to be women who *are* "he-men" or women who worship "he/she-men."

The film narrative attempts to circumvent the stigma of homosexuality evoked by Bev's muscles by having her repeatedly insist that she is a woman, not a man, and by repeatedly showing her accompanied by her trainer/ boyfriend, Steve Weinberger. But these narrative strategies cannot be successful in allaying male castration anxieties and/or homophobia in general, especially since they are reinforced by a fear of loss of love. Where men are concerned, Freud mentions this fear only in passing:[16] for him women, far more than men, are concerned about the loss of love attendant on the abolition of visible difference. Indeed, in Freudian terms, loss of love, not castration, constitutes the most significant *female* anxiety.[17] Adrienne Rich, in contrast, argues that: "it seems more probable that men really fear . . . that women could be indifferent to them altogether" than that "the male need to control women's sexuality results from some primal male 'fear of women'."[18]

In *Pumping Iron II*, the association of muscularity, masculinity, and lesbianism invokes these fears of a loss of love for spectators of both sexes, though in different ways. If heterosexual men see Bev as a lesbian, she is threatening: lesbians incarnate sexual indifference to men. If heterosexual women see Bev as a lesbian, they must reject her: to like her would mean admitting that they themselves might be lesbian, which would in turn entail the abnegation of traditionally feminine powers and privileges.

The overwhelming majority of the female characters in *Pumping Iron II*, from the bodybuilders themselves to the one female judge, fear that a redefinition of femininity will entail the loss of love, power, and privilege.[19] It is fear of loss of love that motivates one of the women to say, rather inanely, but nonetheless quite sincerely and even persuasively, "I hope really that they stick with the feminine look. . . . I mean, really, a woman's a woman. That's my philosophy. I think she should look like a woman. And I think that when you lose that, what's the point of being a woman?"

Most of the images in *Pumping Iron II* espouse the same philosophy. In general, they function to defuse rather than provoke male and female spectators' anxieties about muscular women by fetishizing women's bodies and by making them the objects of heterosexual desire. The differences between the two *Pumping Iron* films illuminate how these strategies work. In four areas in particular – mise-en-scene; costume and props; development of secondary characters; and framing and camera movements – sexuality is surreptitiously linked with sex and gender in such a way as to support heterosexual and patriarchal ideologies.

The settings of both films consist largely of gyms and competition stages. In addition, the "stars" of each film are interviewed at home, in their hotel rooms, and backstage before the final, climactic contest. *Pumping Iron II* adds something more, however. In two sequences involving groups of women bodybuilders, the beauty of the female body is evoked via lyrical images, even as individual women debate the essence of femininity. The first of these is set in Gold's Gym in California. It opens with a series of shots of women lifting weights. Then the camera moves with the women through the door marked "Ladies Only" into the shower room. There, through lather and steam, naked female bodies are glimpsed. The scene is a fetishist's delight: the camera pans and cuts from torsos to biceps to necks to breasts to heads. The second sequence again involves a group of women and is shot in a pool outside of Caesar's Palace. The camera movements, editing, even the lighting, echo those of the Gold's Gym sequence, only here doubly frozen bodies – the female statues – add to the camera's/spectator's titillation and admiration of muscular but distinctly feminine women's bodies, portrayed as so many water nymphs. In each sequence, the images counteract the threat posed by muscular, active women by placing them in traditionally sexy, feminine environments (showers and pools) and by showing them in stereotypical ways (frozen, fragmented, or both). Needless to say, Bev Francis and Carla Dunlap are not present in either group: they represent alternative possibilities of femininity.

The costumes and props used in both films further align sexuality, nature, and the body. The most striking example of this process occurs in the photo sessions for bodybuilding magazines included in each film. Rachel McLish flexes for the camera, holding dumbbells and wearing feathers, chains, and a tiger suit; Arnold Schwarzenegger "wades" knee deep in women, then plays in the ocean and poses against the sky; Lou Ferrigno, Schwarzenegger's chief competitor, crouches somewhat awkwardly next to a cheetah. While the shots of Rachel add a spice of sadism missing from the shots of the men, all testify to an imbrication of sexuality, sex, gender, and nature.

Pumping Iron II again differs from *Pumping Iron*, however, in its creation of a category of secondary characters, "boyfriends," with no equivalent in the first film. Again and again not only Bev, but also Rachel and Lori Bowen are shown with their men. Lori's fiancé (a male go-go dancer – the object par excellence of a certain, class-linked, heterosexual female desire) even proposes to her in front of the camera. Throughout, the film imperceptibly but inflexibly imposes what Adrienne Rich would call a "compulsory heterosexual orientation" on the female bodybuilders.[20] Only Carla is seen in an all-female environment, accompanied by her mother and sister and without a boyfriend or male trainer. In an interview, she described how she told George Butler she would be seen with her boyfriend, who was married, only if Butler were willing to pay for the divorce costs.[21] In *Pumping Iron*, on the other hand, only Arnold Schwarzenegger is constantly surrounded by women, glorying in his super-masculinity. But these women are nameless and interchangeable bodies, not secondary characters of note.

Figure 1.2 Arnold Schwarzenegger in *Pumping Iron* (White Mountain Productions, 1976). Courtesy of the Kobal Collection.

Finally, the way in which the two films are shot differs radically. As is obvious in the discussion above of the Gold's Gym and Caesar's Palace pool sequences, *Pumping Iron* positions women as fetishized objects of the camera's and spectator's gaze far more than it does men. Except in the case of scenes involving Bev, the camera movements, editing strategies, framing and lighting, resemble those of soft-core pornographic films. It comes as a surprise to learn that the camera person in *Pumping Iron II* is a woman, Dyanna Taylor, best known for a documentary about the first women's team to climb Mount Annapurna. Although in interviews she has said she wanted to capture the excitement of bodybuilding by using lightweight cameras and multiple setups, this has very little impact on how the spectator, and the film, look at near-naked women. Though muscular, breasts and buttocks still appear as tits and ass. Marcia Pally graphically describes the voyeurism of the opening shots as follows:

> Close to the woman's skin, the camera slides along her nude body. It runs down a leg, around the soft, flat stomach, and over the hip bones like a steeplechaser barely acknowledging a shrub. It sweeps

across her back to the nape of her neck, and then to an arm more venous than most. It circles a shapely thigh brushing her body with a motion that is part caress but more a search. It scans her surface and takes note; like the cop in any *policier*, it knows what to remember and what to reveal. The case under investigation is the nature of femininity; the female body lies here in evidence.[22]

The men's bodies in *Pumping Iron* are not filmed in the same way: they are not panned or framed like this, nor is lighting used to the same effect. Because the male body in patriarchal societies is not *acknowledged* to be either mysterious or problematic, it is simply not displayed for the spectator's investigation and consumption to the same extent as the female body. In actuality, however, it is intensely problematic: the threat of castration is everywhere present and everywhere hidden. Repressions of, and allusions to, the precarious status of the male body permeate the visual strategies of *Pumping Iron*. These male bodybuilders are freaks just as Bev Francis is: they are *all* too muscular. Lou Ferrigno's subsequent casting as the Hulk and Arnold Schwarzenegger's success as Conan the Barbarian and the Terminator are not coincidental. Their excessive muscularity has made them oddities and has only increased male anxiety and awareness that, to quote Richard Dyer again, "the penis is not a patch on the phallus."[23] This is why, unlike the emphasis on tits and ass in *Pumping Iron*, the camera never focuses on the bulge in Arnold's or Lou's bikinis or pans their naked bodies in the shower: to look might reveal too much or too little, threatening the tenuous equation established between masculinity, muscularity, and men.

The fear of visible difference joined with the fear of an abolition of visible difference thus make it exceedingly difficult to separate sexuality, sex, and gender in the *Pumping Iron* films and in society as a whole.[24] Although *Pumping Iron II* relies for its dramatic tension on the possibility of a separation between sex and sexuality, the contradictions between and within narrative and image reassure us of the continuation of the status quo: sex, gender, and sexuality are one, indivisible.

A similar politics of conflation operates in the films' representation of race. Yet there are significant differences between the way sex and sexuality, and race and sexuality are linked both in these films and in the society they portray and address. Visible difference based on sex must be determined according to secondary characteristics like muscularity due to the fact that the primary characteristic, ownership or lack of a penis is hidden. Although, or maybe paradoxically *because* it is there in plain sight, racial difference is not incessantly discussed and examined the way sexual difference is. In the Reagan U.S., as opposed to in past or present colonial societies, race is ignored and overlooked, hidden by discourse the way sexual difference is hidden on the body. A significant number of Americans prefer to "export" racial discrimination overseas – to South Africa, for example –

rather than acknowledge it at home. When race is discussed, it is often presented via stereotypes, as it would be in colonial discourse.[25]

The *Pumping Iron* films incorporate both strategies – silencing and stereo-typing – in the relationships they establish among race, body, and power. Neither is about racial difference but, again especially in *Pumping Iron II*, race plays a significant role. In *Pumping Iron* race is not regarded as an issue, even though the Mr Olympia competition takes place in South Africa. Here blacks are simply minor characters of no real importance to either the narrative or the images. In *Pumping Iron II*, however, race is constantly visible in the person of Carla Dunlap, one of the four major women characters and the winner of the Miss Olympia title. Yet the film narrative and images and Carla herself downplay her color, concentrating instead on the issues of sex, sexuality, and the body. Carla stands out less because she is black than because she spearheads the revolt against enforced femininity and because, as mentioned earlier, she is the only woman who is not involved with men.[26] Her articulateness, her sensitivity towards and support of the other women athletes, and her interactions with her mother and sister make her extremely appealing to both feminists and non-feminists. What is interesting is that, despite her autonomy and despite the fact that she is more muscular than many of the other women, she never poses a threat of homo-sexuality the way Bev does because, by comparison with Bev, she still looks and moves like a woman. Carla plainly knows how to apply make-up and how to dress seductively. Because images override narrative, the possibility that she might actually be a lesbian or that she might be the object of lesbian desire is passed over, silenced: only the most visible lesbians are recognized as such, in the film and in society as a whole. If anything, *Pumping Iron II* underlines Carla's grace and femininity: a sequence showing her practicing synchronized swimming – that most graceful of sports, one of the few Olympic events so far open only to women – is inserted, not coincidentally, right after she challenges the judges' authority to define women's bodybuilding according to their ideas of what women should be. Accompanied by melodic, andante piano music she swims, slowly and sensu-ously, in an azure pool. The setting and the sounds could not be more romantic. The dual threat posed by her muscularity and her feminism is contained and displaced by an emphasis on her femininity and sexuality.

But the most ambivalent sequence involving race, sex, and sexuality is Carla's free-form posing routine, performed to Grace Jones' song "Feel Up." The song begins with jungle noises, moves on to a sexy, upbeat message of independence and strength, and ends with jungle noises again. Carla's choreography complements the two moods of the song, passing from mystery and bewilderment to flashy self-confidence to mystery again. Although neither the song nor Carla's routine are racist, the jungle sounds and Carla's seductive posing routine might easily be reabsorbed within the framework of racist images and attitudes that permeate mass media representations of blacks. As Gloria Josephs says, "the very presence of black women shrouded in sexual suggestiveness is loaded in particularly racist ways" because racists conceive of black women as "being intrinsically nothing but sexual."[27] The combination of exoticism, blackness, femininity, and sexuality is also, as Sander L. Gilman points out, reminiscent of Freud's equation of female sexuality and the dark continent.[28]

Given the tensions within the film and within society, the judges' choice of Carla as Miss Olympia can be seen, in Foucauldian terms, as a response by the power apparatus to an urgent need in society.[29] Threatened by the spectre of the abolition of visible difference (muscular women), the male judges consciously and unconsciously affirm their need for visible difference by choosing a woman who still looks like a woman (different) and who is black (different). The judges' decision can be seen as a simultaneous recognition and disavowal of racial difference. This ambivalence, as Homi Bhabha provocatively argues in "The Other Question," links the racial stereotype with the sexual fetish:

> [F]etishism is always a "play" or vacillation between the archaic affirmation of wholeness/similarity – in Freud's terms: "All men have penises"; in ours "All men have the same skin/race/culture" – and the anxiety associated with lack or difference – again, for Freud, "Some do not have penises"; for us "Some do not have the same skin/race/culture." . . . The fetish or stereotype gives access to an "identity" which is predicated as much on mastery and pleasure as it is on anxiety and defence.[30]

Most importantly, however, the "identity" of the fetish or the stereotype masks history. It is synchronic, not diachronic. Edward Said offers another, potentially more historical, version of the ambivalence which characterizes how the racial other (in his analysis, the Oriental other) is seen: "The Orient at large vacillates between the West's contempt for what is familiar and its shivers of delight in – or fear of – novelty."[31]

Here, in the appeal to, and the denial of, history, is the key to how and why *Pumping Iron* and *Pumping Iron II* confront both the threat of sexual and racial difference and the threat of the abolition of sexual and racial difference. The muscular bodies we see, whether black or white, male or female, are all sold to us as new and improved versions of an old product. *Pumping Iron* downplays visible difference in its search for the ultimate meaning of generic "man." The film spectator and the audience at the Mr Olympia competition take it for granted that Arnold Schwarzenegger should and will win the contest: after all, he is the most muscular, most articulate, most virile, and most Aryan man around. *Pumping Iron II* plays up the visible differences of sex and race in its search for the new woman who can still be admired and loved. The title song, heard at the beginning and again at the end, betrays the film's preference for a male-oriented, heterosexual eroticism, especially because the start of the film combines the suggestively seductive lyrics with slow pans of a woman's naked body on a tanning bed: "I am the future/Beyond your dreams . . ./I got the muscles/Future sex/I got the motion/Future sex/I got the body/Future sex/Touch this body/Feel this body." From the start, therefore, it is clear that women bodybuilders will be defined by their feminine sex appeal. The men who profit from the sport of bodybuilding, including director George Butler, know that the future of women's bodybuilding depends on "how well it can be marketed to the general public – on how many women can be made to want to look like . . . Rachel McLish, and, to a lesser degree, on how many men can be made to want to sleep with them."[32]

The strategy behind *Pumping Iron II* is thus a marketing strategy. As a film, it wants to make, package, and sell history, not just watch it. *Pumping Iron II* aspires to be more than the chronicle of a contest, more than a sequel subtitled "The Women." In his eagerness to promote and sell women's bodybuilding, director George Butler staged not only the events leading up to the contest, but also the contest itself. He spent months booking Caesar's Palace and convincing Bev Francis to participate, confident that Caesar's was the last frontier and that Bev would inevitably cross it. As in television coverage of sports events, "the worlds of sport and show business meet upon the ground of stardom and competition" in both *Pumping Iron* films.[33] Unique to these films, however, is the way the spectacle of the competition and the spectacle of the film are merged with the spectacle of the near-naked, and therefore supposedly natural, body.

In the final analysis, because they emphasize and appeal to the body, the *Pumping Iron* films resemble advertising far more than sports documentaries or show business dramas. As Marcia Pally says, watching *Pumping Iron II* is like watching one long Virginia Slims commercial: "You've come a long way, baby."[34] The skillful combination of sex, gender, and sexuality, the silencing or stereotyping of race, and the complete bracketing of class readily recall basic advertising principles. In both films slick images and hip music repetitively say the same thing: there is no history, there is no work, there is only leisure and sex. Both films repress the history of bodybuilding and the largely working-class affiliation of its contestants and audiences, choosing instead to emphasize the body as art, sculpture, and timeless spectacle.[35] Only a few sepia stills of nineteenth-century strong men, glimpsed at the beginning and end of *Pumping Iron*, testify to the popular and fairground origins of the sport. No mention is made in *Pumping Iron II* of early strong women like Mme Minerva, Mme Montagna, the Great Vulcana, or Katie Sandwina, the Lady Hercules. While it is obvious in *Pumping Iron II* that the Miss Olympia competition in many ways resembles striptease shows and beauty contests, no mention is made of the very recent (1970s) history of female bodybuilding contests, where models and strippers posed only to titillate the largely male audiences of the men's competitions.

Today female bodybuilding has moved closer to being a sport. Nonetheless the nagging suspicion remains that the "long way" traveled by the women of *Pumping Iron II* deadends in the chance to be treated, once again, as advertising objects. Now attractive white female as well as male body-builders motivate spectators to buy protein and vitamin supplements, to use certain bodybuilding machines, to join health clubs, and to consume magazines, books and, of course, movies.[36] As always, sales are more impor-tant than sports, and much more important than social commentary. Far from abolishing stereotypes based on visible difference, *Pumping Iron II* and *Pumping Iron* as well, visually position the body as spectacle, then sell it as big business. In both films, the threat of visible difference and the threat of the abolition of visible difference are contained and marketed – as flex appeal.

2

WHEN IS A LESBIAN NOT A LESBIAN?

The lesbian continuum and the mainstream femme film

Figure 2.1   Mariel Hemingway as Chris Cahill in *Personal Best* (Warner Bros, 1982).
Courtesy of the Kobal Collection.

In the early to mid-1980s, a hybrid subgenre of the woman's film and the lesbian drama flourished briefly in the United States and Western Europe: the mainstream femme film.[1] Merging female friendship and lesbian sexuality in a skillful cinematic adaptation of what Adrienne Rich has called the "lesbian continuum," these films managed to be popular with heterosexual and lesbian and gay audiences alike.[2] *Personal Best* (Robert Towne, 1982), *Lianna* (John Sayles, 1983), *Entre Nous* (Diane Kurys, 1983), and *Desert Hearts* (Donna Deitch, 1986) all feature lesbians and straight female characters who, on the whole, are femmes rather than butches. Heterosexuals threatened and/or titillated by lesbianism could reassure themselves that the female characters on the screen were "just friends" and/or find voyeuristic satisfaction in watching two beautiful women together. Lesbians too could take pleasure in looking at, and fantasizing about, female characters they saw as lovers, not just as friends.

In these femme films, three specific strategies are used to foster a diversity of audience responses: (1) making the female lead a femme, which allows both heterosexual and lesbian responses/identifications; (2) focusing on the exchange of female looks that can be variously read as erotic (especially when the looking turns into a love scene) or "just friendly"; and (3) referring ambiguously and allusively to what may or may not be lesbianism and/or lesbian lifestyles. Because the range of reception of the characters' sexuality emerges most clearly in the debates over how to read the love scenes and looks, I discuss this topic in detail. But because it is impossible to appreciate the various ways the femme loves and looks without referring to how she dresses and lives, I frame this section with two shorter sections on character and community.

While reception varied wildly among both lesbians and heterosexuals, it is striking the extent to which there were overlaps as well as differences between gay and straight, alternative and mainstream reception, a phenomenon that can be seen more clearly in this study than in Elizabeth Ellsworth's and Chris Straayer's earlier, groundbreaking, analyses of lesbian and feminist reactions to *Personal Best*, or from Straayer's recent discussion of *Entre Nous*

and *Voyage en douce*.[3] Ellsworth's study of feminist response remains important in that it shows how creative lesbian responses to a film text can be. But
because Ellsworth adopts categories of feminist reception popularized in the
early 1980s, which divided feminists into lesbian feminists, socialist feminists and liberal feminists, she tends to treat lesbian response as both unitary
and empathically different from heterosexual feminist response. Straayer does
a better job bringing out the variations in lesbian and feminist identity and
identification in her first article; in the second she at times argues that there
is "*a* lesbian look of exchange" and "*a* lesbian aesthetics."

I argue, instead, that while we may still find it useful or necessary to insist
on the fact of specifically *lesbian* readings and pleasures, it is imperative that
we recognize that lesbian readings are *readings* not inherent in a text, not
unitary, and not solely oppositional. Examining *Personal Best*, *Lianna*, *Entre
Nous*, and *Desert Hearts* as femme films on a cinematic lesbian continuum permits a better appreciation of this fact, at the same time as it forces an acknow-
ledgment of how widespread assumptions of heterosexuality actually are.

Because Rich treated lesbian sexuality so tentatively in her essay, the idea
of the "lesbian continuum," like other slogans adopted by lesbian and gay
activists in the 1970s and 1980s, was criticized from some quarters as
romantic, desexualizing and, in the final analysis, ahistorical.[4] Nonetheless,
Rich's lyrical evocation of lesbian relationships as the epitome of close female
friendships undeniably influenced 1980s feminist literary and film theory,
focusing attention on female bonding and encouraging redefinitions of both
"woman" and "lesbian." Some feminist critics began to ask questions about
the most visibly different lesbian, the butch, the lesbian who adopts male
clothing and sometimes male mannerisms.[5] Should the lesbian, and particularly the butch, be considered masculine? Or should she instead be thought
of as the ultimate woman, because by looking at and desiring other women
she signals the possibility, even the existence, of an active *female* gaze, a
consciously female voice, and a different, feminine, kind of exchange, outside
the bounds of the phallocentric discourse articulated and promoted by most
classical Hollywood cinema?[6] A few critics, notably Esther Newton, Joan
Nestle, Gayle Rubin, and Judith Butler, have offered still a third interpretation, and argue that to read the butch as either masculine or feminine,
as a man or as the ultimate woman, is in fact to conflate gender and sexuality once again, for both gender identity and sexual preference are at issue
in the butch's masquerade of masculinity.[7]

With the exception of Joan Nestle, however, almost no one has looked
at the femme. But the femme, the lesbian who can pass as straight, who
seems not to be a lesbian, forces us to think and see sexuality and gender,
representation and reception, in other ways. The femme does not cross-
dress. Hers is a masquerade of femininity, not of masculinity. Moreover,
unlike the anxious, self-protective, even aggressive masquerade of femininity
adopted by the heterosexual women intellectuals Joan Riviere studied in

"Womanliness as a Masquerade,"[8] the femme flaunts her femininity in order to make "a visual gift of herself for the woman she loves and for her own pleasure."[9] Although she reserves the right to dress as a boy when she feels the urge, she delights in decking herself out as a girl, and thereby suggests that femininity is neither necessarily heterosexual nor necessarily masochistic.

Admittedly the femme's lesbianism is most visible when she is in the arms of her lover, whereas the butch, as Joan Nestle points out, is "known by [her] appearance."[10] For most observers, the assumption of heterosexuality is so strong that the femme is easily seen as just another woman's friend. But for those who know where, when, and how to look, the femme's sexual preference is as unmistakable as her gender. With the femme, far more than with the butch, then, it is obvious that images can be misleading, and clear that reception and context are key.

There can be no simple answers to the questions posed by the femme or to the debates raised by the lesbian continuum. Nor, and this is crucial for feminist theory, should we expect them. We should not continue to insist that authorial intent and/or textual structures in and of themselves define what is a "woman" or when a "lesbian" is a lesbian. But neither should we argue that viewers control mass media texts, let alone that lesbian and gay readings provide uniquely progressive alternatives where straight readings do not. The profit motives behind the mainstreaming of lesbianism in these films that I am going to discuss are enough to render such black-and-white judgments suspect, for the images of lesbians they present are necessarily air-brushed to appeal to as diverse an audience as possible.

Let us instead acknowledge the diversity of the meanings accorded to friendship and sexuality, sameness and difference, not just between gay and straight communities but also within lesbian communities themselves, for a variety of concrete, historically determined reasons. This study of the differing readings, given the sexuality, not just the gender, of the lead characters of these 1980s mainstream femme films highlights the limitations of discussing masculinity and femininity without reference to homosexuality and heterosexuality. Only if we do so can we begin to understand the complex processes of spectator identification with mass media texts.

A new subgenre: the "femme" film

In the space of four years, four films about lesbianism appeared, all ending happily and all portraying lesbian relationships as sincere and loving. The representations of lesbianism these films offered constituted a major shift. Earlier mainstream art films with lesbian characters had always ended with the disease or death of either or both partners and/or had viewed lesbian relationships as predatory or pornographic.[11] Even the female buddy movies of the 1970s like *Julia*, *Girlfriends*, and *The Turning Point* were generally homophobic.[12]

The production histories and plots of *Personal Best*, *Lianna*, *Entre Nous*, and *Desert Hearts* testify to the interest in, if not always acceptance of, gay and lesbian issues in Hollywood as elsewhere, in the early to mid-1980s, the "pre-AIDS" era. Though only *Personal Best* was a studio production and the other three were independents, they can all be considered mainstream films, in that four were widely distributed and all four were, on the whole, favorably received by mainstream and alternative critics. (*Entre Nous* was even nominated for an Academy Award as best foreign film.)

Like earlier films about lesbians, all four films enjoyed a cult status among lesbian audiences. Now, however, that cult status had a different basis: in the past gossip about stars' and/or directors' sexual preferences helped fuel lesbian and gay "readings against the grain." These four films could be read directly as gay films because all of them deal relatively openly and favorably with homosexuality.[13] *Desert Hearts* already had an advance reputation as a lesbian text because the film was a reworking of Jane Rule's popular 1964 romance novel, *Desert of the Heart*. Indeed, many lesbians helped finance the film because it was based on a book they loved.

The films' plots were crucial to their success with straight audiences as well, although not always for the same reasons. All are love stories, framed within the genre conventions of the woman's film. All therefore focus on crises between individuals rather than social groups. Problems are personal, not economic, and so, necessarily, are solutions. Nevertheless, as the directors' and stars' comments about each film make clear, this emphasis on the personal was intended to guarantee the films' market appeal to lesbian and gay audiences as well as to heterosexual audiences.

Personal Best (1982), first directorial effort by screenwriter Robert Towne (then known for his work on *Shampoo* [Hal Ashby, 1975], *Bonnie and Clyde* [Arthur Penn, 1967] and *Chinatown* [Roman Polanski, 1974]) is about two women pentathletes, Tory Skinner (Patrice Donnelly) and Chris Cahill (Mariel Hemingway) who meet and fall in and, in Chris's case, out of love, while competing for a spot on the U.S. Olympic team. The film offers two crises – sports and romance – for the price of one, but resolves both by having Chris and Tory help each other on to victory as friends, not lovers. By the end of the film, Tory is redefined as asexual and Chris as heterosexual. Despite an early emphasis on the women's affair, Towne and others who worked on the film insisted it was *not* about lesbianism. For Towne, the film was about "two children . . . discovering who they are with their bodies."[14] For actress Patrice Donnelly, Tory was not a lesbian: "I had to believe that I could be attracted to Mariel's character in order to play those scenes, but that doesn't make either me or my character a lesbian. I think Tory may have affairs with men after she gets over Chris."[15] Production publicity further displaced the issue of homosexuality by emphasizing Donnelly's status as an ex-pentathlete and Hemingway's assiduous athletic training for her role.

Lianna (1983), in contrast, explicitly deals with coming out – in fact, it is more unequivocally about coming out than any of the other films, including *Desert Hearts*. Directed and scripted by John Sayles (then known as the screenwriter for *The Howling* [Joe Dante, 1981] and *Alligator* [Lewis Teague, 1980] and as the director of *Return of the Secaucus Seven* [John Sayles, 1980]), the film's focus is clear. But it too places lesbianism in a heterosexual context by having Lianna Massey (Linda Griffiths) reject her marriage to have a lesbian relationship with Ruth Brennan (Jane Hallaren). As in *Personal Best* and *Entre Nous*, the film ends with female friendship rather than sexuality when Lianna loses Ruth to another woman, and her closest female friend comforts her. Unlike Towne, however, Sayles never backed away from calling *Lianna* a lesbian film, although in interviews he generally added that it was also "a film about divorce, about growing up."[16]

Of all four films, *Entre Nous* (1983), originally titled *Coup de Foudre*, is the least overtly lesbian. The change in title in the United States and England from "love at first sight" to "between us" desexualized the film still further, while retaining the suggestion of eroticism/exoticism associated with the French language. As director and screenwriter, Diane Kurys (*Peppermint Soda*, 1977, and *Cocktail Molotov*, 1980) drew on her own mother's life to tell the tale of two women friends in 1950s France, Lena (Isabelle Huppert) and Madeleine (Miou-Miou). The two friends ultimately leave their husbands to raise their children on their own. Whether as friends or as lovers is unclear, however, because the story is told by one of Lena's daughters, a stand-in for Kurys herself. In interviews Kurys insisted on the ambiguity of her mother's relationship, and noted that she had refused to include explicitly lesbian scenes that the film's backers wanted, because they "would narrow or skew her audience and blind viewers to the intensity of the story."[17]

No such ambiguity exists in *Desert Hearts* (1986), the first feature film by Donna Deitch, previously a documentary director. *Desert Hearts* centers on a lesbian romance between Vivian Bell (Helen Shaver), a school teacher seeking a divorce in 1950s Reno, and Cay Rivers (Patricia Charbonneau), an openly and happily lesbian casino "change apron." Although the end of the film does not guarantee that the two will live happily ever after, the last shots of them riding off into the sunset on a train do at least promise more sexuality, not just friendship. Unlike Towne and Kurys, Deitch consciously set out to make a happy and explicitly lesbian movie, although she admitted she also tried to "mainstream" this lesbian story as a film about "people at turning points."[18] The actresses, too, were insistent that their characters were lesbians,[19] although some of the publicity downplayed the lesbian subject matter, billing the film as about "friendship, love, and self-discovery between two women."[20]

But while plot summaries focusing on crises and endings may place these films as a lesbian subgenre within the woman's film, and while directors' and stars' comments may indicate how profitable "mainstreaming" can be, neither can fully account for the multiple ways in which audiences and critics saw these films as about female friendship and/or lesbian sexuality, and they are especially unable to account for lesbian response to the films.

Lovely lesbians

All four films mark their major female characters as feminine in various ways, even when they are also identified as lesbians. Without exception, these "lesbians" can easily pass as straight: they are femmes rather than butches. In contrast to many earlier screen portrayals of lesbians as ugly, undesirable bull dykes, all these women are conventionally attractive. All fit nicely within the current bounds of Hollywood femininity: they are white, middle class, young, nicely dressed, with slim bodies and good complexions. Chris, Lianna, Lena, and Vivian are coded as more "feminine" and even as "heterosexual" because they wear skirts, suits, dresses, and make-up and have long hair. Tory, Ruth, Madeline, and Cay are comparatively more "butch" in that they are more independent, more active, more experienced, and often, though not always, older than their lovers. Nonetheless, no woman ever really looks masculine: all are more femme than they are butch.

Pauline Kael's catty comment that Lena's and Madeleine's friendship in *Entre Nous* "seems to be about their great profiles and an interest in clothes" might be considered equally applicable to all the films.[21] In all four, sexuality is contained within fashionable femininity: the title of the *New Statesman* review of *Entre Nous*, "Chic to Chic," sums them all up quite nicely.[22] For many mainstream critics, the basically feminine attributes of all the female characters made these films all the more easily digestible as fictions about "every woman." So too, the fact that Lena and Madeleine are always surrounded by their children encouraged viewers to see them as "just friends"; in the heterosexist conflation of femininity and motherhood, lesbians cannot be mothers – a misconception Sayles challenges when he has Lianna confront family and friends confidently, if naively, with her lesbianism.[23]

Lesbians, in contrast, drew on their daily negotiations of life in two worlds, one gay, one straight, to make the most of the contradictions and ambiguities in these cinematic images of femininity. Many lesbians, after all, have been or are wives and mothers. With *Desert Hearts*, many lesbians liked the fact that, as one woman in a *Gay Community News* survey put it, "neither woman looks like a truck driver."[24] For others, psychologist Barbara Nichols suggests, the reemergence of femmes in the 1980s represented a welcome change from the oppressively narrow range of dress styles and behaviors tolerated within politically correct lesbian communities in the 1970s.[25] In either case, gay pleasures were at work. To paraphrase Joseph Bristow's analysis of the butch gay man, the femme style "is pleasurable because it achieves sexual contact by negotiating a cultural form . . . that is predicated upon homophobia."[26] Clearly some women in the audience *desired* these screen images of women as women, not as men, or as Chris Straayer bluntly puts it, as "transvestites."[27]

To argue that voyeurism is a uniquely male or a uniquely heterosexual pleasure is to wind up, once again, in the "impasse . . . related to the blind spot of lesbianism." Patricia White argues that feminist film theories that fail to distinguish between gender and sexuality, aim and object choice or to ask questions about fantasy, identification, and power from the diverse points of view of lesbian as well as heterosexual male and female spectators, will inevitably reach this dead end.[28] Neither lesbians nor heterosexual women simply "identified" with these female characters. At times they wove elaborate fantasies around them, searched for subtextual and intertextual clues as to the actresses' and/or directors' sexual preference, and even, as was the case with some of the feminist and lesbian feminist reviews of *Personal Best* that Ellsworth analyzed, imagined alternative conclusions.[29]

Languid love and longing looks

Because these films include languid love scenes and longing looks between women, they encourage, more than most women's films, readings of their "feminine" female characters as lesbians, not just as friends. The femme is most visibly a lesbian when making love with another woman, and thus both gay and straight viewers found that the love scenes in particular subverted the traditional equation of sexuality with heterosexuality. During these love scenes, a space for homosexual desires for, and identification with, characters who openly acknowledge and live their homosexuality emerges in a way that it does not in most Hollywood films.

But the femme's sexuality is often ignored or misjudged, just as the status of female and/or lesbian looks is frequently contested. Because these four femme films are mainstream films that aim to market their message to the widest possible audience, they are often consciously restrained by the conventions of love scenes in the heterosexual woman's film. Lighting is never harsh. The use of close-ups and medium shots shows a distinct preference for the caress, the kiss, and the gaze over anything else. Cunnilingus is, of course, out of the question. Sex, when shown at all, is never rough, and always takes place in relatively tame and traditional places: in bed (*Lianna, Desert Hearts*) or at home in front of the fire (*Personal Best*). And all the films, with the exception of *Desert Hearts*, offer heterosexual as well as lesbian love scenes. The place and duration of these heterosexual love scenes typically serve to shift these cinematic lesbian continuums toward friendship and away from homosexuality.

The films' point of view sequences are similarly ambiguous. For although the films occasionally mock male voyeurism and fetishism of women's bodies, male and female looks alternate in them, with the exception of *Desert Hearts*. Some of the female looks are erotically charged, but many others are not. Since the films are on the whole so discrete, it was up to the critic or the audience member to define these film femmes as either lovers or just friends and decide whether these languid scenes and longing looks were progressive or exploitative. No one pattern of response, whether male or female, straight or gay, mainstream or alternative, stood out.

The case of *Personal Best* illustrates how skilled lesbians can be at raiding basically heterosexual texts for their own purposes, at the same time that it demonstrates how pervasive heterosexual assumptions are, and how much disagreement there is over what constitutes exploitation and voyeurism. The film moves quickly from lesbian to heterosexual sex. The lesbian love scene occurs near the beginning of the film. Shot in a yellow light, it begins with Chris and Tory lying on the floor, sharing a joint and drinking as they watch television news coverage of the day's track events. Until they start to arm wrestle, however, Tory looks at Chris more often than Chris looks at Tory. As they match stares and strain to win, the camera moves in and around them, offering close-ups, then extreme close-ups of their eyes, their lips, their throats, their arms, their wrists. When Tory wins, she tentatively kisses Chris. Both laugh. The scene dissolves to the two, now naked, in a bunk bed. First Chris, then Tory, tickles and massages the other. Finally, Tory kisses Chris again and gets on top of her as Chris hugs Tory and caresses her legs with her foot. A fade leaves in doubt what, if anything, happens next.

This single lesbian love scene is then replaced by several heterosexual love scenes between Chris and Coach Tingloff (Scott Glenn) and Chris and her boyfriend Denny. Throughout the film the sound track attenuates still further the impact of the initial lesbian romance, consistently displacing the sound of female pleasure from lesbian lovemaking to sports exertion. A similar transition from homosexuality to heterosexuality occurs in the film's inscription of female looks: the two women's early amorous glances are first recoded as jealous stares, then supplanted altogether by male looks, usually directed at Chris, not at Tory. Although there are point of view shots throughout the film, the ending leaves no doubt that the film wants to reclaim the more "femmey" of the two women for heterosexuality. The moral of this story is: a lesbian, and especially a femme, is *not* a lesbian when there's a man around.

Because lesbian sex in this film is so restrained, mainstream critics like David Denby and Pauline Kael were able to downplay, even excuse, Chris's and Tory's homosexual relationship, although both acknowledged in passing that there was a lesbian love scene.[30] Lesbian audience members, however, often insisted on the characters' lesbianism and refused to accept the film's heterosexual conclusion as "the end." But lesbian response to both the love sequence and the film's point of view structures was not unified. Many women whistled and cheered through the love scene. As coach Thelma

Catalano put it, Tory's and Chris's encounter displayed "an awesome sensuality up on the screen."[31] Other women disagreed. In interviews they said that they found the lesbian sex insultingly tame, and the tickling inappropriate, commenting, "So that's what they think we do?"[32]

The constant close-ups of women's crotches, asses, thighs, legs, and breasts led many critics in both the mainstream and the alternative press to comment on the film as voyeuristic, even to label it soft core pornography. In Vincent Canby's words, "Robert Towne . . . loves women . . . especially their pelvic regions."[33] Yet a significant number of critics in both the mainstream and the alternative presses did not find the film voyeuristic.

These mixed responses to *Personal Best* are sufficiently varied, I think, to give us pause before we argue with Catalano that a male look is voyeuristic, a lesbian look merely appreciative. The reactions to John Sayles' attempts to promote lesbian relationships and replace male voyeurism with a female gaze in *Lianna* suggest still other complications at work. Here the vehemence of the responses evinces a general discomfort with representations of female and lesbian sexuality, but it also shows a fairly widespread recognition of the need for such representations.

Like *Personal Best*, *Lianna* includes heterosexual as well as homosexual love scenes, but here the love scene between Lianna and her film professor husband is brightly lit and thoroughly devoid of eroticism. He is aroused by her enthusiasm for the psychology course she is taking with Ruth. The single love scene between Lianna and Ruth is far more evocative. It begins with the two women drinking wine and exchanging lesbian fantasies. As in *Personal Best*, as soon as Ruth kisses Lianna, the scene shifts to the bedroom. There close-ups of their silhouetted arms, heads, hands, and bodies are shot through a blue filter and linked by slow dissolves to signal tenderness and romance. Murmured endearments in French, taken from the heterosexual love story, *Hiroshima, mon amour* (Resnais, 1959), convey a soothing

Figure 2.2   Linda Griffiths as Lianna and Jane Halleren as Ruth in *Lianna* (Winwood, 1983). Courtesy of the Kobal Collection.

eroticism.[34] The last overt representation of sexuality comes in a montage sequence near the end of the film. Here heterosexuality and homosexuality are given equal time as, in flashback, Lianna recalls key scenes from her relationship with Ruth while she watches a man and woman dance the story of a heterosexual breakup to Otis Redding's "I've Been Loving You Too Long."

More energy emerges from Sayles' inscriptions of female and lesbian looks than from any of the love scenes. Unlike *Personal Best*, *Lianna* consistently privileges women's looks over men's looks. In one early sequence, Lianna, hiding outside in the bushes, watches her husband make love to one of his female students at a faculty party. She is not particularly jealous – her marriage is already on the rocks. After she becomes involved with Ruth she goes to a lesbian bar where several women look at her and at each other. As Lianna starts to enjoy being in a gay bar, rapid long shots and medium two-shots of women having a good time, dancing, hugging, drinking, and smoking are intercut with extreme close-ups of an unidentified pair of female eyes. Perhaps these eyes belong to Ruth who, smiling, watches Lianna dance with other women, perhaps not. It does not really matter: the rapid editing and upbeat rhythms and feminist lyrics of the disco music intimate that what counts is the exhilaration and sense of solidarity women who love women feel. The next sequence continues to emphasize lesbian looks. As Lianna walks down the street, she turns to look at other women or looks them up and down, and they smile and look back at her. Suddenly, it seems, she sees all women, whether alone, with other women, or with babies, as potential lesbians and possible lovers.

Although Sayles tried to inscribe female and lesbian looks sympathetically and to portray lesbian love scenes in non-titillating ways, *Lianna* met with as much criticism as the far more heterosexist and voyeuristic *Personal Best*. Again, reactions to the love scenes varied, and again, not simply according to the gender, sexual preference or political ideology of the reviewer or the paper. *Gay Community News* liked *Lianna*'s love scenes because they were "realistic"; *New Statesman* lauded the film's "fierce eroticism"; in *Jump Cut* Lisa di Caprio wrote of the film's "absence of any real passion."[35]

Critics disagreed most sharply over how to interpret the female and lesbian looks. *Spare Rib* spoke of Sayles' "embarrassingly voyeuristic sex scene" while the *off our backs'* reviewer called the bar and street scenes "lecherous" and worried that women might be scared off by stereotypes of lesbians as predators.[36] Mandy Merck found the fragmentation of the women's bodies in the love scene objectionable.[37] And Chris Straayer maintained that *Lianna* fostered a traditional objectification of women because it split a lesbian exchange of looks into two uni-directional looks.[38] Yet several other feminist and/or lesbian critics and some mainstream reviewers as well argued that the film *did* inscribe a non-voyeuristic female gaze. Lucy Fischer, for example, maintained that "there are certain scenes in *Lianna* . . . [that] invert the normal paradigm of men looking at women, but . . . do not seem to convey the same sense of voyeurism and control. Rather, they connote woman empowered to gaze in a new way."[39]

The range and intensity of critical debate over Sayles' inscriptions of lesbian looks indicate how thorny a question of female voyeurism is. As with *Personal Best*, many of the lesbian and feminist critics who reviewed the film wanted to posit a lesbian look as different from, and better than, a male look, whether or not they liked the looks in *Lianna*. Often their evaluations of the film's point of view structures depended on whom they saw as the viewers – men, women, lesbians, potential lesbians.

Given the heated debates over female voyeurism and lesbian sexuality, it is perhaps not surprising that reviewers generally preferred *Entre Nous'* more subtle portrayals of lesbian looks and languid love to *Personal Best*'s and *Lianna*'s more overt representations. Shortly after the film begins, we see Lena and her husband exchange looks. She invites him into bed, and they begin to make love. Kurys immediately cuts to a medium close-up of Madeleine on top of her fiancé, kissing him. Later in the film Madeleine has an affair with her former art teacher and sleeps with Lena's husband. In the film's most titillating scene, we see a series of quick medium close-ups of Lena's breasts and legs shot from the point of view of two young soldiers, while she makes love with a third soldier in a train compartment. The explicitly male voyeurism continues when Lena and Madeleine dance a mambo together in a nightclub, while two men again watch, their gaze in close-ups fixed on the women's wriggling "behinds."

But throughout the film traces of lesbian sexuality and unmistakably female point of view shots subvert male control. As Chris Straayer notes, female bonding structures the entire film, from the parallel editing of the early sequences, to the two-shots that frame Lena and Madeleine as a couple, to the female voice overs of each reading letters written by the other.[40] Certain scenes stand out. In one scene, Lena, her head on Madeleine's shoulder, tells her friend, "I feel like kissing you." In another, the two women stand in front of a mirror. Madeleine, wearing only a slip, tells Lena, who is wearing nothing at all, "You have a magnificent body." When Lena confesses she thinks her breasts are too small Madeleine turns, looks at her, and says, "They're adorable. Why do I feel so good with you?"

Nevertheless, because *Entre Nous* only hints at, but never shows, lesbian sexuality, it is small wonder that critical perception of the "love" scenes between Lena and Madeleine was so mixed. Many critics saw Lena and Madeleine as early 1950s feminists rather than as lesbian femmes, substantiating Joan Nestle's charge that the term "lesbian" is often only applied to the butch, while "*feminist* [is] the emotional equivalent of the stereotyped femme, the image that can stand the light of day."[41] In this film female voyeurism was not seen as an issue, because the film pokes fun at a male voyeuristic look without replacing it with an aggressively feminist or lewdly lesbian look. Unlike the characters in *Lianna*, Lena's and Madeleine's looks transgress neither heterosexual norms nor butch boundaries: they look at each other in private, not in public, while discussing their children, their husbands, their lovers, their clothes, and their weight. Their looks pleased everyone by threatening no one.[42]

In *Desert Hearts*, on the other hand, women's looks and lesbian love are expressly associated. There are no heterosexual love scenes at all and virtually no male looks. Instead the film is filled with shots of Cay, Vivian, and other women looking at each other. The heterosexual love songs that Buddy Holly and Patsy Cline croon on the sound track in accompaniment acquire a lesbian dimension as a result, although they also help move the love story safely into the past. For once, however, this film intimates that there has been more than one lesbian love scene: early in the film Vivian discovers a naked woman, obviously Cay's lover, in her bed.

As with the other femme films, *Desert Hearts* contains only one explicit lesbian love scene, but since it occurs three-quarters of the way through the movie, this scene is clearly intended to be climactic. Again, though, as in *Personal Best* and *Lianna*, the caress, the kiss, and the gaze are all that count. In a slow progression of shots moving ever closer, occasionally punctuated by Vivian's sighs and shivers, the two kiss each other on the lips and on the breasts, first one, then the other on top, and, that's it, the scene fades to black.

Critics diverged sharply over the love scene. A reviewer for *Body Politic* wrote that *Desert Hearts* was just "another example of the hygienic American attitude toward sex . . . painfully naive, reactionary, and sentimental."[43] Yet another reviewer in *Gay Community News*, and the critics in *The Advocate* and *off our backs* as well, all raved about *Desert Hearts'* sizzling passion, saying things like "one of the hottest bed romps in recent memory," and "a love scene that could melt an igloo."[44]

Such extreme discrepancies along with overlaps in the critical responses to these film femmes may be related to different viewing histories. In general, lesbian and gay critics and audience members saw these films against a backdrop of earlier screen representations of lesbians, and found them, as a result, more positive and more provocative than most. After all, these film femmes *were* at times naked, and they *did* go to bed together. The films' collective silence on what they did once they got there was accepted, even at times appreciated, because, like many heterosexual women, many lesbians take pleasure in suggestive rather than explicit sex, preferring love and romance over sexuality.[45] As Eleanor Rapping pointed out in *The Guardian*, while "gay male culture has been marked by a sexual openness," – at least pre-AIDS – "lesbian culture has been far less visible or stereotypically 'sex'."[46] At the time these films were released, moreover, lesbian and feminist communities were bitterly divided over what constituted acceptable sex.[47]

Whether gay or straight, men or women, almost all reviewers concentrated on the films' love scenes and what they show or fail to show because the films *do* deviate, however cautiously, from the dominant heterosexual paradigm, and because in all of them except *Lianna* a broader context for the character's lesbianism is missing. Yet for most of the critics surveyed, a little went a long way. Where female looks were concerned, the critical differences over whether these films' point of view structures were voyeuristic had several sources as well. Some reviewers were obviously keenly aware of what Diane Waldman calls "the power of patriarchal representations and patriarchal interpretive strategies to construct male spectators out of all of us."[48] In all cases, critical and audience identification with and/or of these film femmes, their looks, and their love scenes as lesbian was never simply determined by the individual film text. Clearly, then, one cannot speak of *a* female or *a* lesbian look in or at these film femmes. "The" lesbian spectator or "homosexual" identification are just as much imaginary constructs as "the" female spectator or "heterosexual" identification.

Community and consciousness

Except for Lianna and Ruth, all of the female characters in these films interact outside the context of a lesbian community, so lesbian readers and critics had to draw on their own experiences to find or create contextual clues pointing to a particular character's homosexuality. It is no coincidence, therefore, that reviewers in the alternative press often invoked "realism" when deciding whether these film femmes were bona fide lesbians or not. But this by no means meant they agreed in their assessments. Some sided with those mainstream critics who bent over backwards to universalize these lesbian characters' dramas as "for everyone," and some did not.

Of the four films, *Personal Best* is the most extreme in its denial of community and consciousness. With the exception of one anti-gay joke, there are no direct references to homosexuality, even though Tory and Chris live together and are quite openly involved with each other. Chris and Tory themselves never talk about their relationship. Chris is so ashamed about her involvement with a woman that she cannot even tell her boyfriend that she was involved in a lesbian relationship. Chris and Tory encounter no economic or social problems when they openly demonstrate physical affection for each other. By not calling attention to lesbianism as a problem, the film thus makes it easy to see sports, not sexuality, as the key to these women's identity.[49]

Since *Personal Best* so obviously opted for sports over lesbian sexuality, not surprisingly a significant number of mainstream critics described it as a sports film, although many also mentioned in some way that it dealt with homosexuality, perhaps because, as Vito Russo suggests throughout *The Celluloid Closet*, films about gay characters are consumed by straight audiences as being "about" homosexuality. The majority of lesbians and feminists that Chris Straayer surveyed, however, felt the film was *not* about lesbianism at all, but only about sports: although 64 percent had initially gone to the film because they had heard it was about lesbians, 42 percent felt it was about sports after seeing it, and only 10 percent felt it was about lesbianism.[50] Because naming and community were so important to lesbian identity in the 1970s and 1980s, alternative reviewers and lesbian audience members found the absence of a lesbian context a particularly glaring omission.

In contrast, most alternative reviewers agreed that *Lianna* functioned, in the words of *Gay Community News'* critic, as a "perfect collage of coming out scenes" and unequivocally labeled it a lesbian film. By so doing, however, they merely followed the film's own lead: in *Lianna* lesbianism is clearly neither shameful nor silenced. Humorous dialog and delivery signal that the fears about lesbianism voiced by Lianna's family and friends are based on stereotypes. Her daughter, for example, says "like that with their tongues? Ugh!" Her son, trying to be cool, blurts out, "So my old lady's a dyke. Big deal!" And her friend, Sandy, fears lesbianism is "catching." Eventually everyone learns to accept Lianna as a lesbian. The film is structured around a kind of checklist of things-you-do-as-you're-coming-out: going to the library to look up "lesbian" ("See homosexual"); reading *The Well of Loneliness*; checking out the bar scene; telling stories from the past that show you always had lesbian tendencies; looking at women in the street; and having a casual affair to confirm you're really gay.[51]

Most feminist, lesbian feminist, and gay critics felt *Lianna* was limited, however, despite the accuracy of its portrayal of a woman's coming out, because it evaded deeper problems and daily life. Mainstream critics all described *Lianna* as a lesbian film, but several alternative reviewers faulted Sayles for his choice of situations like falling in love, loneliness, and boredom to which anyone, gay or straight, could relate. As *off our backs'* reviewer put it, *Lianna* is "about how homosexuals aren't really all that different . . . [A]bout and not for lesbians."[52]

Entre Nous made it much easier for critics to equate gender and sexuality than *Lianna* did. Lena and Madeleine have no visible sexual contact with each other and make no direct mention of the nature of their love for each other. Lena's husband is the only character who ever explicitly refers to lesbianism, jealously accusing the two women of being dykes.

Most reviewers consequently concluded that the film was more about friendship than sexuality, though only mainstream critics made no mention of its hints at lesbianism. For lesbian reviewers and audiences to say the film is about "friendship," however, means something quite different from what it means for heterosexual reviewers and audiences: in lesbian communities lovers frequently become friends and friends, lovers; indeed, a common passing strategy is to introduce lovers as friends. As a result, whether they called Lena and Madeleine "friends" or "lovers," lesbian audiences and critics invariably claimed *Entre Nous* was a lesbian film.

With *Desert Hearts* there was no need to interpret friends as lovers, for sexuality was in no danger of being swallowed up by friendship. Even though, as in *Entre Nous*, no mention is made of a lesbian community, Cay frequently and proudly refers to her lesbianism. She tells Vivian she does so not "to change the world . . . [but] so it god damn well won't change me." She even refuses the advances of a man at the casino where she works on the grounds that she prefers women. She is so at ease with, even out about, her sexuality that her less sexually successful brother teases her, "Beats me how you get all that traffic without any equipment." Like Lianna and Ruth, Cay and Vivian know no real social or economic hardships. Cay's only real problem is her stepmother, Frances (Audra Lindley), who has difficulty accepting Cay's lifestyle.

For *The Body Politic*'s reviewer, this rift, coupled with what he saw as the "straightforward and conventional" development of the lesbian affair, indicated the "ordinariness" of the relationship.[53] Some reviewers took pleasure in seeing lesbians live openly and happily outside the sometimes confining context of a lesbian community. Others noted with disapproval what Mary Colbert called "the blandness of the social context."[54]

In both mainstream and alternative reviews, *Desert Hearts'* "ordinariness" was often seen as universality, despite the simultaneous recognition that *Desert Hearts* was a film about lesbians. *Newsweek*, for example, described *Desert Hearts* as a film where "homosexuality is not an 'issue' . . . but a fact of life," where *Gay Community News* stressed the film's cross-over potential because of "the universality of falling in love."[55]

But "universality" and "sameness" or "identity" meant different things to different people. For the mainstream press to review a lesbian film as

Figure 2.3   Gwen Welles as Gwen, Patricia Charbonneau as Cay Rivvers, Helen Shaver as Vivian Bell, and Dean Butler as Darrell, in *Desert Hearts* (Desert Heart Productions, 1985). Courtesy of the Kobal Collection.

universal marked a liberal stance, a contestation of the traditional dismissal of lesbianism as "just for lesbians." It did not, however, necessarily entail a questioning of heterosexual privilege or assumptions of identity, rather it merely extended "equal rights." The blurring of friendship and sexuality compounds the problems, making it easy for Pauline Kael, for example, to recommend *Personal Best* as "one of the best dating movies of all time."[56] Because sexuality slid into, and under, gender, lesbians and heterosexual women became, in the final analysis, one and the same. *Christian Century*'s assessment of Kurys as "a major artist . . . [because] she escapes ideology and creates rich, real people about whom we can care" is representative of the denial of lesbianism at work in many mainstream reviews.[57]

The alternative press, however, generally continued to acknowledge difference and, especially, different *readings*, but then claimed "universality" as a kind of strategic move, as in B. Ruby Rich's comment: "*Desert Hearts* is not just a lesbian, but a truly universal film. . . . [B]ut what's really amazing is that [the film] *is* a lesbian heartthrob movie."[58]

Conclusion

Distinctions between mainstream reception and lesbian/gay/feminist reception thus hinged on two issues: (1) whether these film femmes were recognized as different from, as well as similar to, heterosexual women, and (2) whether these film femmes were found to be attractive *as* lesbians, that is, whether lesbianism and, more generally, female desire, became for once, not just possible, but realized.

Context, then, was key to assessments of the political implications and impact of the film femme and the cinematic lesbian continuum. But defining "context" is no simple matter. Both mainstream and alternative critics split, after all, over whether these films merely reinscribed a male voyeurism when they displayed attractive women, or whether they managed to articulate a non-voyeuristic and/or lesbian look. In most cases, because these films valued romance over sexuality and downplayed references to community and consciousness, following the conventions of the woman's film, the burden of deciding whether these film femmes were friends or lovers fell on the individual audience member.

But the fact that all these films, not just *Desert Hearts*, were and are lesbian cult movies sometimes added a consciously communal dimension to spectatorship missing from most filmgoing experiences. Where there were significant numbers of lesbians in the audience, as there often were, the "universal," "normal" heterosexual public space of most movie theaters was temporarily redefined as an extension of lesbian community space. Lesbians met other lesbians, and even, according to one critic in *Gay Community News*, exchanged phone numbers. They subverted and supplemented the narratives of all four films, vocally and as a group, demonstrating preferences for one character over another through catcalls and whistles, correcting what were considered to be inappropriate heterosexual responses.[59] For once, the presence of lesbian looks and desires – in the audience, if not the text – and the eagerness of lesbian audiences to look at and see themselves in movies were hard to ignore.

There was, however, no *one* way to evaluate the film femme and the cinematic lesbian continuum. Thus, I would argue, for feminist film theory to militate on behalf of an imaginary lesbian reader who, like father, always knows best, would be to ignore the diversity, variability, and tenuousness of the necessary identities and identifications that structure viewing and other social practices. We need to recognize just how much the invisibility and fluidity of gayness, in Richard Dyer's words, are "unsettling to the rigidity of social categorization and to the maintenance of heterosexual hegemony," for all of us.[60] If we overlook the questions posed by lesbians, whether or not butches or femmes, we confront, once again, the binary oppositions of heterosexual masculinity and femininity where "woman," formulated as the sole foundational category of feminist analysis, "effects a political closure on the kinds of experiences articulable as part of a feminist discourse."[61]

This is not, however, to argue that "lesbian," "butch," or "femme" replace "woman." "Coming out" and identity politics in general are often useful, even necessary, as strategies but they are also problematic, for several reasons: they presume a stable identity; they focus on sexual preference to the exclusion of economic, racial, and social differences; they ignore the fact that living one's life around one's sexual orientation is a very recent and culturally limited phenomenon; and they assume that, as Jeff Minson puts it, "speaking one's identity is the most appropriate form of knowing it."[62] Nor are there any guarantees that the femme's or the butch's masquerades of femininity and masculinity will be perceived as masquerades outside lesbian and gay communities. "Subversiveness," as Andrew Britton rightly says, "needs to be assessed not in terms of a quality which is supposedly proper to a phenomenon, but as a relationship between a phenomenon and its context – that is, dynamically."[63]

What we need is a more flexible approach to the implications of how we locate and define ourselves and others on the lesbian continuum. Arguments that lesbians and straight women are the same and that lesbian sexuality and female friendship are equivalent often minimize lesbian visibility, and reduce romantic and sexual possibilities for both lesbians and straight women. Because these films present such a standardized and homogenized view of lesbianism, the danger that difference will be denied through a relatively asexual definition of lesbian love is even greater in the cinematic lesbian continuum of the 1980s than it was in Rich's original concept.

Nonetheless, it is sometimes polemically useful to maintain that lesbians are the same as, or similar to, straight women, and that lesbian sexuality is equivalent to, or another form of, female bonding and friendship.

Unfortunately, we still need to increase lesbian visibility and to criticize the categories "feminine" and "woman." As Angela Partington says, "The 'feminine' is *not* in itself *bad*. . . . [U]nder certain circumstances, in certain contexts, the celebration of femininity is a highly appropriate and useful strategy."[64] And, of course, among femmes and butches, there can be no doubt that joyous masquerades of femininity are savored to the fullest.

The range of audience reactions demonstrates how much the meanings attributed to sameness and difference, friendship and sexuality, differ between and even within communities. This range highlights why, as feminist activists, critics, and theorists, we cannot afford to lose sight of variations in class, race, and sexuality when analyzing gender. Especially now, when a woman's right to abortion is placed on the same footing as a fetus's right to life, and when AIDS is taken as proof of gay men's damnable difference, it is imperative that we realize that the task of specifying what historian Joan Scott calls "the contingent and specific nature of our political claims"[65] is *not* just an academic exercise.

NOUVEAUX WESTERNS FOR THE 1990S

Genre offshoots, audience reroutes

Figure 3.1   Antonio Banderas as El Mariachi in *Desperado* (Columbia Pictures, 1995). Courtesy of the Kobal Collection.

Introductory round-up

Pronounced dead twice in the last quarter century – first in the early 1970s with shifts in Hollywood organization, then again in 1980 after the box office bust of *Heaven's Gate* (Michael Cimino) – the western seemed the most impossible of Hollywood genres.[1] The 1990s witnessed a mini-renaissance triggered by the success of *Pale Rider* (Clint Eastwood, 1985), *Silverado* (Lawrence Kasdan, 1985), and *Young Guns* (Christopher Cain, 1988): more than three times as many westerns were released in the 1990s as in the 1970s and 1980s combined. More importantly for marketing departments, a few – *Dances with Wolves* (Kevin Costner, 1990), *Last of the Mohicans* (Michael Mann, 1992), and *Unforgiven* (Clint Eastwood, 1994) – have done well at the box office.

Such numbers are nevertheless small: as Richard Slotkin says, "the terms of [western] cultural presence have drastically altered." Today the genre is "relegated to the margins of the 'genre map'."[2] A homespun example: a "round-up" of westerns in the biggest and "best" video store in Knoxville (28,000 titles; many foreign and older films) corralled only 100 tapes, huddled together on a single "western" aisle. Yet careful scouting uncovered additional titles lurking in the many action aisles. And of course, as Anne Thompson argues, U.S. audiences "know plenty of western plots and motifs from TV and from countless action movies . . . that have assimilated them."[3]

This chapter zeroes in on 1990s western influence and "retro-*activity*," arguing that most recent productions are not "new" but rather "nouveau," a designer repackaging of earlier western retro-strategies. Like "classic" westerns set "from about 1865 to 1890 or so,"[4] today's films repeat plots and reprise fictional and/or historical characters, often literally via "bio-pics."[5] They also reformat earlier subjects for emerging (previously often "impossible") markets, via fresh (before sometimes "unthinkable") genre mixes.

To examine the sociological and economic factors that underpin and shape nouveau western ideology I target five films: *Posse* (Mario van Peebles, 1993),

The Quick and the Dead (Sam Raimi, 1995), *Last Man Standing* (Walter Hill, 1996), *Desperado* (Robert Rodríguez, 1995), and *John Carpenter's Escape from L.A.* (John Carpenter, 1996).[6] That the five seem anomalous is in part the point, because a closer look reveals striking similarities: (1) the lead actors all transform themselves into young Clint Eastwood clones; (2) the films are otherwise influenced by Sergio Leone's spaghetti westerns as well.

Who better than Clint to take as a model for western resurrection? Think of all the times *his* characters have returned from the dead! Talk about "impossible!" All five of the films, moreover, are nouveaux westerns because they blaze promotional trails via genre offshoots and audience "reroutes." All are made by known directors, if not necessarily by "A list" directors, most of whom have no experience of making a western.[7] All include recognizable but not western stars, many of whom participated in producing and/or scripting the films.[8] Aging western actors appear in secondary roles or bit parts.[9] Verbal and visual allusions to earlier films, not just Leone's westerns, are ubiquitous. All five increase the amount of screen time accorded spectacular violence and often feature special effects and rapid editing. Tightly bound up with such explosions of blood and guts are the impossibly built, quasi-"buff" bodies of the stars, sculpted by breeches and buckskins, rippling under shirts or below necklines.

Since each film employs different tactics to recruit jaded and/or juvenile audiences and remap genre territories I treat each separately, emphasizing the lead actors' performances as Clint clones. The overall title for the next section is "Role call"; the homonym "roll" hopefully suggests how much today's westerns owe to action and martial arts films. Following a historical trajectory suggested by the narratives, I begin with *Posse* and *The Quick and the Dead* (both primarily set during the "Old West"), cruise on to *Last Man Standing* (the 1930s), burst into *Desperado* (the present) and terminate with *Escape from L.A.* (the first intertitle reads: "2013: NOW").

The conclusion returns to the general questions about 1990s western impossibility and retro-*activity* set forth in this introductory "round-up," studying how nouveaux westerns interact with earlier films. The title, "Final tally: missing in action," gestures toward exchanges with war and action movies, and signals that, despite 1990s script alterations, casting innovations, and marketing modulations, certain groups and topics remain impossible in today's "shoot 'em ups."

Role call

Cowboy 'n' the Hood: Posse

People forget their past, and they forget the truth, but the pictures don't lie . . . [P]eople forget that almost one out of every three cowboys was black, 'cuz when the slaves was freed, a lot of 'em

Figure 3.2 Stephen Baldwin as Jimmy J. Teeters, Big Daddy Kane as Father Time, Mario van Peebles as Jesse Lee, Tiny Lister as Obobo, Charles Lane as Weezie, and Tone Loc as Angel in *Posse* (Universal Pictures, 1993). Courtesy of the Kobal Collection.

headed out west, built their own towns. . . . Over half of the original settlers of Los Angeles were black. But for some reason, we never hear their stories.

Posse opens with a monolog about invisibility ("impossibility") delivered by aging western sidekick Woody Strode.[10] Photographs of African American cowboys ranged on the desk behind him support his claims. The stills become moving pictures, and a tale of black buddies looking for good times and gold, romance and revenge, begins. Van Peebles' film adds a white "token" cowboy (Stephen Baldwin); other nouveaux westerns – *Silverado*, *Tombstone*, *Unforgiven*, *Young Guns*, and *Young Guns II* (Geoff Murphy, 1990) – foreground racial mixes but remain predominantly white. Primarily set during Reconstruction, *Posse* nonetheless exceeds classical western spaces and times: the main narrative begins in 1898 Cuba; the film ends with a present day coda where Strode reappears.

As director and star, Mario van Peebles fashions hero "Jesse Lee" on several Eastwood characters, mixing spaghetti westerns with *Two Mules for Sister Sara* (Don Siegel, 1970), *High Plains Drifter* (Clint Eastwood, 1973), *Pale Rider*, and *Heartbreak Ridge* (Clint Eastwood, 1986). At one point, a character surprised to see Jesse Lee comments, "I thought you were dead." Jesse Lee tersely replies, "So did I." Like the young Clint, van Peebles combines grace and agility, in the final shoot-out leaping onto his horse, dynamite in mouth, and loading gold bullets into his big gun as he gallops. He taunts his white nemesis: "When you get there, tell 'em Jesse Lee sent you. . . . We all gotta go to hell someday."

But van Peebles' avenging angel utilizes swords as well as guns, whips, knives, dynamite, and fists: Clint has never, to my knowledge, parried and thrust with a blade.[11] Van Peebles is also more narcissistic than Eastwood ever was, reflecting 1980s and 1990s absorption with "built" male bodies.[12] During the first half of the film especially, the camera lingers on Jesse Lee. At one point, he pauses in a doorway, sleeve torn, shirt open to the waist, oiled muscles bulging. At another, naked save for his black hat, he looks lazily on as his merry band of naked men frolic in a river and joke about penis size. During the second half of the film, a beautiful girlfriend named Lana (Salli Richardson) affords Jesse Lee "better" reasons to take off his clothes.

Certainly, Lana's capture by evil whites fuels Jesse Lee's drive to avenge his father's murder and save the beleaguered black settlers of Freemanville. The combination of motives suggests how many genres – swashbucklers, romances, action, war films – *Posse* drapes over van Peebles' shapely shoulders. The opening sequences look and sound like *Heartbreak Ridge* (where van Peebles co-starred with Clint), ensuring that *Posse* replays Vietnam worries about victory and loss, if from a critical, Black, perspective.[13] More obliquely, *Posse* recalls van Peebles' roles in "hood" films like *New Jack City* (Mario van Peebles, 1991). Sidney Poitier's *Buck and the Preacher* (1970) is a major influence: *Posse* repeats *Buck*'s emphases on black pioneers and settlements; its designation of white capitalists as villains; its insistence on alliances with Native Americans.[14]

Like Poitier, van Peebles casts prominent black cultural figures: here father-director-actor Melvin van Peebles, director-actors Charles Lane and the Hudlin brothers, actors Pam Grier and Blair Underwood, actor-singer Isaac Hayes, wrestling champ Tiny Lister Jr, blues artist Vesta Williams, crooner Aaron Neville, hip hop idol Tone Loc, and reigning rap star-sex god Big Daddy Kane. The film also alludes to issues that resonate with African American communities, among them the L.A. riots, attacks on black churches, the importance of schools. Recasting western conventions, black male generational continuity is stressed.[15]

Yet *Posse* also strives to please cross-over publics via multiple genre references, a lively sound track, a white sidekick, a black villain (Underwood), and Native American allies. The only black western to achieve widespread release,[16] *Posse* is thus multiply retro-*active*, grounded in earlier white westerns but incorporating elements from black counter-westerns as well.[17]

Lady in Limbo: The Quick and the Dead

SCARS: "I need a woman."
THE LADY: "You need a bath."

The Quick and the Dead manifests a similar nostalgia for classic westerns. But because Sharon Stone is so obviously a white woman, her campy performance as a young Clint clone demonstrates more clearly than do van Peebles' star turns how much most nouveaux westerns utilize ethnic and racial differ-

Figure 3.3   Sharon Stone as the Lady in *The Quick and the Dead* (Tri-Star Pictures, 1995). Courtesy of the Kobal Collection.

ences at best as marketing ploys while venerating *machismo*. Newly arrived in town, Ellen (Stone) makes short shrift of the leering, one-eyed ex-con who tries to force himself on her after killing a man – his fifteenth – and notching his arm instead of his gun. Shortly afterwards, she demonstrates that she can place a bullet as precisely as a barb. As the Lady, Stone's line readings are slow and deliberate, her movements controlled and cat-like. Coolly surveying the action from the sidelines, chomping on an unlit cigarillo, grimacing from under a broad-brimmed black cowboy hat, she nails Clint's ready-for-anything poise in repose. Yet tight buckskins and plunging necklines leave no doubt that she is endowed with boobs, not balls.

Raimi's film playfully reprises several spaghetti western elements. The opening repeats the Man with No Name's entrance into town past a row of coffins; that the undertaker (Woody Strode in his last performance) sizes up a woman's measurements merely provides a different erotic kick. The final sequence similarly showcases her miraculous reappearance, phenomenal gunplay, and casual departure. Throughout, music serves as punctuation, not accompaniment. *Quick*'s scenario is more tautly constructed than *Posse*'s, but it too incorporates flashbacks and fuses genres. Actors familiar from previous westerns (Gene Hackman as the evil mayor, Herrod; Pat Hingle as the bartender) have substantial parts. Other westerns – *High Noon* (Fred Zinnemann, 1952), *The Wild Bunch* (Sam Peckinpah, 1969), *Once Upon a Time in the West* (Sergio Leone, 1968) – are constantly cited. The main plot centers on competition for money and survival; subplots suggest Oedipal rivalries. Gunfighters include a white card shark, a Swede, a hillbilly, a Native American, and an African American; the townspeople are primarily Anglos, although some Mexicans appear on the sidelines.

Spectacle is key: Raimi's films are known for virtuoso camera movements, inventive special effects, and rapid editing. Horror elements like canted angles, unexpected inserts, and ghoulish costuming creep in to darken western skies. Claustrophobia is pervasive, thanks to dim interiors (the bar, Herrod's private dining room), fractured exteriors (the dusty central street and main plaza), and extreme close-ups on body parts, especially eyes. Though *Fistful of Dollars* also emphasizes vision, most famously via shots of Clint's eyes looking out from a coffin where he hides, the effect is quite different. There his omnipotence is underlined; here, accent is on uncertainty.

Surprisingly, Herrod's ex-lieutenant turned wanna-be Preacher, Cort (Russell Crowe), gets most physical abuse. Herrod also treats the Kid (Leonardo di Caprio) very badly: when the Kid defies the mayor's authority, Herrod coldly kills him, then denies that the Kid is his son. As Clint clone and horror heroine, Stone should be the prime target for torture. Yet, as if in deference to her gender, the Lady remains untouched.[18] As in *Posse*, the narrative and visuals insist on heterosexual relationships. Exchanges of looks between Ellen and Cort repeatedly mark them as partners. Ellen's costuming is carefully designed to attract attention: when the Kid rouses her from sleep, she is clad only in boots and a nightshirt tantalizingly positioned just above her crotch.[19] Later she dons a décolleté red dress and black lace gloves to dine with Herrod, pinning up her usually tousled hair so that only a few tendrils tumble onto her bare shoulders. "Naturally" she finds herself unable to fire the little pearl revolver she carries in her handbag.

Just before the final shoot-out we learn through a flashback why she has come to Redemption in search of revenge: when she was young, Herrod forced her to fire at the rope hanging her innocent sheriff-father. Never having shot a pistol, she missed and hit her dad. As an adult, will her gender continue to corset her courage? Hair tightly braided, body hidden under buckskins, the Lady does ultimately blow Herrod away, but power and activity remain linked to male bodies. In a parting gesture, Ellen tosses her father's badge to Cort, ensuring male inheritance of power and position.

Marketed as a seductively revisionist girl western,[20] Stone's kittenish pastiche of Clint's macho prowess is not really intended to be a gender-based corrective to the western. On the contrary, the roles accorded other female characters as white prostitutes and Mexican mothers make clear the film's attachment to macho, racist, codes.[21] Not surprisingly, then, *The Quick and the Dead* was rarely received as a feminist western by mainstream critics, although several admired Stone's acting and the film's energy.[22]

Desperado Dud/e: Last Man Standing

> I was coming through Texas on my way to Mexico. . . . I spent
> most of my life on the dodge. . . . For the most part I was a big
> city guy. . . . I figured this little burg was just the kind of place
> you gassed up the car and got something to eat. . . . Then I got a
> look at her, and that's when all the fun started.

Last Man Standing's macho intentions were more widely, if derisively, recognized by critics, many of whom labeled it the "worst film of the year." Walter
Hill's revision of *Fistful of Dollars* drags the nouveau western into the twentieth century, restaging western gunfights as bootleg battles fought in west
Texas by Italian and Irish mobsters. Bruce Willis's opening voice over about
a woman who turns out to be Trouble is pure film noir. He is first seen from
behind, drinking whiskey from a flask, his face shaded by a fedora. As he
drives into town, he passes a dead horse, covered by flies, much as Clint did
in *Fistful of Dollars*. From then on, however, only dust, an occasional twangy
guitar riff in Ry Cooder's score, and the appearance of Bruce Dern as the
corrupt sheriff signal "western-ness."[23] Save for the Yaqui Indian "moll,"
Felina (Karina Lombard), who provokes the "fun," the faces we see are white,
and the thugs who accost Willis wave machine guns, not rifles.

Offhand quotes from other films, so common in *Posse* and *The Quick and
the Dead*, are rarely found here. Most importantly, the short, stocky Willis
is an unlikely western hero, more reminiscent of the cocky Jimmy Cagney
than of the rangy Eastwood, even though Willis occasionally clenches one
eye in a Clint-like squint. Yet *Last Man Standing* faithfully reprises core
elements from *Fistful of Dollars'* plot. Like Clint's "Joe," Willis's "John
Smith" shuttles back and forth between rival "families" led by Strazzi (Ned
Eisenberg) and Doyle (David Patrick Kelly). The two are flanked by cousin
Giorgio (Michael Imperioli) and the ominous Hickey (Christopher Walken),
respectively. Strazzi falls for dumb Polish blondes like Lucy (Alexandra
Powers), brought from "Chicago" "to keep up his morale"; Doyle prefers
devout brunettes like Felina. Smith has a weakness for any and all dames:
indeed, the sheriff warns him that, "When you go down, it's gonna be over
a skirt." But even when Willis takes his clothes off – and he does so much
more frequently than Clint ever did – he always keeps his cool. Already in
the second scene we see him wanking away on a prostitute named Wanda
(Leslie Mann). Suddenly he rolls off her, grabs two guns, and kills two of
Doyle's men who are sneaking up on him.

Per gangster tradition dictating that women are to be at best protected,
more often collected, most frequently rejected, Willis ends up without a
woman, though at least he *is* standing at the end of the film. Given the
amount of torture he undergoes, this is a feat, but then he is obviously a
very tough guy, capable, he confesses, even of not drinking for two days

when push comes to shove. Violence is ubiquitous: bullets zoom and bodies crumple or fly in most scenes. A high point for action buffs comes when Smith escapes from a freezer room where he has hidden. One eye swollen shut, several ribs broken after being kicked, punched, and stomped, he mumbles, as ever off screen: "But all I needed was a gun and some time to heal."

The gang members and leaders are neither as lucky nor as macho. Strazzi's gang is barbecued to death, their ranch house torched by Doyle's mobsters. For several minutes, carefully superimposed layers of writhing, flaming bodies fill the screen. Willis watches, then helped by the sheriff, he and a half wit bartender named Joe (William Sanderson) take refuge in a burnt-out roadhouse. At dawn, Doyle, Hickey, and a third cohort pull up. Joe shoots the third man, Willis downs Doyle, and Hickey fakes a surrender because he "doesn't want to die in Texas, maybe Chicago." Willis terminates him, too.

Although macho protocol demands that *the* "best" man win, *two* men are thus left standing at film's end: the star-oriented focus of the title masks the actual finale. Unlike *Posse*'s insistence on justice, education, and representation, unlike even *The Quick and the Dead*'s fleeting explorations of violence against women, moreover, *Last Man Standing* is unconcerned with moral or political issues: alcoholic that he is, Smith has no real objections to bootlegging, and his salvation of Felina has nothing to do with inter-racial solidarity.

Border Brujo: Desperado

BUSCEMI: "And in walks the biggest Mexican I've ever seen. Big as shit. Just walks in like he owns the place. No one knew quite what to make of him, or quite what to think. But there he was . . . and in he walked."

FLASHBACK: Stranger (Mariachi) rises from the ground surrounded by angry scum and he levels what appears to be the BIGGEST FIREARM you've ever seen. It spits blinding FIRE so fast you can't get a good look at it, nor the damage it does as BODIES FLY about the room, crashing into this and that. KNIVES FLASH and get BURIED in the wrong chests, BULLETS FLY and take out the wrong men. The place is a mad house and in the middle of it is the faceless stranger doing unspeakably impressive acts of violence, too fast for the human eye to register, but enough to make you wonder if he's the devil himself . . . and where'd he learn all those tricks?[24]

In contrast, Richard Rodríguez' *Desperado* puts Latino actors, singers, and musicians center stage and references Latino customs and concerns. Yet as a studio picture with a sizeable budget (almost $7 million), *Desperado* pointedly targets mixed audiences. In this remake *cum* sequel of Rodríguez' first film, *El Mariachi* (1993), Antonio Banderas replaces Rodríguez' childhood friend, Carlos Gallardo, as the Mariachi, a Latin lover and border *brujo* (sorcerer). Set in contemporary Mexico, the film ups the action ante considerably. A key sequence revolves around a duel in the dust fought with grenades and rocket launchers.

Steve Buscemi's introductory story (screenplay quoted above) nonetheless reiterates western concerns with history and myth. Glowering out from under long, greasy, hair that renders any hat superfluous, face shadowed to highlight lowering brows, "only Clint looks as good on a poster," wrote Amy Taubin of marketing that intentionally evoked spaghetti western publicity.[25] Shot in Mexico, in what Taubin calls "sun bleached and burnished" colors ("weathered greens, dirt browns, dried-blood reds"),[26] the film limits "western" sounds to jingling spurs. The story is tangentially indebted to *Fistful of Dollars*: there are two rival drug lords, one the Mexican Bucho (Joaquim de Almeida), the other an unseen Colombian represented by a knife-throwing henchman.

Like *Posse* and *The Quick and the Dead*, *Desperado* draws on many Eastwood films, including *Pale Rider*, *High Plains Drifter*, and *Two Mules for Sister Sara*. In passing it refers to other Westerns as well, among them *Once Upon a Time in the West*, *The Magnificent Seven* (John Sturges, 1960), and *The Outlaw* (Howard Hughes, 1943). Like many of Clint's characters, the Mariachi is an other-worldly presence returned somehow "from the dead." The teasing relationship between Salma Hayek and Banderas owes most to *Two Mules for Sister Sara*: Hayek's torturous tending of the wounded Banderas (she blithely pours alcohol on him after removing a bullet, then cauterizes her "surgery" with her cigarette) reprises Shirley Maclaine's earlier salvation of Clint (she cheerfully pounded a poisoned arrow through his shoulder). In every action scene, as Banderas shoots, his mouth promises more: lips push forward and round into a provocative "o." Unlike Willis, he shifts easily from smoldering romance to wry comedy to incendiary action. Stretched out on a table, one leg dangling, seemingly asleep after Carolina's "operation," he suddenly bolts upright. He looks particularly appealing when vulnerable, stumbling gracefully down a street despite the multiple knives piercing his back, for example.

Desperado relies most heavily on *El Mariachi*, however,[27] in turn based primarily on action films like *Road Warrior* (George Miller, 1981) and John Woo's martial arts films.[28] With the infusion of Hollywood capital and attendant cross-marketing demands, the "*rascuachismo*" (the ironic use of found, often kitsch, objects and family members to evoke Chicano life and empower Chicano culture) of the original disappears.[29] Instead *Desperado*'s action sequences become literally explosive: so many thugs die that during filming "killed to date, to be killed today, yet to be killed" lists had to be consulted.[30] More screen time is also devoted to the love affair. Opposite Banderas, Hayek matches his charm and poise, though her part often devolves into spectacle. Sporting uneven hemlines, bare midriffs, revealing necklines, and spike heels, she literally stops traffic in one sequence. Bucho's girlfriend (Angel Aviles) is likewise a spitfire.

Obviously Rodríguez does not question *machismo*, but his casting of two Latin leads is exceptional for Hollywood, as is his awarding of prize roles to Latino actors, among them Cheech Marin as the scuzzy bartender. The crew, too, is predominantly Latino. In response to pressure from studio executives, *Desperado* designates Bucho, a Latin American, as chief villain; *El Mariachi* made Moco (the name means "snot") an American because, Rodríguez says, "I didn't want the character to be Mexican; there's enough bad guy Mexicans in movies."[31] In the final sequence, Bucho is revealed to be the Mariachi's brother.

That *Desperado* was made is a tribute to Rodríguez' talent, technical wizardry, and hard work. He was virtually a one-man crew on *El Mariachi* (he claims the film cost $7,000); here he wrote the screenplay, directed, served as steadicam operator and assisted with editing. Marketed to both Latino and cross-over audiences, *Desperado* did well at the box office and became a cult hit on video. The sound track, an energetic mix of Tejano/Latin rock and ballads performed by some of the most popular L.A. and Texas bands (Tito and the Tarantulas, the Latin Playboys, Los Lobos, Link Wray, Roger and the Gypsies) helped guarantee success. Critics were divided: some found the film boring and unnecessarily gory; some relished its playfulness ("bloody good fun," wrote *Time Out*'s Geoff Andrew).[32]

American Spirit: Escape from L.A.

Snake Plissken is cornered in a debris-filled alley. A half dozen Latino gang members close in on him. Slowly Snake reaches down and picks up an empty coffee can.

SNAKE: "What do you say we play a little Bangkok roulette? Nobody draws until this hits the ground. You ready?"

Cautiously the gang backs away. Snake tosses the can high into the air. Before anyone pulls his gun, before the can hits the ground, he draws two huge pistols and fires, killing everyone.

The can hits the ground.

SNAKE: "Draw."

More typically John Carpenter's *Escape from L.A.* includes Latinos and Latin Americans in secondary and bit parts. Like *Desperado* both a sequel and a

Figure 3.4   Kurt Russell as Snake Plissken in John Carpenter's *Escape from L.A.* (Paramount Pictures, 1996). Courtesy of the Kobal Collection.

remake, it moves the western into a science fiction-horror future, while returning to Clint's original portrayal of the Man with No Name as a macho loner, not a lover. The above sequence is carefully calibrated on the Man with No Name's initial face off with the Baxter family. Snake (Kurt Russell) is a modern-day gunslinger who ends up fighting on the side of justice. His outfit – black leather pants, long coat, huge guns – recalls Clint's later westerns. Russell's breathless delivery of terse one-liners is obviously modeled on Eastwood's characters: "Call me Snake"; "I used to be a gunfighter."[33] Such self-deprecation is, of course, designed to fake out enemies who threaten "you may have survived Cleveland, you may have escaped from New York, but this is L.A., *vato*, and you're about to find out that this fuckin' city can kill anybody!"

Carpenter maintains that all of his films are "really westerns underneath." He readily admits to being influenced by Leone but cites several genres (including martial arts films), and directors (first and foremost Howard Hawks) as important to his filmmaking.[34] Co-screenwriter and co-producer Russell is similarly known for his work in a range of genres; *Escape from L.A.* is his fifth film with Carpenter.[35] Not surprisingly, then, *Escape from L.A.* mixes genres and contemporary critiques with abandon. Set in 2013, post the L.A. earthquake and tidal wave of the year 2000, a right-wing theocracy headed by a former televangelist (Cliff Robertson) is poised to take over the world. As the film begins, Snake is infected with the (supposedly) lethal virus "Plutoxin 7." To receive the antidote in time, he has 24 hours to bring back a nuclear black box that the President's daughter Utopia (A. J. Langer) stole when she ran away to live with Cuervo Jones (George Corraface). L.A. is the last zone of free thought, free love, and free enterprise in the U.S., home to hustlers like Map to the Stars Eddie (Steve Buscemi), surfer-bikers like Pipeline (Peter Fonda), Latino, Korean and African gangs, and white actors (look-alikes for Bette Davis, Karen Black, and more) kept alive by repeated plastic surgeries.

References to other movies abound,[36] but Carpenter's devotion to horror in particular emerges in his concern for framing and editing. Focus shifts complicate identification of characters at the back or sides of the frame, heightening a sense of eeriness: the sequence featuring Bruce Campbell (of *Evil Dead* series fame) as the fiendish plastic surgeon who carves up street people to refurbish decaying actors is a good example. The science fiction narrative facilitates references to contemporary obsessions and fears, including lethal viruses, miscegenation, illegal immigration, terrorism, evangelical religions, electronic surveillance, alien invasion, and nuclear disaster. At one point Snake is chained to a fitness machine, condemned to work out; at another he encounters an mtf transsexual named Hershe (Pam Grier, her voice altered to resemble a man's) he had known in Cleveland as Carjack Mallone. Sets feature semi-destroyed landmarks like the L.A. freeways (half-standing), Sunset Boulevard (covered with rubble), Universal Studios (under water), the Santa Anas and Hollywood (in flames). The special effects generally look tacky, however, making *Escape from L.A.* more camp send-up than straightforward adventure.

Following *Escape from New York*'s blueprint, *Escape from L.A.* mocks but ultimately maintains macho masculinity: that the film's most powerful female character is a transsexual at best tweaks western conventions requiring female gunslingers to dress like men. Snake is the epitome of a macho hero, even though – or because – he is barely interested in girls. His reputation precedes him. Other key white characters – Map to the Stars Eddie, Malloy (Stacey Keach), and the President – are solely reprehensible. Cuervo, in contrast, at least fights for ideals.

Despite its "multi-cultural look," *Escape from L.A.* was not marketed as a cross-over film. Promotional material capitalized on the cult status of *Escape from New York* and featured Russell's imitation of Clint. Critics split, some admiring the stylish look and relishing in-jokes, others finding the story too predictable. The final sequence offers ample examples why. Through flames reminiscent of *High Plains Drifter*, Snake confronts the President.

The President orders him shot, but the Snake he sees is only a hologram. Aghast, all watch as the real Snake programs the black box with the code that will shut down all energy sources and send humanity back to the dark ages. As satellites explode and lights dim, Snake reaches down and grabs a discarded cigarette pack, another L.A. marker of liberty (elsewhere smoking is forbidden). Clenching an American Spirit cigarillo between his teeth, he looks into the camera, lights a match, then blows it out. "Welcome to the human race," he says, as credits roll in total darkness. The ultimate incarnation of an American Spirit, Snake is ready to puff and die for his beliefs.

Final tally: missing in action

Today's western stars may sound and act like Clint, but they often do not look like him. More importantly, the principal villains of these five films vary. In *Posse* the worst guys are white capitalists and colonels; in *The Quick and the Dead*, a wealthy white, sadistic, "deadbeat dad"; in *Last Man Standing*, Polish and Italian Mafia members; in *Desperado*, Colombian and Mexican drug lords; in *Escape from L.A.* white religious fanatics. In the absence of a single clear-cut enemy, it becomes impossible to advance a unifying national myth. Indeed, as Tom Engelhardt notes in *The End of Victory Culture*, it is profoundly questionable "whether a national story [such as the one told by earlier Hollywood westerns] will . . . be sustainable for a superpower in a world of transnational media entities intent on their own styles of global storytelling."[37]

The classical western's nation-building mission is also impossible today because the "identity politics" these films tap do not aim to unite all Americans. Critical response illuminates the ideological dilemma: (1) when whites are in front, as with *Last Man Standing*, *The Quick and the Dead*, and *Escape from L.A.*, reviewers ignore other racial and ethnic groups; (2) when blacks or Latinos are in front, as in *Posse* and *Desperado*, critics treat the films as "special interest" vehicles.

But even if these films no longer promote a single myth or build an indivisible nation, they still sell American obsessions. Following the kick-ass examples of action films, all feature a post-Rambo recombinant who functions as Victim, Rebel, *and* Savior, making the films more torturously but defiantly "macho-centric" than earlier westerns.[38] All reinforce western associations of activity and masculinity: even Stone must cross-dress to kill. Mario van Peebles' and Antonio Banderas' characters receive especially large injections of testosterone: arguably, they are more attractive; clearly, they are studs.

Does the escalation of spectacular violence pack a bigger homoerotic bang for audience buck than the 1960s spaghetti westerns Steve Neale scrutinized or the 1950s Anthony Mann psychological westerns Paul Willemen eyed?[39] Whatever the answer, all five films reassure spectators that the lead characters are healthy heterosexuals, often by including explicit sex scenes. Other 1990s westerns employ similar strategies. Having looked at roughly thirty, I must therefore disagree with Jim Kitses' claim that "films that in whole or part interrogate aspects of the genre such as its traditional representations of history and myth, heroism and violence, masculinity and minorities, can be seen now to make up the primary focus of the genre."[40]

To summarize my findings:

> Axiom A: Macho rules. Corollary 1: Recent film and made-for-TV biopics "toughen up" historical figures like Wyatt Earp, the James Brothers, the Mastersons, Doc Holliday, and Wild Bill Hickok, Geronimo, and Calamity Jane. Corollary 2: Other nouveaux westerns designate fictional groups as collective tough guys.

> Axiom B: White men dominate. Corollary 1: Several films and made-for-TV movies feature older, still fit, white western actors like Clint, Jack Palance, Lee Van Cleef, Sam Elliott, Robert Duval, Willie Nelson, and Kris Kristofferson. Corollary 2: A smaller subgroup showcases younger white stars like Kevin Costner and Kevin Kline.

> Axiom C: Action triumphs. Corollary 1: Comedy westerns (the *City Slickers* films; *Back to the Future, Part III*) are exceptions. Corollary 2: A few independent films like *Dead Man* and *The Ballad of Little Jo* offer "queer" counter-examples.

Crucially, certain populations and concerns are "missing in action," a.k.a. "impossible," in most nouveaux westerns. Significant absences include:

(1) Asians and Asian Americans. When Asian characters do appear, as is the case in *Posse* and *Escape from L.A.*, it is only in bit parts, in the background, exactly as before. (*The Ballad of Little Jo* is an exception.) This is astonishing for several reasons: Hong Kong martial art films are a strong influence on many nouveaux westerns; Asians constituted a significant population in many areas of the Old West; Asians are today the second largest group of new immigrants in the U.S.

(2) Children. Pre-teens are almost entirely excluded, visible only in crowd scenes. Although mining camps and cattle towns historically catered to adult men, children were vital members of the community in every farming region.[41]

(3) Workers and work. In the 1970s and 1980s, independent films like *The Emigrants* (Jan Troell, 1971), *The New Land* (Jan Troell, 1972), *Days of Heaven* (Terence Malick, 1978), *Northern Lights* (John Hanson, 1979), and *Heartland* (Richard Pearce, 1979) focused on both. Classic Holly-

wood westerns, too, routinely pitted lazy capitalists against hard-working homesteaders. Today only independents like *Dead Man* and *The Ballad of Little Jo* foreground soot or feature grime, and only feminist experimental films examine everyday tasks and feelings. Holly Fisher's 1992 *Bullets for Breakfast*, for example, juxtaposes sequences from *My Darling Clementine* (John Ford, 1946) against shots of women working in a herring-smoking house; Gunvor Nelson's 1984 *Red Shift* weaves Calamity Jane's letters to her absent daughter together with footage exploring the mixed emotions that she, her mother, her daughter, and three fictional women characters of three generations experience.

That such lacunae occur not only in mainstream movies but also, new western historians warn, in historical accounts, suggests salient pressure points for retro-activ*ism*.

To close, tongue-in-cheek, along such lines, I note a final, startling, omission in all the Clint clone films: the absence of any mention of animal rights. Other nouveaux westerns, in contrast, foremost among them *Dances with Wolves* and *Unforgiven*, acknowledge the need to save the buffalo, dance with the wolves, take it from the horse you used to mistreat. *Fistful of Dollars* was equally explicit, and more succinct. Shortly after riding into town, legs dangling on either side of his mule, the young Clint confronts the gang of toughs who mocked him. "My mule doesn't like you laughing at him," he snarls, cigarillo in mouth, hands hovering ominously near his hips. "My mule wants you to apologize to him." The gang looks perplexed: *my mule . . . ???!!!* Too slowly, they reach for their guns. Clint blows them all away, then walks past the undertaker. "My mistake," he breathes, "four coffins."

Part II

SIDING WITH SIDEKICKS

4

CRUISIN' FOR A BRUISIN'

Hollywood's deadly (lesbian) dolls

Figure 4.1   Sharon Stone as Catherine Tramell and Michael Douglas as Nick Curran
in *Basic Instinct* (Carolco, 1991). Courtesy of the Kobal Collection.

In the last decade, more deadly dolls have fueled Hollywood's – and our – imagination than ever before.[1] Around the United States, in the biggest of cities and smallest of towns, movie theaters and video stores offer up box office blockbusters and straight-to-video releases featuring young, sexy, female killers. Many of today's lethal lovelies are central characters, not just sidekicks, and they kill using a variety of weapons, for any number of reasons, in a plethora of genres and genre mixes. Sometimes – as in *Single White Female* (Barbet Schroeder, 1992), *Thelma and Louise* (Ridley Scott, 1991), *Mortal Thoughts* (Alan Rudolph, 1991), *The Grifters* (Stephen Frears, 1990), *Heathers* (Michael Lehman, 1989), *Black Widow* (Bob Rafelson, 1986), *Aliens* (James Cameron, 1986) and *The Hunger* (Tony Scott, 1983) (the list grows longer every day) – they are killed and/or convicted for their crimes; more frequently – as in *Jennifer 8* (Bruce Robinson, 1992), *The Hand that Rocks the Cradle* (Curtis Hanson, 1992), *Buffy the Vampire Slayer* (Fran Rubel Kuzui, 1992), *Switch* (Blake Edwards, 1991), *Silence of the Lambs* (Jonathan Demme, 1991), *Blue Steel* (Kathryn Bigelow, 1990), *The Handmaid's Tale* (Volker Schlondorff, 1990), *Parents* (Bob Balaban, 1989), *The Accused* (Jonathan Kaplan, 1988), *Fatal Attraction* (Adrien Lyne, 1987), *Nuts* (Martin Ritt, 1987), *Surf Nazis Must Die* (Peter George, 1987), *Jagged Edge* (Richard Marquand, 1985), *Aliens*, *Sudden Impact* (Clint Eastwood, 1983), and *Eating Raoul* (Paul Bartel, 1982) – they are not.[2] Whether or not they are killed or convicted, however, many of these women "cruise" because they have been "bruised," and most are in some way "bruised" as a result of having "cruised."

That these deadly doll films constitute a cinematic cycle cannot be appreciated within the framework of classical female genres like film noir and melodrama, however. In such genres cruising is too often made synonymous with aggression and bruising too often conflated with victimization: film noir's bad girls appear primarily as predators, while melodrama's good girls are seen mainly as martyrs. Of course, much like the long-suffering heroines of classic melodrama, today's deadly dolls are often bruised, both in the sense of being physically injured and in the sense of being morally flawed. But now they also cruise like the vicious, violent vamps of film noir, and they even actively bruise. Indeed, so varied have the meanings accorded cruising and bruising become that it is frequently difficult to distinguish pleasure from pain.

Not surprisingly then, these deadly dolls' motives for murder are also more diverse than those of yesteryear's martyrs and molls. Like their most imme- diate movie "mothers," the heroines of 1970s rape-revenge horror movies, this decade's violent femmes often destroy others in self-defense.[3] In addi- tion, however, they now kill in the line of duty, to protect adoptive or bio- logical family members, even, as in *Eating Raoul* or *Parents*, for fun and/or profit. Many are given multiple reasons to murder because Hollywood and its audiences are both fascinated by, yet uncomfortable with, violent women.[4]

Because the distinctions between "born victim" and "born killer" are becoming increasingly blurred, it is no coincidence that my list of deadly dolls includes as many befuddled dames as crazed psycho bitches.[5] In order to explore these changes, I will focus in what follows on two deadly doll films from 1992 that represent generic end points on this contemporary cinematic continuum: *Fried Green Tomatoes* (Jon Avnet) and *Basic Instinct* (Paul Verhoeven). For me, comparing these two films makes it easier to understand deadly doll films as a cycle and easier to recognize that, as a word and as a phenomenon, women's *rage* is always caught up with both *race* and *age*. Of course, the fact that both films feature cruising and bruising also highlights how much all films, not just horror movies, revolve around the "exploitation of the pain/pleasure response."[6]

I concede that, at first sight, these two films appear to have little in com- mon besides their box office success, the critical and public attention they provoked, and the fact that in each the weapon of choice is, rather unreal- istically, a kitchen utensil: an ice pick and a frying pan.[7] A deadly doll film where almost everyone kills, *Basic Instinct* is a thriller cum soft core porn film, containing elements of both the slasher and rape-revenge sub- genres of horror. Set in the present in swinging San Francisco, it features a middle-aged male detective (Michael Douglas) who falls in lust with a bisexual murder mystery writer (Sharon Stone). In *Fried Green Tomatoes*, in contrast, only a seldom seen and virtually silent secondary character (Cicely Tyson) kills, though for most of the film we suspect one of the main char- acters. A female buddy movie cum melodrama cum mystery cum romance, *Fried Green Tomatoes* offers two narratives for the price of one: a present- tense frame story set in the suburban New South and a past-tense main story set in the rural Old South. The present-tense story focuses on a middle- aged woman (Kathy Bates) and her 83-year-old friend (Jessica Tandy); the past-tense story centers on the loving friendship of two younger women (Mary Stuart Masterson and Mary-Louise Parker).

Despite these differences, however, the presence of a kitchen utensil as the murder weapon in each film reveals how much both – and, indeed, deadly

Figure 4.2   Kathy Bates as Evelyn Couch and Jessica Tandy as Ninny
Threadgoode in *Fried Green Tomatoes* (BFI/Film on Four International/
Sankofa Film & Video, 1992). Courtesy of the Kobal Collection.

doll films in general – participate in a fundamentally old-fashioned patriarchal ideology: where else should women be, after all, but in the kitchen?[8]
That to varying degrees both films portray women as sexually threatening
and killing men is part of the same resolutely heterosexual package.

Nevertheless, as in most deadly doll films, in both these movies a murmured fear of lesbianism lurks beneath the general discomfort with violent
women – hence the parentheses of my subtitle.[9] Lesbian and gay audiences
found it easy to "see" the lead characters of these two films as lesbians
because, as I will show in the first of three readings of these films, both
revolve around tropes that haunt "queer" as well as "straight" imaginaries,
portraying lesbians as mirrors (of each other), as mothers (to each other),
and as men (for each other).

Unlike most deadly doll films, however, differences of race and age are
fairly strongly marked in these films, and especially in *Fried Green Tomatoes*.
Typically, a terror of racial difference and miscegenation remains unspoken
in the deadly doll cycle, camouflaged by the brouhaha around comely white
superheroines who are more frequently viewed as sexually desirable objects
than as sexually desiring subjects.[10] My second reading thus analyzes how
Basic Instinct and *Fried Green Tomatoes* depart from this model and explores
what such deviations may mean for portrayals and perceptions of hetero-
and homosexuality.

Finally, in a third reading, I argue that the entire cycle's obsession with
death, dying, and lethal lovelies masks a more deep-seated denial of age
and aging. Although both films participate in this denial, each takes the
mid-life crisis of its protagonist as a narrative point of departure, and each
prominently displays older bodies. Nevertheless, each continues to associate
sexual desirability with youthful femininity.

75

My own desire to analyze these two films was, I confess, triggered by the warm and heated responses they provoked, respectively, among lesbians, gays, and straight feminists. Admittedly, reactions to the films' representations of sexuality among and within these groups differed quite a bit. Still, I was concerned by how often queer and feminist activists concurred with the mainstream movie reviewers and industry publicists they sought to critique and persuade, discussing both films largely in terms of their representations (or not) of women and/or lesbians who are, according to Hollywood's standards, a priori young and white. Because I agree with Isaac Julien and Kobena Mercer that, as activists and as critics, we must acknowledge how much our own perceptions are caught up in and confined by those "relations of power/ knowledge that determine which cultural issues are intellectually prioritized in the first place,"[11] I will consequently preface my three readings of these films with an analysis of critical and activist response.

By offering three readings of these two films, the first focusing on sexuality, the second on race, and the third on age, I do not mean to imply that identities are simply additive or solely fragmented. Rather, my goal is to highlight modes of response and areas of intervention which do exist and should exist, but were and are often not recognized. After all, as Martha Gever reminds us, "naming oneself never occurs divorced from other, contingent cultural identities."[12] I conclude therefore that if we are to forge political alliances (and I believe we must if we are to be more effective), those of us who theorize and act on the basis of *any* kind of identity politics need to see our own and others' identities as hybrids, emerging and dissolving in time and over time.

On the range of reception: from good ole home-cooking to "ice pick envy"[13]

Like the print reception of other lucrative deadly doll films made in the last decade, most of the critical and activist response to *Basic Instinct* and *Fried Green Tomatoes* was gender-based and gender-biased.[14] What female violence meant for men was hotly debated, while male violence against women was largely ignored. Sexual orientation was discussed, if often downplayed, but race and age went virtually unnoticed in trade press coverage, in interviews with stars, directors, and screenwriters, in mainstream and alternative reviews, and even in the comments from demonstrators included within news stories.[15]

Typically, mainstream critics of *Fried Green Tomatoes* took little notice of what lesbian and gay activists said. In contrast, because demonstrations against *Basic Instinct* began in response to Joe Eszterhas's script and garnered a great deal of attention, they established a framework for subsequent debates in both the mainstream and the alternative press.

In retrospect, however, the relatively sparse discussion of *Fried Green*

Tomatoes in many ways presaged the furor around *Basic Instinct.*[16] Most critics labeled *Fried Green Tomatoes* a "woman's film" but usually also stressed its appeal to men, insisting on the fact that Idgie (Mary Stuart Masterson) and Ruth (Mary-Louise Parker) are not only helped by men but also have close male friends. As John Simon wrote in the *National Review*, "not even feminism, of which there is plenty in this movie, can drive any undislodgeable wedge between men and women."[17]

Critics failed to mention the bruising inflicted on the main female characters, I submit, because melodrama is one of the key generic components of *Fried Green Tomatoes*. Very few reviewers discussed the performances of African American actors or acknowledged how important African American characters were to the narrative.[18] Almost all backed away from discussing age or disease, even though both are prominent in the film.[19] The film's marketing changed to target male as well as female audiences and to highlight the younger female stars.[20]

Perhaps because the white female characters were not perceived as threats, all but one reviewer criticized the film's "cowardice" in avoiding the lesbian attachment between Idgie and Ruth.[21] A few cited lesbian and gay protests in support of their charges.[22] But not all lesbians and gays objected to the omission: GLAAD (Gay and Lesbian Alliance Against Defamation) even awarded director Jon Avnet a prize for his positive portrayal of lesbians.

In contrast, and much as was the case a decade earlier with *Cruising* (William Friedkin, 1980), *Dressed to Kill* (Brian de Palma, 1980), and *Windows* (Gordon Willis, 1980), *Basic Instinct* became a prime locus for lesbian, gay, and feminist organizations protesting pejorative media representations, including Queer Nation, ACT-UP, GLAAD, Community United Against Violence, Catherine Did It, and NOW. The 1990s round of activist protests were formulated somewhat differently from the 1980s protests, in part because new coalitions had been forged between lesbians and gay men under the rubric of "queer" in response to governmental failure to support AIDS research and in an effort to stop rising homophobic violence. Thanks moreover to two-plus decades of organizing, lesbians and gays were more visible, in Hollywood and elsewhere, more practiced in media manipulation, and more aware of their own consumer clout.

Yet there were many similarities between the critiques raised in the 1980s and those voiced in the 1990s, primarily because much had *not* changed for lesbians and gays during 12 years of Republican rule. As with the 1980s protests, demonstrations against *Basic Instinct* centered around charges that the film was homophobic and/or misogynist. Not surprisingly, of course, what constituted "homophobic" and "misogynist" varied by individual and group. One set of complaints revolved around a perceived lack of realism. Some activists objected to the absence of ordinary lesbian/gay characters; others denounced the distortion of their "true queer lives."[23] A second, related set of criticisms focused on the stereotyping of lesbians as man-haters.[24] Now, however, a lesbian member of Queer Nation added, "The girl never gets the girl. I'm tired of that."[25] A third set of objections engaged directly with the issue of bruising, maintaining that *Basic Instinct* would fuel the upsurge in gay bashing.[26]

Those who called the film misogynist did so primarily because they felt the female characters were bruised. Some women articulated contemporary feminist concerns, charging that the sex scene between Nick and Beth was a date rape. Others felt the entire film implied women like violence, a decades-old feminist critique. The president of LA-NOW, for example, indicted the film because for her "the message [was] that women like violence, women want to be used, women want to be raped."[27]

Where Friedkin refused to meet with the *Cruising* protestors in 1980, 1990s activists drew on Hollywood connections and talked with Eszterhas.[28] They demanded he rewrite the script, cutting all homophobic remarks and the "date rape" scene, having two of the victims be women instead of men, and – my favorite – recasting Michael Douglas's character as a lesbian to be played by Kathleen Turner.[29] Eszterhas drafted some changes, but the production company, Carolco, and Verhoeven argued they could not implement them because the film's "artistic integrity" was at stake.[30]

Although not successful in altering the film, the demonstrators received so much coverage that mainstream and alternative critics alike found themselves responding to activist charges.[31] The majority of mainstream critics, however, lectured activists for what they saw as overreactions. A few agreed the film was misogynist, while refuting claims it was homophobic.[32] Most simply "proved" the protesters wrong by comparing *Basic Instinct* to other Hollywood films and correcting what they saw as mistaken interpretations.[33]

A small segment of male mainstream and leftist critics acknowledged that the film was basically a male mirage.[34] Many women, in contrast, insisted on just this point, and a few criticized male reviewers for not bothering to ask women what they did or did not like about the film.[35] Several insisted they were delighted with *Basic Instinct*, and especially with Sharon Stone's lascivious cruising and powerful bruising. Amy Taubin, for example, "thought it was a gas to see a woman on the screen in a powerful enough position to let it all hang out and not be punished for it in the end."[36] Ruth Picardie wrote: "a dyke with two Ferraris who kills men? Now that's a positive image!"[37] And Liz Gaist gleefully noted that "dykes, or should I say bisexuals, are portrayed as more beautiful than the average girl, which in the skewed world of Hollywood means that we are on the verge of becoming respectable."[38]

Tellingly, only Gaist acknowledged how important the simultaneous representation and denial of aging is to *Basic Instinct*, describing the film as "simply another vehicle to prove the irresistability [*sic*] of Michael Douglas' *40-plus* body and soul."[39] With the single exception of Sharon

Stone, no one reflected in print on how "white" a film it is,[40] and no one, including Sharon Stone, examined how this whiteness plays in the images and the plot.

That the imbrication of gender, race, and age was rarely acknowledged in the print coverage of mainstream and activist responses to either film is understandable: sexual difference is, after all, the dominant fiction of our time, for mass media, mainstream critics, and marginal movements alike. Nevertheless, as Julien and Mercer argue, because it is "a recurring site upon which categories of race and gender [and age] intersect . . . the representation of sexuality" *should* prove a privileged point of departure for an "analysis [that will] take account of the intersections of differences."[41]

And what better place to undertake the analysis Julien and Mercer call for than *Basic Instinct*, which offers more explicit sexuality than most R-rated Hollywood films do, and *Fried Green Tomatoes*, which, with its PG-rating, is guaranteed to offer less? So . . . here goes.

Lesbians as mirrors, mothers, and men

That activists and critics alike discussed these two deadly doll films in terms of sexuality, and often labeled this sexuality "lesbian," is not surprising for a variety of reasons. Both films suggest the presence of lesbian desire through what are rapidly becoming clichéd counter-conventions of continuity editing: shot/reverse shots where two women look longingly at one another, point-of-view shots where one woman spies on another, and two-shots where two women hug, romp, or dance together. *Basic Instinct* frequently shows and/or talks about the pleasure Roxy takes in spying on or looking at Catherine. The disco sequence is particularly explicit, with the two French kissing, then dancing seductively together under Michael Douglas's lecherous gaze. *Fried Green Tomatoes* removes the male gaze while keeping a certain number of female looks. Here the most sexually suggestive shots occur in playful contexts: Idgie and Ruth are physically closest during a water fight and a food fight.

More important, however, both *Basic Instinct* and *Fried Green Tomatoes* are readily seen as "about lesbians" because they are structured around an unholy trinity of lesbian tropes: lesbians are mirrors (to each other), mothers (of each other), and/or men (for each other). Queers may, or may not, react differently to these tropes than straights do; my point here is that, on some level and in some way, we all recognize and reply to them. Of course since *Basic Instinct* and *Fried Green Tomatoes* are Hollywood films, concerned with marketing their messages to as many people as possible, they also distance themselves from even the relatively safe space of metaphor, recoding the lesbians they portray as mirror-mother-men as "bisexuals" (*Basic Instinct*'s ploy) or "just friends" (*Fried Green Tomatoes*' solution).[42] It is this hide-and-seek strategy that in turn triggers such a range of responses, from charges of "delesbianization" to applause for "assimilation"; from protests that butches are not butchers to cheers for broads with brains.[43]

In *Basic Instinct* and *Fried Green Tomatoes*, as in many films and novels about "lesbians," all three tropes coexist, linked through narrative line and visual display to lead and supporting characters alike. In *Basic Instinct*, every female character, not just Sharon Stone's character, Catherine, embodies at least one of these three lesbian tropes. All are mirrors of each other: all are, or were, bleached blondes, and all are or were killers. Catherine Tramell and her lover, Roxy (Leilani Sarelle), are look-alike "lipstick" lesbians. Roxy is slightly more "mannish": she always wears pants while Catherine often wears dresses without, Verhoeven's camera and screenwriter Eszterhas's dialog insist, any underwear. At one point detective Nick Curran (Michael Douglas) even jealously refers to Roxy as "Rocky," though of course it is Catherine, not Roxy, who has the ever-ready, ever-erect ice pick and who knows how to use it far better than Nick does.

In the cases of Catherine and Beth Garner (Jeanne Tripplehorne), who was the original and who the copy depends on which one is telling the story: according to Catherine, Beth was so obsessed with her she dyed her hair blonde and began to follow her around; according to Beth, she was the model and Catherine the make-over. The only older female character, 60-ish Hazel Dobkins (Dorothy Malone), is portrayed as an aging mirror and possible stand-in "mother" lover of Catherine as mirror/"daughter" lover – why else would she appear on the stairs at Catherine's house in one of the final sequences, much as Roxy had earlier?[44]

Significantly, all these mirror-mother-men kill family members: Catherine probably murdered her parents as well as a string of male lovers; Roxy killed her two brothers; Beth may have killed her husband, and either she or Catherine murdered their college psychology professor; Hazel hacked up her husband and children with a carving knife she received as a wedding present. *Basic Instinct*'s mirror imagery thereby reinforces with a vengeance the "popular perceptions of lesbians and gays as people without social ties or family, a species set apart" that anthropologist Kath Weston so eloquently contradicts in *Families We Choose*.[45]

The same three tropes exist in both book and film versions of *Fried Green Tomatoes*. Because "mirrors can reflect inversion as well as likeness,"[46] however, this film (like many other cinematic and print narratives) offers a slight variation on the reflection trope, depicting the members of its "lesbian" couple as opposites, butches and femmes, brunettes and blondes. In Avnet's film, although both Idgie and Ruth are conventionally attractive and somewhat unconventionally spunky, Idgie (Mary Stuart Masterson) is blonde and Ruth (Mary-Louise Parker) is brunette. Ruth wears the dresses and Idgie the pants – not to mention the bow ties, suspenders, shorts, and bowlers. The film attributes Idgie's fondness for cross-dressing to an unconscious identification with her dead older brother, Buddy (Chris O'Donnell). Ruth, in contrast, incarnates the last of the three basic lesbian tropes, lesbian-as-mother, doing the female Freudian right thing and giving birth to Buddy, Jr. (Grayson Fricke).

Fried Green Tomatoes grants Idgie and Ruth a relatively blissful if asexual life of longing looks together, whereas *Basic Instinct* casts Catherine's lesbian affairs as titillating and temporary phenomena played out for Nick's staunchly heterosexual gaze. But in both films the lead "lesbian" characters cruise because they have been bruised and are bruised because they cruise. Aggression and victimization, satisfaction and punishment are narratively and visually interwoven.

Exceptionally, *Fried Green Tomatoes* is one of the few deadly doll films to broach the question of spousal abuse: Idgie brings Ruth back to Whistle Stop to protect her from her husband, Frank's (Nick Searcy) beatings. To date, only *Mortal Thoughts* has gone further, suggesting that battery might be the reason behind the central murder. In each film, however, both women are "punished" for being with another woman. During *Fried Green Tomatoes*, Idgie is tried for Frank's murder, while Ruth dies from a painful and debilitating illness; at the end of *Mortal Thoughts*, Joyce (Glenne Headley) and Cynthia (Demi Moore) are sent to jail. Significantly, in neither film does a deadly (lesbian) doll actually kill her husband: in *Mortal Thoughts* revenge for rape is really the motive and the wife's friend, not the wife, the murderer; in *Fried Green Tomatoes* Idgie is acquitted, while Ruth is at best a dead (lesbian) doll, never a deadly (lesbian) doll. At the end of *Mortal Thoughts* Joyce and Cynthia stand a chance of "getting it on" in that "hotbed" of lesbian passion – prison. In *Fried Green Tomatoes*, by contrast, once the film's femme

Figure 4.3   Mary Louise Parker as Ruth and Mary Stuart Masterson as Idgie
Threadgoode in *Fried Green Tomatoes* (BFI/Film on Four International/
Sankofa Film & Video, 1992). Courtesy of the Kobal Collection.

81

is transformed into an angel, its butch necessarily becomes always only a tomboy: death guarantees the "delesbianization" of their relationship.[47]

Suffering and punishment pervade *Basic Instinct* as well, though here they are more overtly associated with sadomasochistic pleasure and pain. The plot consistently connects perversion with inversion and both with what is "basic," as lesbians and bisexual women help heterosexual men understand that good cruising involves a little bruising. For many spectators, the spectacle of murderous cruising was so lavishly and lovingly chronicled that the women's own victimization was hard to perceive. Yet their lives are littered with deaths, not all of their own making or desire. Even Catherine, the ice maiden with the ice pick, sobs because she always loses those she loves. Then these deadly dolls themselves start dying: the most clearly lesbian, Roxy, goes up in flames in her car, while Beth is shot to death by Nick, the man whom she ostensibly loves.

In the case of *Fried Green Tomatoes*, the majority of activists and critics alike overlooked the lead characters' bruising by concentrating on their refined cruising, a.k.a. reciprocal "mothering." Most of the "queer" and some of the feminist activists focused on bruising in *Basic Instinct*, taking umbrage at seeing lesbians cast as murdering men and s/m practices equated with homosexuality.[48] In contrast, mainstream critics and certain feminist critics and activists as well (if for different reasons) relished Sharon Stone's cruising. In both films "lesbian" reflections served as deflections: attention was so centered on the similarities and differences within "lesbian" couples that the presence – or absence – of other female pairs went unnoticed. How acute this short-sightedness was emerged more dramatically with respect to *Fried Green Tomatoes*, for here the failure to recognize that race is a component of rage made it impossible for most people to begin to see this film as a deadly doll film. *Basic Instinct*, in contrast, was easily classified as such, for there all eyes were glued to Sharon Stone's feminine curves and bisexual exploits, while her blondness and youth were simply taken for granted, as necessary but secondary attributes.

Of bleached blondes and blacks

The linkage of lily-white, look-alike, lipstick "lesbians" with mayhem, mystery, and murder thus meant that in both films, though differently, race vanished from view. Most white critics and activists failed to "see" *Fried Green Tomatoes'* "murderer" because she is a secondary character, African American, female, and not otherwise associated with criminality. Racial issues went even more unnoticed in *Basic Instinct* because there are no major African American characters to call attention to the fact that white, too, is a color. As Richard Dyer bluntly put it, "[It is] as if only non-whiteness [could] give whiteness any substance."[49]

But *Basic Instinct* is probably more concerned with whiteness than any other deadly doll film released in the last decade. The settings are predominantly or exclusively white: luxury San Francisco beach homes and apartments, small northern California towns, discotheques and country western bars. Only one African American actor has a speaking part, as a police investigator. Others are visible, but only in the background.

Female whiteness is a particular obsession: bleached, tinted, frosted, and dyed blondes are everywhere, in the past as in the present. Their ubiquity is reminiscent of the Aryan Valkyries in Leni Riefenstahl's films and is, I suspect, caught up with similar anxieties regarding racial origins and ethnic lacks. Indeed, so hysterically does *Basic Instinct* insist that whiteness equals blondness that Sharon Stone's exposure of blonde pubic hair can perhaps be taken as "proof" of her racial, not just sexual, superiority.[50] And I am tempted to suggest, further, that Roxy and Beth die not just because they are lesbian and bisexual, respectively, but also because their roots are showing. According to the visual logic of this film, Beth certainly deserves to die: though she used to bleach her hair, she has become the film's only brunette.

Race is more readily recognizable in *Fried Green Tomatoes* than in *Basic Instinct* for two reasons: first, there are black as well as white characters and, as Dyer says, "black people are always marked as black,"[51] and second, the film is set in the South, *the* region Hollywood films associate with race. Nevertheless, the present-tense sections of the film are largely unconcerned with race as a marker of anything other than class difference: Ninny (Jessica Tandy) seems to be a favorite of the black women on the nursing home staff and she refers in passing to an elderly black woman friend.

On the whole, "rac*ism*" is confined to the past, though here too the film paints a relatively rosy picture of black servitude, for the most part equating racism with "tradition." The principal African American characters are nonetheless usually shown as part of the white family, as servants working in and around the "Big House" or in and around Idgie and Ruth's café. Their homes are never shown and their familial relations are touched on only in passing: not until the last third of the film do we learn that Big George (Stan Shaw) is Sipsey's (Cicely Tyson) son and that the young black girl we see, Naughty Bird (Lashondra Phillips), is Sipsey's younger sister.[52]

Each of these three major African American characters is built around a stereotype, with Sipsey incarnating the "mammy," Big George the "buck," and Naughty Bird the "pickaninny." Visually, all three are coded as less important than any of the principal white characters. For the first half of the film, Sipsey is only visible at the side or in the background of a shot, her head bowed over her cooking or sewing. She says little, never looks at the camera, and only looks obliquely at the white characters. We see her take care of the white children but not her own children. Barbara Christian's description of the mammy of white Southern literature is quite applicable: "She relates to the world as an all-embracing figure, and she herself needs or demands little, her identity derived mainly from a nurturing service."[53]

As the film progresses Sipsey speaks somewhat more frequently and becomes a bit more "uppity," slyly pointing out to the Georgia sheriff who is searching for Frank, for example, that the "secret's in the sauce." Nevertheless, like Whoopi Goldberg's character in *Ghost*, Sipsey still functions "centrally and crucially to enable the fantasy of the white participants."[54] And like Big George she always appears as a protector, helper, and nurse, never as a sexual subject in her own right.

Big George is more often framed, muscles bulging, in the center or close to the center of a shot, but he too is usually seen "helping" the white characters: whether chopping wood, taking care of little Idgie, cooking the barbecue, or helping Ruth flee her abusive husband. He is more asexual than his "big" white counterpart, Grady (Gary Balarama). In love with Idgie, Grady at least gets to fight with her and at one point to dress as a woman to her "man." And though the only cruising Big George does is as Idgie's driver, of all the characters he is the most bruised, first bull-whipped by the "bad" Georgia Klan for having helped Ruth escape (the "good" Arkansas Klan merely engages in verbal threats), then, with Idgie, put on trial for Frank's murder. As Manthia Diawara succinctly says, "Hollywood requires that [a] black character . . . be punished after he has behaved like a hero."[55]

The penultimate sequence reveals that Sipsey, not Idgie, was the real murderer but intimates that her "murder" was really accidental homicide: she hit Frank on the head with a frying pan to keep him from stealing Ruth's baby. Though Sipsey thereby becomes one of the few black deadly dolls of the last decade, neither she nor the murder are at any point sexualized.[56] At the end of the film, moreover, the mystery of Sipsey is subsumed by the enigma of Ninny. Narratively the crucial question becomes not *where* is Ninny, though she has disappeared from the nursing home, but *who* is she, a riddle only an exploration of age and aging can solve.

Most white critics and activists acquiesced in this narrative shell game. For them, Sipsey figured merely as a "strong black woman," floating, like the black feminist described by Michele Wallace, "above our heads like one of the cartoon characters in a Macy's Christmas Parade, a form larger than life and yet a deformation powerless to speak."[57] Only Janet Maslin felt Cicely Tyson's forceful and dignified performance accused her character's silence, reproaching rather than supporting the feminist politics of inclusiveness proffered by the film.[58]

The shift in focus from race to age made it doubly hard for most people to see *Fried Green Tomatoes* as a deadly doll film. Most of us view older people as the victims, not the perpetrators, of violence and rarely think of them as the purveyors of sexual pleasure. *Basic Instinct*'s sleight of hand functions somewhat differently, for here the focus on voluptuous young women offered ample opportunity for all, but especially for men, to escape anxieties about aging by fixating on (another) gender and (another) generation.

Age spots as blind spots

Most blatantly, however, the emphases on death and dying in both films mask how much each is structured around age and aging. In *Basic Instinct* in particular, as in most action adventure and many horror films, the spectacle of violent death substitutes for the narrative exploration of psychic and physical processes. Yet both films feature middle-aged characters who fixate on a murder mystery as a way to postpone dealing with mid-life crises. What constitutes a mid-life crisis varies depending on whether the film protagonist is male or female: in *Basic Instinct*, Nick's (Michael Douglas) dilemma is presented as "failed masculinity"; in *Fried Green Tomatoes*, Evelyn's (Kathy Bates) quandary is portrayed as "inflated femininity."

At the beginning of *Basic Instinct* Nick Curran's career is on the skids, his wife has killed herself, and his ex-girlfriend is literally his psychiatrist. Although he has presumably faced up to his alcohol and drug abuse, he represses his anxieties about aging and failure by focusing on sexuality and murder. The first shots encourage us to adopt this position as well, offering a breathless display of violent love-making, then brutal death. Moments later the camera pans blood- and come-stained sheets and the corpse of a naked middle-aged man, revealing in the process his limp penis.[59] The male detectives on the scene of the crime joke about the dead man's sexual prowess: "at least he got off before he got offed," Nick's best friend, Gus (George Dzundza), comments approvingly.

Nick and Gus's preoccupation with sexual performance in the face of death is shaped and shared by Freudian psychoanalysis. What Kathleen Woodward says of Freud holds for Nick and Gus, too: "aging is associated with a lack of sexual activity" and therefore "represents a threat more serious than that of death itself." For heterosexual men, "youth is valued . . . even more in women than it is desired for themselves" because it allows them to disguise their anxieties and disappointments about aging onto and as heterosexual desire.[60] In the case of *Basic Instinct*, Nick's conquest of women through rough sex thus functions as a kind of double proof of his virility and youth. Not coincidentally, Nick's nickname is "Shooter," a double entendre if ever there was one. That the women he "shoots" are young and beautiful is, of course, key to his – and to the extent we identify with him, our – successful denial of middle age and failure. After all we, like Freud, often find it easier to associate activity with sadism and both with masculinity.

Figure 4.4 Michael Douglas as Nick Curran and George Dzundza as Gus in *Basic Instinct* (Carolco, 1991). Courtesy of the Kobal Collection.

Female threats – *is* her "Picasso" bigger than his, as Gus maintains? – are therefore equally thrills and guarantee both Nick's youth and his heterosexuality, a must given how frequently Michael Douglas bares his still fairly shapely butt.[61] Beside him Gus looms as an ominous reminder of what the middle-aged male body can become, left untended and unattended. Ultimately, the narrative and Nick simply avoid the perils of aging, killing off Gus, then looking beyond Michael Douglas's crow's feet and love handles toward lascivious, if rapacious, young women. The closing shots show Nick and Catherine again in bed, again engaging in ultra-athletic sex. Nick even envisions a future where they will "fuck like minks, raise rug rats, and live happily ever after." Only when Catherine says, "I don't like rug rats" does he relinquish the idea of babies.

Fried Green Tomatoes proposes a different solution to its middle-aged female protagonist's fears of an inflated femininity, brought on by overeating and, the film suggests, linked to the menopause. Where Nick denies the past by focusing on a future of younger lovers and babies, Evelyn Couch learns to recognize that both past and future are contained within the self. For much of the film, however, she worries about her changing body and dissolving marriage. Seeking a solution, she joins a women's consciousness-raising group. But when the other women start to look at their vaginas using pocket mirrors, she finds she has grown too fat to even see her own genitalia.

Ninny's (Jessica Tandy) tales of love, death, and the caloric delights of yesteryear offer a welcome escape. Evelyn stops going to her women's group and starts to make herself over using diet, exercise, hormone therapy, new clothes, and Mary Kay cosmetics. Yet at no point is she presented as glamorous or seductive. Instead, the film constantly pokes fun at her attempts to recapture her youth, and nowhere more so than in the scene where she greets her husband wrapped in cellophane. Evelyn does, however, learn to be more assertive. In the parking lot outside the local supermarket, two young women steal her parking space and call her names. She simply smashes her car into their car, then says smugly, "Face it girls, I'm older and I have more insurance." Although still comic, for once the connection among cruising, age, and women's rage is made to seem appealing.

Eventually Evelyn's husband, Ed (Gailand Sartain), notices her "makeover" and starts to bring her flowers. But while reassured that she is not yet old and not yet unattractive, Evelyn still worries about the future. A pan of a corridor in Ninny's nursing home from her point of view makes it clear she sees age as a period of inevitable bruising, decline, and decay: the hall is lined with old people, all confined to wheelchairs. Ninny comforts her, saying *she* doesn't feel 83, "it sort of slipped up on me." As far as Ninny is concerned, old people can and do still cruise: without question her decision to color her white hair pink for Christmas constitutes what Woodward would call a "masquerade of defiance."[62]

More important, Ninny's voice-over segues between the past and present sections of the film hint that age is a continuum wherein past and present are connected. But because past and present are visually disjunctive (the film frequently cuts from intimate two-shots in the nursing home to distant establishing shots of Whistle Stop), youth and age seem opposed. Who Ninny really is thus remains a riddle, at least to Evelyn, until the very end.

The final images solve this mystery and resolve Evelyn's fears of a lonely infirm old age. Ninny is Idgie, and Evelyn will bring her to live with her and her husband.[63] The very last frames may display a deserted place – the boarded-up Whistle Stop Cafe – but the narrative promises that since she is spry, loveable, and lucid, Ninny/Idgie will have a room – and a family – of her own. As grandmother/mother, she will take the place of Ed and Evelyn's son, now away at college.

The solutions the two films post to the mysteries of age and aging could not be more opposed: denial and displacement are a far cry from acceptance and integration. Nonetheless, because the aging body is a disintegrating body, and because to look at and identify with aging bodies jeopardizes the narcissistic pleasures of a lifetime, for young and old alike, age spots remained blind spots, for critics and spectators of all ages.

Beyond the valley of the – deadly (lesbian) – dolls

The critical and activist hoopla around lithe, lovely, lily-white "lipstick" lesbians is thus eminently understandable. But, as I mentioned in my introduction, I consider it urgent that queer and feminist responses emerge from the straitjackets of mainstream models. Like other activist-critics, I believe that protests based on "positive" images and/or "true" representations have severe limitations. "Positive" images are not positive for everyone, and "truth" is very much in the eye of the beholder. Too often what Douglas Crimp says of protests against AIDS misrepresentations holds for mobilizations against film femmes fatales as well: "One problem of opposing a stereotype . . . is that we tacitly side with those who would distance themselves from the image portrayed. We tacitly agree that it is other. . . . [W]e must . . . recognize that every image . . . is a *representation* and formulate our activist demands not in response to the 'truth' of the image but in relation to the conditions of its construction and to its social effects."[64]

We need, in other words, to remember that "campaigns to challenge cultural representations" are often predicated on "a surprisingly benign view of power. . . . If only Hollywood would show positive role models, life for lesbians and gays in this country would improve."[65] Of course, many of those who protested against *Basic Instinct* were fully aware of such limitations. For them this film was "the gimmick of a lifetime," a rare opportunity "to get our message across about what life is like for queers in this country."[66]

But what kind of "message" do gimmicks and slogans actually get across? When activists talk about "what life is like for queers in this country," whose "queer" life are they describing? How much do such arguments "presuppose the very phenomena to be interrogated, and thereby foreclose the very issues that should serve as the subject matter to be investigated?"[67] Is not Carol Clover right to argue that "the operation whereby female figures are made to stand for, and act out, a psychosexual posture that in fact knows no sex . . . for a variety of reasons . . . add[s] up to male dominance?"[68]

Without a doubt, critics, spectators, and/or activists interested in increasing lesbian visibility must still insist that no matter how wonderful representations of female friendship may be, they are not acceptable substitutes for representations of lesbian sexuality and love. But if we are ever to get beyond the unholy trinity of lesbian tropes, we need to insist on the diversity of lesbian lives. Necessarily, I believe, we must also learn to see "whiteness" and bleached blondness, not just "blackness," as colors, and we must begin to treat age spots as something other than blind spots. There are, after all, links as well as disjunctions among homophobia, sexism, racism, and ageism. As Audre Lorde reminds us, "difference must not merely be tolerated, but seen as a fund of necessary polarities between which our creativity can spark like a dialectic. Only then does the necessity for interdependency become unthreatening."[69] To which I would add, after Kathleen Woodward, "it is as important to stress continuity as difference." After all, "we both are and are not identical to ourselves throughout our lives."[70]

Only because ours is such a youth-oriented, white-dominated, heterosexually fixated society do so many of us miss the extent to which representations of women's rage revolve around race and age as well as gender and sexuality in films as different as *Basic Instinct* and *Fried Green Tomatoes*.[71] If we really want to expand the ways we cruise or are cruised, and if we really want to limit the ways we bruise or are bruised, race, age, and aging *must* become integral parts of any analyses and activism hooked on film representations.

5

SWEDE AS "OTHER"

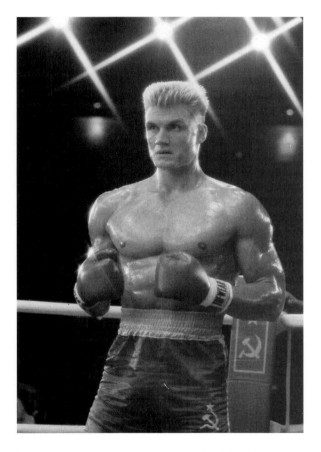

Figure 5.1   Dolph Lundgren as Drago in *Rocky IV* (MGM/UA, 1985). Courtesy of the Kobal Collection.

The hole at the heart of whiteness

"Swedes in this country, they keep popping up like jack-rabbits," says the villain played by Sebastian Cabot in the 1958 western *Terror in a Texas Town* (Joseph Lewis). In reality, "there's only Sterling Hayden and his father" playing a seafarer turned farmer and a homesteader, respectively. Nonetheless, per the entry on "Swedes" in the *BFI Companion to the Western*, the western is one of the few genres where characters designated as Swedes by name and/or accent can be found, typically played by non-Swedish actors cast in minor roles.[1]

Swedish actors, in contrast, so often play other nationalities that they would seem to exemplify Richard Dyer's argument that, as a racial category, "white" does not appear marked by ethnicity. Yet the "overarching hegemonic whiteness" Dyer explores in *White* has assumed different configurations over the course of the last century.[2] At the beginning of the century, "race" was commonly used to describe what are now thought of as "ethnic" or "national" subgroups: people spoke of the "Anglo-Saxon race," the "Nordic race," the "Aryan race," the "Japanese race," and so on.[3] Today "ethnicity" is more often associated with "choice" and for whites indicates a voluntary affiliation with a national and/or cultural heritage. "Race," in contrast, entails "discrimination" based on arbitrary physical or cultural characteristics without much regard for national or cultural distinctions.[4]

Scandinavians, Germans, and Anglo Saxons remain the quintessential Aryans, the ideal "whites," in U.S. popular imagination. On screen, Swedish male bodies are nonetheless doubly "impossible": it is axiomatic that Swedish actors do not play Swedes and that Swedish characters be subordinate to Anglo-American leads. Key examples: Nils Asther, who made his mark playing Orientals in the 1920s and 1930s; Dolph Lundgren who plays Americans, Germans, and Russians in action films of the 1980s and 1990s; non-Swedish actors who play Swedes as silly sidekicks in 1950s to 1960s westerns.

That I take Swedes as exemplary Scandinavians is motivated by personal as well as political considerations: while Swedes represent over half of all

Scandinavians in the U.S., among them were my paternal grandfather, grandmother, and mother.[5] But I can only comment on male screen Swedes with a sense of humility, for in my case studies Swedish men in particular function as a "hole" at the heart of whiteness. To put it bluntly, male screen Swedes are always "Others," even though as whites – at least "underneath" – all are privileged in ways that "non-white" characters are not.[6]

The first section of this chapter, "Beauty and the b/east," explores Asther's casting as a tall, sexy Oriental aristocrat who seduces the beautiful Anglo-Saxon heroines of *Wild Orchids* (Sydney Franklin, 1928) and *The Bitter Tea of General Yen* (Frank Capra, 1934). These exotic melodramas were among Asther's most popular films, thanks not only to the renown of co-stars Greta Garbo and Barbara Stanwyck, but also to the juxtaposition of the commanding Asther with shorter Anglo-American actors. Asther's characters can afford to be alternately macho and effeminate: their appeal is assured.

A second section examines the Swedish immigrants played by non-Swedes in *Shane* (George Stevens, 1952), *The Searchers* (John Ford, 1956), and *The Man Who Shot Liberty Valance* (John Ford, 1962). Next to the virile, violent Anglos who make or break the laws, they seem effeminate and pacific. Like other minor characters – Mexicans, African Americans, Native Americans – most are not particularly memorable and most live "Ho-hum on the range" lives. Only *Terror*'s Sterling Hayden is brave, tall, and tragic, a classic hero.

Big is "baaaack" in the 1980s and 1990s "hard body" films where Dolph Lundgren looms large as East Germans, Soviets, or Americans. In several movies, *glasnost* and *perestroika* shape who he fights, together with whom. Few female and no feminized characters appear. "Partnered" with – and often more "Asian," "African" or "African American" than – smaller male buddies, Lundgren as lead becomes "Swede as (br)other," witness roles in *Rocky IV* (John Avila, 1986), *Red Scorpion* (Joseph Zito, 1989), *The Punisher* (Mark Goldblatt, 1989), *Showdown in Little Tokyo* (Mark Lester, 1991), *Universal Soldier* (Roland Emmerich, 1992), *Johnny Mnemonic* (Robert Longo, 1995), *Pentathlon* (Bruce Malmuth, 1994), and *Silent Trigger* (Russell Mulcahy, 1997).

The conclusion's title, "Scandinavian humor and other myths," is borrowed from one of my 6-foot-plus father's and brother's favorite books. For my purposes it is perfect, since although race and ethnicity are experienced differently today in the U.S., "whiteness" continues to be more strongly marked as Anglo-Saxon than as Nordic, while Swedes, whether as actors or characters, continue to appear in Hollywood films as "Others," restricted to certain roles and confined to particular genres – comedy not among them.

Beauty and the b/east

"There is nothing I so bitterly regret as my decision to leave Sweden and give myself over to the film world's violence. [M]ost of all [I regret] that

I let myself be captured by Hollywood's lying dream factory," writes Nils Asther in his autobiography, *Narrens Väg (The Jester's Way)*.[7] His fortunes fluctuated wildly during the 31 years he lived in the U.S., largely due to his mismanagement of money. In late middle age he was blackmailed by a Philadelphia gang that threatened to expose him as a homosexual (he was bisexual).[8] Out of work, sick, and broke, he left shortly thereafter for a welfare state Sweden now guaranteeing pension plans and free medical coverage. He hoped to continue working as an actor but had been away from the tight-knit Swedish theater/film system too long: when he died in 1981 he had appeared in only four more films. In Hollywood, however, being a Swede with a slight accent worked *for* him, as it did for compatriots Ingrid Bergman, Greta Garbo, Anna Q. Nilsson, and Warner Oland.[9] At the height of his popularity, Asther received mountains of fan mail, hobnobbed with stars and starlets, and lived luxuriously. U.S. credits include forty-two sound films and twelve silents, mostly as a European seducer and/or spy.

On the face of it, Asther would thus seem to stand at the center of unmarked, successful, Nordic cum Anglo-Saxon screen "whiteness." But what to make of the fact that the two films in which he played an Oriental – *Wild Orchids* and *The Bitter Tea of General Yen* – were among his most popular? Surely it is important that both films were made during roughly the same era, when nativism was triumphant in response to earlier Southern European and Asian immigration.[10] Asian immigration, in particular, had been stringently policed: in 1882, Chinese were banned via the Chinese Exclusion Act; subsequent laws targeted Filipinos and Japanese. The first really far-reaching piece of immigration legislation, the Immigration Act of 1924, extended this pro-European, anti-Asian bias via a quota system designed to favor Northern European "races." Racism rather than economic rivalry explains the preference: at the time, only 300,000 Chinese and fewer Japanese and Filipinos had entered the U.S.[11]

White dominance in Hollywood combined with this general mistrust of Asia. The result was a number of silent and early sound films starring Asian characters. Often played by whites in "yellow face," these "Asians" engaged in unhappy, unhealthy, and/or unequal relationships with Caucasian characters.[12] Both *Wild Orchids* and *The Bitter Tea of General Yen* fit this pattern, warning against miscegenation while celebrating heterosexual romance in stories told largely from a woman's point of view. Because a good-looking Swedish heartthrob plays the "Asians," they become multi-dimensional, accorded masculine as well as feminine, civilized as well as barbaric, and Western as well as Eastern, traits.

Both films recycle the "beauty and the beast" saga, shifting the tale to the East while continuing the original emphases on capture and rescue, rape and romance. Set during different time frames (*Wild Orchids* is undated but presumably contemporaneous with the time of its release; *Bitter Tea* takes place during the Boxer Rebellion), each features an Anglo woman who travels to the East with (*Wild Orchids*) or to meet (*Bitter Tea*) her Anglo-Saxon partner. En route she encounters an Oriental aristocrat played by Asther. In each film, Asther's character is first seen by the female lead. Both women are initially more repulsed than attracted, but the extent of their aversion is conditioned by whether an Anglo male partner has previously appeared. Shocked when she witnesses the elegantly attired Prince whip his servant on board ship, Lily (Greta Garbo) turns to her kindly, older husband, John (Lewis Stone), for consolation. On her way to marry a man (Gavin Gordon) she has not seen in 11 years, Megan (Barbara Stanwyck) watches Yen's limousine run over a peasant. Yen emerges from his car, kisses Megan's hand, and, bleeding from a head wound, asks if he can borrow her handkerchief. Megan is simultaneously flattered and repelled.

Not surprisingly, more sexual contact occurs between beauty and beast in the pre-Hays Code *Wild Orchids*.[13] John encourages contact between Lily and the Prince, perpetually placing the taller and younger Prince between himself and his wife. Older and stiffer, he looks out of place next to Garbo and Asther who, as tall Swedes with aquiline noses, high cheekbones and foreheads, look like they belong together.[14] Both are also sexually ambiguous: in some scenes she wears tailored suits; he affects "Oriental" accessories like turbans, rings, and wide belts. Where John turns and looks away, the Prince tirelessly looks at, bends over or leans towards Lily. An early dream sequence shows the Prince as a cruel Oriental tyrant superimposed over the sleeping Megan, flailing his whip. Increasingly, however, their attraction is evident. A key moment comes when, off on business, John sends the Prince to the bungalow where Lily is resting to protect her from a leering "native." Jauntily clad in cap, boots, and jodhpurs, the Prince waits until Lily emerges from the bedroom. Architectural design (arches, low ceilings) intimates entrapment. Lily runs back and forth as the Prince tries to catch and kiss her, but their eventual embrace seems ardent, at least from John's point of view. (He has returned unexpectedly and sees them hug silhouetted through curtains.) Lily manages to flee before he enters; the Prince pretends he has been kissing a servant.

Often dressed in Oriental garb, Yen is nevertheless the epitome of European *savoir faire*: that Asther speaks with a slight Swedish accent only underscores the point.[15] A much taller actor than Stanwyck, he looks more threatening as Yen than he does as the Prince, but he again is unfailingly attentive. In contrast, Megan's frumpy fiancé rushes away from his wedding to save a group of Chinese orphans, followed by Megan. Together they ask Yen for a safe conduct pass through the fighting. That Yen writes, "this fool prefers civil war to the loving arms of his bride," only literalizes the obvious: Anglo-Saxon potency and virility are in trouble; indeed, in the next sequence one of Yen's henchmen abducts Megan and kills her husband.

Figure 5.2   Nils Asther as General Yen and Barbara Stanwyck as Megan
Davis in *The Bitter Tea of General Yen* (Columbia Pictures, 1933.
Colour by KHBB). Courtesy of the Kobal Collection.

Love-struck, Yen is ready to do anything for Megan except set her free.
When she lectures him on Christianity, saying, "we're all of one flesh and
blood," he asks, wistfully, "Really? Do you mean that?" A brief close-up
shows him gently place his hand on hers. She pulls away, and he mutters,
despairingly, "Words! Nothing but words!" Other physical contact occurs
only in Megan's dreams: superimpositions and process shots mingle three
different Yens, two threatening (one a vampire with spike nails and pointed
ears, one in a military outfit), the third protective and tender (dressed in
Western clothes and a mask). Megan responds warmly to the last Yen,
taking off his mask, kissing and hugging him.[16]
Both Garbo and Stanwyck cradle Asther in their arms the last time they
meet. Wearing the Oriental gown Yen gave her, Megan embraces him as
he drinks poisoned tea and sadly tells her, "real torture is to be despised
by the one you love." Lily clasps the Prince after he is mauled by a tiger
(the jealous John having removed the bullets from the Prince's gun), then
chides her husband in intertitles: "What right had you to take it for granted
that I loved him? that I was faithless to you? You are blind – blind –

blind!" Yen dies, the Prince lives. Neither Megan nor Lily sees her Oriental suitor again, for racial logic of the time dictates that the Anglo-American partner or his surrogate, not the Oriental beast, appear in the final frame next to the beauty. In *Bitter Tea*, Yen's American partner, then betrayer, Jones (Walter Connolly), stands behind Megan, though she smiles happily at his suggestion that Yen lingers on as the wind in her hair. In *Wild Orchids*, Lily and John sit side by side, kissing, in John's luxury automobile, while the Prince recovers from his wounds inside his palace. Throughout both films, supposedly "Oriental" backdrops and "Asian" extras have reinforced how strange Anglo-Americans look in the East, making it seem only right that they should end up together, on their way home.

The Bitter Tea of General Yen intrigued female audiences during the Depression, argues Gina Marchetti, because it offered women exoticism, wealth, and escape.[17] That the beast is in fact Swedish allows Yen to be seen as attractive. His loss of money and suicide grimly recall the market crash; at the film's end there are no successful Anglo-American characters to turn to, only Jones – a common last name to be sure. In contrast, the pre-Depression *Wild Orchids* leaves the (Swedish) beast alive if without the (Swedish) beauty he resembles, because a rich, reasonably attractive alternative exists: not coincidentally, John's last name is "Sterling."

Both films thus follow a general "racial" logic favoring "native" over "stranger," a logic that dictates that "native" Anglo-Saxons must ultimately supplant any and all foreigners. Dead or alive, however, as (Nordic) Oriental, Asther is at least as powerful as his Anglo male counterparts. Certainly he is more sexy and virile, whether flicking whips or waving fans, clad in military overcoats, Western dinner jackets or Oriental robes. The same cannot be said of the majority of Swedish characters played by non-Swedes in westerns: their erotic appeal, like their earning power, is almost non-existent, particularly by comparison with the macho Anglo gunfighter heroes and villains who prowl the prairies and shoot up the streets.

Ho-hum on the range

"Skål!" says George Hanson (Sterling Hayden) to Molly (Carol Kelly), the whore with the heart of gold, near the end of *Terror in a Texas Town*. The two are drinking whiskey, as good Westerners will. George tries to pump Molly about her evil gunfighter boyfriend, Johnny Crayle (Neil Young). Though it is clear that Molly likes George, she will tell him only: "Stay away from him, he's mean." Swede that he is, George puts her reticence down to the inefficacy of American liquor. "If you were drinking akvavit, you would talk," he mumbles.

As a relatively young, tall actor playing a Swedish hero, Hayden is spared stock phrases like "by golly," "by yiminy mama," "I bet you," and "yust do your yob" that older and shorter actors playing Swedish homesteaders constantly utter in *Shane, The Man Who Shot Liberty Valance*, and *The Searchers*.[18] The portrayal of Swedish pioneers as peace-loving immigrants may be accurate, but their characterization is otherwise cliché. As members of the "Nordic race," Swedes were welcome newcomers and only occasionally the butt of jokes: as Patricia Limerick points out, "race . . . was the key factor in dividing the peoples of Western America" although "[d]ifferences in culture, in language, in religion, meant something" as well.[19] Lured by the 1862 Homestead Act's promises of 160 acres of free land awarded those who settled on and improved it, Swedes constituted the seventh largest group of European immigrants in the U.S. By 1910, almost one-fifth of the world's Swedish population (1.25 million people) lived in the U.S.; most had farming backgrounds.[20]

Frederick Jackson Turner's influential, now discredited, frontier hypothesis described the integration of European immigrants into American society, framing the West as a "crucible" wherein "immigrants were Americanized, liberated, and fused into a mixed race, English in neither nationality nor characteristics."[21] His focus was on white inhabitants at the expense of the "persistent population of Indians, . . . established Hispanic population, as well as one of later Mexican immigrants; Asians . . . black people."[22] Several of Turner's contemporaries, among them Teddy Roosevelt, went further, arguing that white western migration would ensure "progress" because "superior" forms would replace "primitive" races, using violence if necessary.[23]

Contemporaneous literary and film westerns popularized these racist, imperialist theories via narratives where, in Dyer's words, "The greatest threat . . . comes not from the native peoples or Mexicans but from within, from bad whites" because "[t]o make non-whites the greatest threat would accord them qualities of will and skill . . . which would make them the equivalent of white people."[24] In this sense the Swedish sidekick films of the 1950s and 1960s resemble earlier westerns. With an all-white cast, *Shane* pits a group of farmers and a cattle rancher, each represented by a gunfighter, against each other. *The Man Who Shot Liberty Valance* weaves a romantic rivalry between Tom Doniphon (John Wayne) and Ranse Stoddard (Jimmy Stewart) together with the question of how best to protect the town from outlaws like Liberty Valance (Lee Marvin). Mexicans are glimpsed in the background of a cantina and a classroom; an African American, Pompey (Woody Strode), has a supporting role as Tom's devoted, uneducated, servant. *Terror in a Texas Town* opposes George and Johnny because Johnny's fat cat boss (Sebastian Cabot) wants the homesteaders' land for oil; members of a Mexican family appear in supporting roles. Only *The Searchers* centers on race as Ethan (John Wayne) pursues Indian nemesis Scar (Henry Brandon, a blue-eyed white actor). Nonetheless most Indians and Mexicans appear only in crowd or bar scenes and Martin's "squaw" (Beulah Archuletta) is ludicrous, if loyal.

But why do so many Swedes suddenly pop up on the sidelines of 1950s and 1960s westerns when they were virtually absent from earlier films?[25] The time of production is telling. By the 1950s and 1960s, what already were referred to as "ethnic" rather than "racial" distinctions had become less meaningful among first and second generation European immigrants. In contrast, as Brian Henderson argues with respect to *The Searchers*, the question of racial integration had grown to be "an American dilemma."[26] Beginning in the late 1940s liberal sociologists and policy makers argued that the "melting pot" model of Northern European assimilation patterns should be applied to African, Mexican, and Native Americans.[27] By the mid-1950s the popularity of "ethnicity theory" marked film narratives. Swedish farmers who help and/or resemble Mexican, African, and Native American minor characters appear. Too late to save his old father, George helps a Mexican family; Ranse teaches Pompey, the Erikssons, and others how to read. Obsessed with wiping out miscegenation if patronizingly tolerant of Swedes, Ethan, in contrast, is portrayed as a flawed hero.

All four films are set in places where Swedes actually settled – Texas (*The Searchers* and *Terror*), somewhere in the Southwest (*The Man Who Shot Liberty Valance* mentions the Picketwire River), Wyoming (*Shane*). As in most westerns, however, the grimy reality of pioneer life disappears. The Swedes played by Norwegian Canadian character actor John Qualen are accessorized so as to render them ridiculous: Peter Eriksson appears in a stocking night cap in *The Man Who Shot Liberty Valance*; Lars Jorgensen supportively dons reading glasses when his wife reads the letter Martin (Jeffrey Hunter) has written to Laurie (Vera Miles) aloud in *The Searchers*. In both films, Qualen makes a show of his emotions, waving his hands, stumbling over words. *Shane*'s Axel and *Terror in a Texas Town*'s Sven are less silly, but they too are portrayed as meek, weak and/or obliging.

Like most Mexican, African, and Native American characters, male screen Swedes thus figure primarily as foils to Anglo gunfighters who seem braver and more intelligent because they are so constantly compared with "aliens" playing supporting roles or bit parts. Casting emphasizes differences in height and age, with tall, usually youthful or middle-aged men with Anglo features and full heads of hair chosen to play Western heroes and villains, and shorter, older, balding men designated as Swedes. Anglo masculinity and virility are accentuated because Swedish homesteaders are positioned inside or near houses, behind or next to women, in the background or at the side of the film frame. Axel is barely noticeable among the other settlers gathered in Joe's (Van Heflin) log cabin. A restaurant owner and cook, Peter wears an apron and wields a skillet, never a gun. Lars putters around his farm, accompanied by his wife and daughter. Crucially, boys prefer

Anglos: little Joey (Brandon de Wilde) has a crush on Shane; Martin desperately wants to be recognized as "kin" by Ethan; the Jorgensen's son is killed when he, too, follows Ethan.

Only in *Terror in a Texas Town* does a Swedish sailor hero oppose an Anglo gun slinging villain. After 19 years at sea, George is fiercely independent and very strong. Trumpets sound whenever he appears; he is often shot from below, towering over the other characters or marching along in the landscape. When Johnny kills a Mexican settler, George steps in to protect and provide for the family, giving the boy the cow he has inherited from his own father, then seizing a harpoon and stomping off in search of justice. Townspeople massed behind him, he confronts and kills Johnny by harpooning him through the heart from an impossible distance. But George also dies: the final close-ups show his face and the other homesteaders' feet as they file past.

On the brighter side, at least George is not condemned to eek out a ho-hum living on the range as but one more Swedish homesteader in a land where Anglos rule. Real Swede Dolph Lundgren goes Swedish character George Hanson several better in scores of 1980s and 1990s action films. Not only do most of Lundgren's macho characters survive, they become honorary (br)others, not "others," because they adopt and adapt the knowledge and skills of smaller African, African American or Asian sidekicks. Like Asther's Oriental seducers, however, Lundgren's heroes and occasional villains are never Swedes, but now Aryans – Soviets, East Germans, and (Anglo-)Americans.

Swede as (br)other

"The biggest man I've ever been with. *Definitely* the biggest," says Grace Jones, who as Lundgren's ex-girlfriend of many years should know.[28] At 6 foot 6 inches and 230 muscular pounds, Lundgren oozes power and virility. Now married to a Swedish fashion designer, he earlier squired several beautiful women. The child of two Swedish academics, little Dolph was, however, studious, skinny, and prone to severe allergies. Only as a teenager did he begin lifting weights and studying martial arts. Fluent in five languages, he earned a masters in chemical engineering, taught hand-to-hand combat for a year to Swedish marines, then became captain of his country's martial arts team. Eventually he specialized in kick-boxing, winning European competitions in 1980 and 1981. His film career started thanks to Jones with a walk-on part in *A View to a Kill* (John Glen, 1985).[29] Since then he has starred or played major roles in over twenty action films. He is especially popular in Europe and Japan. The U.S. is his weakest market, but he is well known here, too, thanks to video.

Following action rules, Lundgren's figures engage in combat, not courtship. At home or abroad, they often learn from non-white allies, though ultimately the clearly bigger Lundgren always knows best. Of the eight Lundgren vehicles I treat – *Rocky IV*, *Red Scorpion*, *The Punisher*, *Showdown in Little Tokyo*, *Universal Soldier*, *Johnny Mnemonic*, *Pentathlon*, and *Silent Trigger* – only *Showdown* pairs him with a non-white, Brandon Lee. The other seven include African American, African, Japanese American, and Japanese characters in supporting or bit parts, nodding to contemporary demographic trends while appealing to the white working-class men whose jobs are most threatened by new arrivals from Latin America and Asia.[30]

Beginning with the 1952 liberalization of the 1924 Immigration Act, immigration laws have facilitated shifts in population make-up. The 1965 Immigration Act, for example, scrapped national origins quotas in favor of hemispheric caps; today, transnational migration additionally affects the character of intergroup relations.[31] As a result, the "de facto racial dictatorship constituted by the denial of basic democratic rights to racially defined minorities (and to women)" has modified.[32] Nonetheless, Michael Omi and Howard Winant argue, the liberal "ethnicity" paradigm of assimilation popularized in the 1940s to 1960s continues to mask the crucial importance of race, witness the ways census categories like "white," "Asian American," and "Hispanic" are used to decide representation and funding.[33] Meanwhile generational distance from initial immigration, widespread social mobility, and intermarriage among white ethnic groups have made "ethnicity" increasingly "symbolic" for white European Americans.[34]

Because contemporary action films draw so heavily on Western conventions, most of Lundgren's chief opponents are other whites. But only the cryogenetically frozen Vietnam war villain of *Universal Soldier* makes overtly racist comments when recalled to life by U.S. special forces. In every other film, whether made during or after *perestroika* (i.e. in the Reagan-Bush 1980s or the Bush-Clinton 1990s), Lundgren becomes more (br)other than "Other," absorbing the racial and national "markings" of smaller allies into himself in an "assimilation" reminiscent of Ethan's uncanny ability to track and "speak good Comanche" in *The Searchers*. Thanks to his childhood in Japan, for example, *Showdown*'s Detective Kenner (Lundgren) proves himself to be more versed in Japanese culture than his Eurasian partner, Johnny Murata (Lee): though both excel in martial arts, Kenner, not Murata, is fluent in Japanese and knowledgeable about *haiku* and flower-arranging. *Pentathlon*'s Eric Brogar (Lundgren) learns that he has much in common with his African American coach and friend Creese (Roger E. Mosley). Eric complains, "I live in a country run by people I don't understand who don't understand me." Creese replies, "You must be black." The most delicious metamorphosis is that of *Red Scorpion*'s Lieutenant Nikolai (Lundgren) into a bushman: though Nikolai gets a scorpion tattoo and becomes adept at spear-throwing, he draws the line at eating grubs.

Most films feature foreign policy concerns more prominently than domestic debates. In the three films set during *glasnost* and *perestroika* (*Rocky*

IV, *Red Scorpion*, and *Pentathlon*), the bad guys are Aryan authority figures. Each film emphasizes individualism while condemning party machinery.[35] In all, Lundgren disappears into his characters, not only imitating Russian and German accents when speaking English, but occasionally speaking Russian and German as well. His big blondness may appeal to white neo-Nazis and/or racists, but the scripts make concerted efforts to disentangle *his* Soviet and East German characters from any taint of Stalinism or Nazism.[36] In *Rocky IV*, Drago (Lundgren) proves a sympathetic figure because he defies the Politburo's demands that he win for Mother Russia with an "I fight to win! For me!" When Rocky (Sylvester Stallone) wins, all applaud, the crowd with genuine enthusiasm, the party officials because prompted to do so by a chief who looks much like Gorbachev. In *Red Scorpion* Lieutenant Nikolai escapes from a Soviet prison to join forces with African freedom fighters. Soviet troops spray the Namibian desert and the people who live there with poisonous chemicals; Cuban "advisors" excel at tortures even the Soviets cannot imagine. In *Pentathlon* East German superstar Eric Brogar literally jumps to freedom during the Olympic games. The evil Heinrich Mueller (David Soul) is first a Nazi party man, then a Stasi chief, then a neo-Nazi leader who tries to blow up a "Never Again" rally. Perennially clad in black leather, Mueller refuses to shower, preferring to smell, as he puts it, "European." Mueller imprisons Eric's father, stalks his girlfriend, and kills Creese. Small wonder Eric fights back with all the Pentathlon skills at his command. Eventually of course he kills Mueller, and by the film's end earns a place on the 1994 U.S. Olympic team.

The post-Soviet films target no single, clear enemy, though Lundgren's leads frequently fight against drugs and gangs with foreign connections.[37]

Figure 5.3   Dolph Lundgren as Lieutenant Nikolai in *Red Scorpion* (Shapiro Glickenhaus, 1989). Courtesy of the Kobal Collection.

His opponents are almost never Anglos, and in all Lundgren plays an American. In three, his characters have Anglo-American names ("Scott" in *Universal Soldier*, "Detective Kenner" in *Showdown in Little Tokyo*, and "Frank Castle" in *The Punisher*). In all five, his belligerent bluster betrays no hint of a foreign accent. His opponents, in contrast, often have accents, whether "French" (Jean-Claude van Damme as the hero in *Universal Soldier*), "Italian" (Jeroen Krabbe as the villain in *The Punisher*) or "Japanese" (Toshiro Obata and Cary-Hiroyuki Tagawa as the key villains in *Showdown in Little Tokyo*).

In every film, whether set during or post-*perestroika*, nationality thus occupies center stage although nostalgia for a symbolic (Anglo-)American identity lingers on. "White" dominates screen space and time. In all except *Silent Trigger*, women have minor roles, and homo-eroticism rules.[38] Lundgren is often naked or semi-naked, with what Stallone taught him are the prime "movie muscles" – stomach and butt – prominently on display. In *Red Scorpion*, dramatic lighting and sharp camera angles emphasize his determined jaw line and glowering eyes. Thanks to close-ups and framing, his mammoth arms, bulky calves, and massive thighs seem to dwarf the mountains behind him. In *The Punisher*, back and side lighting sculpt his bare body as, crouched on his heels in his underground hide-out, he worships at a make-shift altar. The minimal and/or unappealing spaces in which Lundgren crouches, catapults, and kicks further showcase his body. Sets range from abandoned warehouses (*Silent Trigger*) to claustrophobic sewers (*The Punisher*) to debris-filled streets (*Johnny Mnemonic*) to barren barracks (*Universal Soldier* and *Red Scorpion*) to metallic training facilities (*Rocky IV* and *Pentathlon*). Tight-fitting clothes call attention to his muscularity, and position the characters as proletarians: in most films Lundgren appears in T-shirts, combat boots, and tight jeans; when he changes, it is to sweat pants, as in *Pentathlon*, or boxing shorts, as in *Rocky IV*. Frequently other men look admiringly on.

Unlike Asther's Oriental beasts, however, Lundgren's white (br)others are motivated by masochism as well as sadism. Most films feature torture scenes where male and occasionally female characters have ample opportunity to measure how Lundgren's "movie" – and other – muscles twitch and tense when poked by needles, jolted with electricity or shackled in chains. Yet to a man, Lundgren's heroes – and villains, too – surmount their suffering to "kick ass," following an ancient "white ideal" predicated, Dyer argues, on a "dynamic of aspiration, of striving to be, to transcend."[39] Several are resurrected robots, endowed with hellish rather than heavenly attributes. *Universal Soldier*'s evil Scott is a killing machine. *The Punisher*'s Frank Castle is differently half-human. His wife and children dead, 125 "revenge" murders later, he prays from his subterranean retreat to a God who never answers: "Come on God, answer me. Where is justice, where is punishment? Why are the innocent dead and the guilty alive? Or have you already said to the world, here is justice, here is punishment, here in me?" Robe clad, with shoulder-length blond hair, *Johnny Mnemonic*'s Street Preacher resembles a glued-together, drug-propelled, Sunday School Christ.[40]

Lundgren's big (br)others are all simultaneously gods and monsters: in these films, terror of, and fascination with, technology are omnipresent and intertwined.[41] General Vortek's (K. P. McKenna) description of Lieutenant Nikolai as a "powerful valuable tool if he can be controlled" is typical. Caricatures of macho masculinity, these quasi-human (br)others are working-class warriors, not aristocratic rulers, and certainly not peaceable peasants. Competing with Anglo-American men for Anglo-American women, Asther's Orientals may outmaneuver Lundgren's characters in the bedroom but not beyond; second fiddles to Anglo-American gunfighter heroes, humdrum Swedish homesteaders are tied to their land and their ladies and would never dream of traveling in space or time, as Lundgren's leads do. Nonetheless as a bulky blond (Swedish) (br)other, Lundgren finds himself strait-jacketed in action, forever cast as Soviet, Eastern European or American characters, yet another Swedish hole at the heart of whiteness.

"Scandinavian humor and other myths"

For years Lundgren has dreamt of making a historical film with a good Swedish director: reportedly at the time of *Universal Soldier* he was "trying to write a romantic comedy."[42] Unhappily for him, comedy seems out of the question. Lundgren himself recognizes that "it would be difficult to make me credible in intellectual roles, as it would if Woody Allen wanted to be Rambo."[43]

But fellow "ethnic" big men Sly and Arnold *have* acted in comedies. Why not Dolph? And why was Asther so rarely cast in comic parts? An entry on the Norse "God of Humor," "Kmute" (pronounced "Mute") in *Scandinavian Humor and Other Myths* snidely clarifies why Swedes and comedy are so at odds:

> There is substantial doubt where Kmute . . . ever existed. . . . Some contend that some medieval scholar invented him while transcribing the ancient tales of Nordic cosmology, because he refused to believe that so many people could be so totally lacking in any sort of humor. Other scholars take the opposite viewpoint: Any people who can talk convincingly about the humor in Ingmar Bergman's films have no need of an external power to tell them when to be amused.[44]

The only Hollywood comedy to include Swedes that I can think of is a western, *Blazing Saddles* (Mel Brooks, 1973). As Ella Shohat comments, identities throughout are misaligned: the sheriff (Cleavon Little) is black, the "Indian" chief (Mel Brooks) speaks Yiddish, and so on.[45] She does not mention the town full of Swedish characters played by non-Swedes, however. As the sheriff rides down the main street, all the shop signs read "Johnson"; the town leaders are named "Gaby," "Samuel," "Olson," and . . . "Howard" "Johnson"; the townspeople, together with their cows, gather in church when they need to decide what action to take. Other than these rather vague markers, there are fewer signals of "Swedishness" than in 1950s to 1960s westerns: although the town leaders are fools, none is a bumbling buffoon à la John Qualen in the Ford westerns, and no one speaks English with a Swedish accent. In *Blazing Saddles*, too, then, "Swede" remains an empty sign: being "Swedish" is less visible – and less funny – than being Jewish or black.

Nonetheless the ways Swedes have – and have not – been cast and portrayed over the last six decades has changed from marked difference (Swedish actor as Oriental beast) in the 1920s and 1930s to supportive backdrop (Swedish characters as humdrum homesteaders, played by non-Swedes) in the 1950s and 1960s to unmarked focus and effacement (Swedish actor as Soviet, Eastern European or American [br]other) in the 1980s and 1990s. (*Blazing Saddles'* vaguely marked "Swedes" constitute a 1970s bridge.)

Such shifts are, of course, funneled through genre conventions. Asther's depiction as a commanding, sadistic, Oriental aristocrat who is alternatively masculine and feminine is shaped by the fact that *Wild Orchids* and *The Bitter Tea of General Yen* are exotic melodramas designed to intrigue white women just before and during the Depression. That Swedish characters in 1950s and 1960s westerns are so frequently represented as feminized, pacific, farmers is triggered by western requirements that heroes and villains be Anglo gunfighters who appeal to white men. Today's action formulae dictate Lundgren's casting as macho if/and masochistic working-class hero or villain who functions, thanks to global television and rental systems, as an intimidating white – and increasingly "American" – model for Asian, European, *and* American male audiences.

Bottom line, though Anglos continue to reign supreme in film representation, they now do so in more tenuous ways. To quote Richard Alba, today the "conception of ethnicity . . . depends . . . on voluntary commitments to ethnic identities," at least where white European Americans are concerned.[46] At the same time, "far from decreasing, the significance of race in American life has expanded, and the racial dimensions of politics and culture have proliferated."[47]

Consider one last time the shifts and continuities in race and ethnicity manifest in my case studies: first, tall attractive (Swede as) Asian vied with Anglo-American lead or his surrogate, while smaller Asian characters cringed or crowded in the background. Then, small "Swedish" farmers took refuge indoors while Anglo-American cowboys roamed the range and Mexicans and Native Americans lurked in the background. Now a big Swede is first clearly labeled Soviet and German, then vaguely designated (Anglo-)American; he wins against other whites and, occasionally, Japanese, by internalizing the customs and expertise of African Americans, Africans, Asian Americans, and Asians.

Lamentably, then, all three of my examples of Swedes as Others offer photographic "proof" that, in Dyer's words, "white people [broadly speaking] lead humanity forward because of their temperamental qualities of leadership: will power, far-sightedness, [and] energy."[48] Yet they also point to the existence of frictions, contradictions, and restrictions within, and on, whiteness. And if I am right that Swedes form a hole at heart of whiteness, as with empty spaces in general, they will necessarily elicit varying interpretations. As Winant argues, to combat racism, we must pay attention to race, and emphasize what he terms "the volatility of contemporary white identities."[49] Certainly male screen Swedes demonstrate how much "whiteness" is "unclear and unstable," marked by shifting borders and internal hierarchies.[50]

6

LATINAS IN LA-LA LAND

From bit part to starlet in "indie" and mainstream films

Figure 6.1   Rosie Perez as Tina and Spike Lee as Mookie in *Do the Right Thing* (Universal Pictures, 1989). Courtesy of the Kobal Collection.

Of spitfires, maids, and mamas

Latino directors, writers, and producers were key to late 1970s and 1980s independent film formations. Like other newcomers to film at the time, these "auteurs" made a point of telling stories not previously heard or misrepresented in Hollywood, often drawing on their experiences in groups on the margins of U.S. society.[1] In the mid- to late 1980s, several Latino "indie" directors, among them Gregory Nava, Cheech Marin, and Luis Valdez moved mainstream; fleetingly, critics spoke of a "Hispanic Hollywood."[2] Since then, however, there have been few Latino-acted, -directed, or -oriented films, even though Latinos now constitute over 11 percent of the total U.S. population and are among the more dedicated movie-going publics.

And what of Latinas in La-La Land? How have *they* fared in the last two decades of independent and studio features? To date, only Rose Troche (*Go Fish*, 1994; *Bedrooms and Hallways,* 1999), Kim Flores (*Vocessitas,* 1997), and Ela Troyano (*Latin Boys Go to Hell*, 1997) have directed feature fiction films, and only Lourdes Portillo (*El Diablo nunca duerme*, 1996) and Jennifer Maytorena Taylor (*Paulina*, 1997) have made feature length documentaries. Most Latinas working today in the cinema, as earlier, are actresses, cast in bit parts to boot. A few dozen are featured as third wheels in triangular relationships and/or as supporting players; a handful are promoted as starlets.

But since ensemble and/or character acting were widely held to help shape 1980s independent films, what better place to tackle questions of possibility and impossibility for Latinas in La-La Land? This chapter focuses on three actresses, exploring whether independent films grant them greater freedom than do mainstream movies, and examining how audiences understand the "service" roles they often play as spitfires, maids, and mamas asked to provide sexual favors, perform household chores, and proffer emotional glue. I choose Lupe Ontiveros, Rosie Perez, and Jennifer Lopez as subjects because their films span the gamut of 1980s and 1990s production and distribution possibilities, and because between them they have worked with many of the leading male directors who began as "independents": Gregory Nava

111

(Ontiveros and Lopez), Cheech Marin (Ontiveros), Spike Lee, Peter Weir, and Jim Jarmusch (Perez), Oliver Stone, Bob Rafelson, Frances Ford Coppola, and Steven Soderbergh (Lopez), if often in decidedly mainstream films produced by major studios. I refer in passing to other films in which these actresses have worked. I concentrate on nine Latino-themed and/or -directed features that are box office and/or critical successes and either independently produced or "authored" by a director known for his independent work. With Ontiveros, I study *El Norte* (Gregory Nava, 1983), *Bound by Honor* (Taylor Hackford, 1993) and . . . *And the Earth Did Not Swallow Him* (Severo Perez, 1994); with Pérez, *Do the Right Thing* (Spike Lee, 1989), *Night on Earth* (Jim Jarmusch, 1991), and *Somebody to Love* (Alexandre Rockwell, 1995); with Lopez, *My Family/Mi Familia* (Nava, 1995), *Blood and Wine* (Bob Rafelson, 1997), and *Selena* (Nava, 1997).

I also pick these three actresses because their *bodies* are all somehow "impossible," both torquing and tempting casting traditions and hence revealing limitations and liberties that Latinas encounter. Ontiveros is short and squat, self-styled the "Chicano Miss Piggy"; Perez is infamous for her "mouth," i.e. foul language, lisp, accent, screech; Lopez has capitalized on her butt: asked about prostheses on talk shows, she proudly pivoted, patted, and proclaimed, "todo es mio!"[3]

I begin with Ontiveros as the oldest of the three, scrutinizing her roles from the early 1980s onwards in a section entitled "Maid to order, Doña to flee." A second section investigates how, starting in the mid-1980s, Perez' performances as "Ghetto girl/drama queen" made her in 1995 the second most popular Hispanic star after Andy Garcia.[4] A third section called "Shake your booty, cash your check" turns to Lopez' mid-1990s rise to fame and fortune playing "noir" heartthrobs and action heroines. Finally, in a conclusion titled "Revolutions in dependence," I compare all three, wondering why the stout Ontiveros continues to be cast in at best supporting roles, though she has "grown" over the years; why the tiny, talkative Perez gets top billing only in "indie" vehicles though she frequently steals the show in mainstream films as third wheel; and why only Lopez burst into star(let)dom, nationally, and cross-media, though reports now proliferate that she has undergone derriere reduction to do so.

Maid to order, Doña to flee

Lupe Ontiveros' 20-year-long career seems girdled by constraints placed on Latina bodies in both studio and independent films. Increasingly overweight, always 4 foot 11 inches, time and again she has played a maid and/or a mother (with older sisters and aunts as variations on the latter). As she has aged and grown heavier the comic and/or horrific aspects of her characters have become more pronounced, in independent and mainstream films alike. In early work in the children's action vehicle, *The Goonies* (Richard Donner,

1985), Ontiveros plays a modestly dressed, hard-working maid named Rosalita who – unlike every other non-Anglo in the cast (and there are several) – speaks no English. A decade later, in the epic *My Family/Mi Familia*, Ontiveros appears as the more foolish sister "Irene." Ruffled blouses and large flowered skirts accentuate her girth as she bustles about, preparing or serving food and eating. And in a smaller part as the maid Nora in James Brooks' romantic comedy, *As Good as It Gets* (1997), her double chins tremble in response to Jack Nicholson's abuse. Here, however, she has the second largest non-white part: all of five minutes.[5]

Yet Ontiveros' acting occasionally fleshes out the clichéd maids and mamas she plays. This is especially true of her participation in Latino-"authored" films like *Zoot Suit* (Luis Valdez, 1981), *El Norte, Born in East L.A.* (Cheech Marin, 1985), . . . *And the Earth Did Not Swallow Him*, and *Bound by Honor* (screenplay by Jimmy Santiago Baca). Some are best labeled independents, others not, but all somehow emphasize the need for social and political engagement, an attitude long-time activist Ontiveros shares.[6] In *El Norte*, for example, Ontiveros' measured performance as an undocumented Mexican maid shapes the character of Nacha into a bilingual voice of protection, conscience, and pan-Latino solidarity. In tones ranging from reserved to comic to explosive, she helps Rosa (Zaide Silvia Gutiérrez) escape an I.N.S. raid in L.A., teaches her where to buy clothes, coaxes her to apply make-up, secures work for them, and tracks down Rosa's brother Ernesto (David Villalpando) to help her when she is hospitalized with typhoid fever. Pitched as an "art film" and "personal statement," by 1984 *El Norte* had become the highest grossing Spanish language picture in the U.S. and an early example of cross-over "indie" marketing.[7] Following Nava's lead, however, critics have on the whole ignored Ontiveros' performance, focusing instead on the film's magical realism and family values.[8]

In contrast to *El Norte*'s success, the cross-over dreams of the $20 million *Bound by Honor* (Hollywood Pictures/Buena Vista) went unrealized, though the film opened in thirty cities nationwide[9] and director Taylor Hackford, crew, and over 90 percent Latino cast went to considerable efforts to produce an "authentically Latino" film, grounded in L.A. locations and undertaken together with the local community.[10] Ontiveros' character occupies little screen time, but her role illuminates the ideological underpinnings of the film because as the drug-dealing matriarch Carmen, Ontiveros operates within the same macho "family" parameters as the male leads. Save for omnipresent statuettes of the Virgin Mary, hers is one of largest female roles, but she is as much if not more a *marimacha* as a "mama."[11] Chomping on a cigar, in pants and short-sleeved knit shirt, with red fingernails and hennaed hair, she confronts the long-haired, bearded, undercover cop named Paco (Benjamin Bratt) over a PCP drug deal. Suspicious, she pokes his crotch with her pistol, crooning "PCP is very explosive! boom! I'd hate to lose such a handsome customer!" With her daughter's help, she literally exposes Paco as a cop; in retaliation for the unmasking of his wired manhood, he kills first the daughter, then Carmen's husband; Carmen is hauled off to jail.

In the made-for-TV movie . . . *And the Earth Did Not Swallow Him*,[12] Ontiveros finally has a supporting role, but again as a bad (now surrogate) mama. As Doña Rosa (her name is simplified from the book's Doña Bonifacia), she is both frightening and sleazy. With her husband, Doña Rosa cares for Marcos (José Alcada) so that he can attend school in Minnesota while the rest of his family goes off to pick beets. Intent on pinching every possible penny, Doña Rosa feeds Marcos rotten meat smothered in chili sauce, clasping him to her large bosom to force him to eat it. One day she orders him to dig a ditch in the lawn, while she lounges in long shot in a chair, fanning herself, smoking, and drinking. That night, with her husband's acquiescence, she sells liquor to an illegal visitor, seduces him, and kills him for his money. Marcos returns from work to find the man's body in his bed, and his guardians make him their accomplice in the burial, giving him the dead man's ring to ensure his silence.

The film underscores the heroism and humanity of Mexican American migrant workers based in 1950s Texas, much as the original 1971 novel by Tomás Rivera does.[13] Recast and tightened to appeal to cross-over public television audiences, however, the film omits some of the book's more horrific events, adds sympathetic Anglo characters, and uses Spanish only as a kind of "environmental" background buzz. Yet Perez had difficulty financing his film, ultimately making it through a combination of NEH grant, regional and Texas-based arts and humanities council grants, and American Playhouse monies. Distribution by American Playhouse Productions was, and is, so limited that Ontiveros' and others' acting remains unnoticed.

Ghetto girl/drama queen

The petite Rosie Perez, in contrast, is always shrilly vocal and hyperkinetically visible, if most frequently as supporting character or third wheel. Although she has several big budget studio films to her credit – among them *White Men Can't Jump* (Ron Shelton, 1992), *Fearless* (Peter Weir, 1993), *Untamed Heart* (Tony Bill, 1993), and *It Could Happen to You* (Andrew Bergman, 1994), she has specialized in "riffs" on "ingenue" roles: to date, her motor mouth, screechy pitch, and slight speech impediment have seemed to make starring roles "impossible" other than in indie films.

Most of Perez' roles, whether mainstream or indie, capitalize on her idiosyncracy, positioning her as a hysteric who is likeable if screwy; most showcase her dancing and talent for ensemble acting.[14] In contrast to Woody Harrelson's boyish charm and Wesley Snipes' "jive" cool in *White Men Can't*

Jump, for example, Perez is flaky yet focused; in counterpoint to Jeff Bridges' bravado and Isabella Rossellini's reserve in *Fearless* she is withdrawn, even timid; by comparison with Nicholas Cage's soft-heartedness and Bridget Fonda's sweetness in *It Could Happen to You*, she becomes money-grubbing and shrill.

Despite these casting coups, however, Perez, like Ontiveros, maintains that her ethnic background constrains her.[15] Most of the characters she plays are identified as of Puerto Rican descent. Critics and interviewers comment tirelessly but affectionately on her "sound," describing her voice as a "buzz-saw ... that ranges from a squealing whine to a whining squeal" and her "elocution" as reminiscent of "a barrio Betty Boop blended with a touch of Elmer Fudd."[16] Though she is widely appreciated for her independence and toughness, some Latinos find her public persona and/or her screen performances problematic: certain groups charge she is "divisive" and "offensive"; others feel that her speech and dress are an embarrassment; still others charge that she promotes herself thanks to an image that the commodity market wants.[17]

In her first supporting part for Universal in *Do the Right Thing*,[18] and in most later roles, Perez plays a working-class character.[19] Though costumes and sets are crucial to her class assignation, language, pitch, cadence, and accent additionally stamp her as "prolo": Lee easily incorporated Perez' own off-color expressions like "your shit is to the curb!" into his screenplay.[20] Stereotypes notwithstanding, Perez incarnates, in Carlos Cortés' words, "a new and somewhat more complex Latina role ... the Latina as conscience to the central [male] character": Tina is more responsible than her common-law husband, Mookie (Spike Lee): indeed, she has to order pizza just to get him to come visit their son.[21] Though a spitfire, she chooses when and if she gets "sexy": at one point Mookie tries to "heat" her up by melting an ice cube over her lips, neck, knees, elbows, thighs, and finally nipples. The opening credit sequence in particular is quintessentially, controversially, "Perez": clad in three differently brightly colored spandex outfits, one including boxing shorts and gloves, she dances frenetically to Public Enemy's "Fight the Power." Different street backdrops appear behind her, but she is always center frame, and cuts are coordinated with her movements. Because the sequence ends by focusing on her "tits and ass," some feminist critics objected; others – including other feminists – viewed it as expressive of female power and creative collaboration.[22]

No feminist furor accompanied Perez' role in Jim Jarmusch's *Night on Earth*, though Angela, too, might be seen as a "bitch," to use hooks' descriptor.[23] In the second of five stories, she strides along a nearly deserted winter street at 11 p.m. wearing an orange jacket, black mini-skirt and stockings, low boots, and large hoop earrings. Her brother-in-law, Yoyo (Giancarlo Esposito), is driving a cab leased to immigrant clown Helmut

Grokenberger (Arman Mueller-Stahl) because Helmut neither knows how to drive nor how to get to Brooklyn, Yoyo's destination. "There she goes, fuckin' up again!" says Yoyo as he brakes and jumps out. He picks up Angela, and throws her, kicking and screaming, into the back of the taxi. The first one can understand of her staccato screaming is: "What is your fuckin' problem, man? . . . YOU my fuckin' problem man! . . . fuck you, fuck you, and FUCK YOU!"

Helmut is enthralled. "She's really beautiful!" he says to Yoyo. "Thanks!" Angela replies, politely. As soon as Yoyo speaks to her, however, she again becomes a banshee. "You're like a fuckin' chihuahua always gnawing at my ankles!" says Yoyo. She lashes back, "Oh yeah, well I'm gonna take a big fuckin' bite out of your fuckin' ass, asshole, so you better watch out for this little girl! Shit!" Bottom line, she refuses male control; her kindness to Helmut and acceptance of his difference make her more of a whore with a heart of gold than a gold-digger.

In contrast, as Mercedes in Alexandre Rockwell's *Somebody to Love*, Perez is decidedly materialistic.[24] *Finally* she has a starring role, albeit again as a "spit-fire": an aspiring actress and taxi dancer involved with lounge lizard Harry Harrelson (Harvey Keitel) and a young Mexican worker named Ernesto (Michael DeLorenzo). While Keitel's name is enough to bankroll most independent pictures, the rest of the supporting cast is also (indie) star-studded: Anthony Quinn plays a Latino "godfather"; Stanley Tucci appears as Mercedes' scummy agent; "indie ingenue" Steve Buscemi plays her drag-queen "girlfriend"; Quentin Tarantino briefly sets up drinks as a jaded bartender.

Living with wife and kids in a suburban rancher, Harry is a somewhat more experienced actor than Mercedes, but he is equally execrable: when he finally gets a job playing a gorilla on a Tarzan TV show, he is so awful that he is fired for not being "animal" enough. But Mercedes admires him, and works assiduously at her own craft, listening to self-help diction tapes as she brushes her teeth, book on her head to improve her posture. Her auditions are miserable flops, however: doors are repeatedly slammed in her face because her "tits are too small" or her "tits are too big."

Yet *as* Mercedes, Perez provides pyrotechnic shifts in tempo and tone. Her opening scene with Stanley Tucci is exemplary: with staccato delivery, she accuses him of sabotaging her career by sending out badly done head shots; when he out-hysterics her, she instantly deflates. Later, as dancer to songs performed by Tito Larriva, she adroitly modulates her movements to convey emotion. Like spitfires past, however, Mercedes' is a tragic tale. Longing for a career *and* a lover, at the movie's end she has neither. Harry hustles her out the window when his wife and children unexpectedly return; Ernesto is shot to death before her eyes because he has stolen mob money so that she will be happy. Bewildered by his death, Mercedes is nonetheless left with the loot. Exceptionally for most of Perez' characters, therefore, at the film's end Mercedes suddenly finds herself rich; more typically for Perez' characters, she is alone.

Shake your booty, cash your check

Unlike her compatriot, Jennifer Lopez usually gets the guy and often the money, too. Coupled with many of Hollywood's leading men – Wesley Snipes, Eric Stoltz, Sean Penn, Jack Nicholson, and George Clooney – her accomplishments are nonetheless so heavily linked to her looks that her success, too, raises questions about the contracts and options tendered Latinas in La-La Land.

Vitally interested in seducing new audiences, providing, of course, that old ones remain titillated, the reigning movie moguls are more than willing to customize costumes and design roles to fit Lopez' curvaceous *cuerpo*. Lopez matches their flexibility by undergoing figurative and literal make-overs, witness not only the range of Latina characters (Cubana, Chicana, Tejana, Mexican, Puerto Riqueña) she plays but also the dietary and training regimens she undergoes to trim her waist and shape her "booty." Captions in English-language print media eagerly focused on her physique: "Actress Jennifer Lopez has backbone. Better yet she's not afraid to show it" appears under a shot of her by a pillar, rear end demonstrably jutting out. "Here is the new American face" boasts *Mirabella*, tongue-in-cheek, under a photo where she poses in lingerie, face in focus, butt more dimly up and out behind. And "Jennifer Lopez Gets Cheeky" promises *Gentlemen's Quarterly* over yet another quasi-salacious portrait.[25] Response from other Latinas and Latinos has been mixed: although Lopez has won several awards for her positive portrayals of Latinos, the National Council of La Raza protested that as a lighter-skinned Puerto Rican actress, she was chosen to play darker-skinned Tejana singing sensation, Selena, over the 22,000 Selena wannabes who flocked to open casting calls.[26]

Framing and foregrounding of her posterior are paramount to Lopez' celluloid success: witness the moves her *culo* makes from "out of sight" to "in" in the short space of two years. The phenomenon is readily apparent in mainstream vehicles. In *Money Train* (Joseph Rubin, 1995), for example, her "caboose" moves slowly, seductively in tandem with Wesley Snipes' sculpted posterior; he is so much more "together" and cool than his white counterpart (Woody Harrelson) that, quite understandably, she prefers chocolate to vanilla.[27] Two years later, as professional spitfire and documentary film director Terri Flores in *Anaconda* (Luis Llosa, 1997), Lopez gets promoted from Big Apple third wheel to Amazonian co-star. Wading through mud and muck beside Ice Cube, her white love interest (Eric Stoltz) conveniently confined to bed, Lopez' *culo* is "naturally" more than once captured in wet pants, the object of both human male *and* giant snake desire.[28]

In more identifiably Latino and/or "independent" films like Gregory

Nava's 1995 *Mi Familia*, Bob Rafelson's 1996 *Blood and Wine*, and Nava's 1997 *Selena,* however, the presence or absence of Lopez' "assets" is even more marked. In Nava's $5.5 million "indie" epic, *My Family/Mi Familia*, Lopez nets only a supporting role playing a young Mexican American matriarch/maid named "Maria": but, after all, her devilish derriere *is* chastely hidden under long, loose-fitting dresses.[29] Unjustly deported to Mexico in 1933, Maria miraculously manages to walk home a year later, crossing a raging Rio Grande and bringing with her a new baby. Virtuously, the camera concentrates on her drenched face as she beams angelically down on her child. Elsewhere she is usually shown in long shot, cast as part of an "authentic" landscape created through colors, locations, and lighting for a film "conceived as a moving Diego Rivera or Orozco mural."[30] Publicizing the movie, Nava was at pains to describe *familia* as "the heart of the Latino cultural experience." Blithely, he predicted that the film would "appeal strongly to Latinos but also [be] the greatest cross-over point because *everybody* comes from a family."[31] Not coincidentally, however, most of the action in *My Family/Mi Familia* centers around the brothers and one grandson rather than on the sisters or the wives.[32]

The bottomless cynicism of Bob Rafelson's $22 million *Blood and Wine*, a caper cum film noir study of two tortured generations in a wealthy white family is, by comparison, refreshing.[33] With the pastel mansions, manicured lawns, sun and sea of the Florida Keys as backdrop, the focus is again on the male characters, with Jack Nicholson in the lead as womanizing wine merchant Alex Gates and Michael Caine as his asthmatic but cigarette-puffing partner in crime Victor. But Lopez has a plum part as Gabrielle, the Cuban governness who tantalizes both Alex and his jet-setting stepson (Stephen Dorff). Framed in profile, in short, tight-fitting, dresses and spike heels she is a "hot tamale" whose amorous associations prove highly lucrative: she squirrels away a magnificent diamond from the necklace Alex and Victor have stolen. Though she hides the fact from Alex, she does return to help him as he lies on a wharf, legs smashed by his jealous stepson's speed boat, at the film's end. Through a combination of serpentine movements and lascivious looks, Lopez thus succeeds in suggesting that her character has soulful as well as smoldering sides, despite jumbled narrative and visual clichés that simultaneously paint her as "an ambitious Latin spitfire and a basically honest immigrant anxious to carve out a better life."[34]

In Warner Brothers $23 million bio-pic, *Selena*, Lopez finally becomes the first Latina to earn $1 million plus deferments, 40 years after Elizabeth Taylor as Cleopatra and only two years after being paid $350,000 for *Money Train*.[35] Not coincidentally, her behind is given such a prominent role in the film that British critics speculated that it "probably had its own agent, trailer and press conference" and "[was] sure to get an Oscar for best supporting role."[36] Indeed, the first time we see Selena/Lopez she is shot

Figure 6.2   Jennifer Lopez as Selena Quintanilla in *Selena* (Esparza/Katz
Productions, 1997). Courtesy of the Kobal Collection.

from behind, her butt looming luminously large in tight cranberry bell
bottoms, back stage before a concert. A basic bio-pic "fit" of star and real
life figure is painstakingly captured throughout, with Lopez assiduously
retracing dance steps and pouring herself into replicas of Selena's trademark
spangled and spandex costumes; interviews at the time made much of how
Selena's mother scolded her for adopting similarly bad eating habits.[37]

   That Nava would frame Selena's life as family narrative was a foregone
conclusion: as Chuck Kleinhans comments, given his earlier film projects,
it was easy to understand why her manager/father, Abraham Quintanilla,
should anoint Nava as director of his baby girl's story, while retaining full
rights to script revision as executive producer with final script approval.[38]
Symbols like bridges, roses, and full moons evoke Selena's cross-over
flowering. The sound track is geared towards both English and Spanish
markets: it begins and ends with English-language pop tunes ("I Will Survive" and "Dreaming of You") and provides almost thirty Spanish-language
hits as well.[39] Selena/Lopez shows occasional flashes of spitfire independence

119

and temper, but on the whole, she appears chaste, even saintly, and her death cinches her ascension.[40] The film's final sequence pays her transcendance tribute, joining documentary footage with staged scenes in order to multiply the number of families who mourn Selena's passing, and projecting a final fusion of Tejana character-subject and Puerto Rican actress-star via concert footage where the real Selena replaces Lopez.

"More hagio-graphy than biography," was the *Village Voice*'s capsule comment; "a Partridge Family vision of the Quintanillas," read the *L.A. New Times* review.[41] Yet as in *El Norte* and *Mi Familia*, Nava, together with a largely Latino cast, and a dedicated crew, set out to give a Latino "feel" to the film.[42] More specifically "Tejano" references end up being relegated to the side of the frame, however, as when a farmworker is glimpsed on the edge of the highway near the beginning or two *cholo* low-riders pop up on the road, mid-way.[43] And with sexy Puerto Rican soap star Jon Seda cast as Selena's devoted rock-guitarist husband, Chris Pérez, pan-Latino clearly takes precedence.

Revolutions in dependence

For Lopez — indeed for any Latina in La-La Land — to be coupled with a sexy Latino actor is nevertheless a highly unusual occurrence. Following current La-La Land logic, Selena, like Ernesto in *Somebody to Love*, *must*, however, die, for partnered Latino happiness is reserved for madonnas like Maria. *Selena* is, admittedly, an extreme example, if authorized by "fact." But must films featuring Latinas necessarily proffer a "discourse of citizenship" wherein, to paraphrase Kathleen Newman, a "trope of [Latina] physical and emotional sacrifice" is operative?[44] Must Latinas continue to be "impossible bodies" within independent and mainstream movies, restricted to "service" roles as spitfires, maids and mamas, inhibited as role models unless they become saints? Within what parameters, in light of what restraints, might other possibilities be emerging for Latinas in La-La Land?

Of these three actresses Rosie Perez not surprisingly speaks most insistently on behalf of her own and others' rights to independence as *role models*:

> If I saw Rita Moreno with a joint in her mouth, I would not be mad at her. That would not take my heart away from what she has contributed and how she's inspired me. . . . I am very flattered when people say I inspire them. . . . But don't get mad at me if you see me in a club, humpin' on some fine-ass man's behind. Because I've got to live my life the way I see fit. I've got to make *me* happy first, before I can make you happy — or inspire you, for that matter.[45]

To date, however, Ontiveros' steady career and Lopez' meteoric success are more illuminative of the limitations Latinas encounter with respect to *roles*, for two rules in particular seem to govern Latina casting and characters: (1) slim, limber bodies are prerequisite for casting in supporting or starring roles, outweighing accents and pitch by far; and (2) a heterosexual imperative holds sway, whether or not the characters played by Latina actresses are married.

A question Nacha/Ontiveros puts to Rosa – way back in 1983 – in *El Norte*, illustrates Rule #1. Rosa gawks admiringly at two tall, thin, glamorous Anglo models who enter the sweatshop where they work; Ontiveros teases: "Don't I look like a model?" Obviously not. Within La-La Land logic, therefore, for the next two decades, she will be confined to bit parts: only in 2000, as L.A. children's theater director Beverly Franco in *Chuck and Buck* (Miguel Arteta), does she find a role worthy of her talents. The good-looking, light-skinned Lopez, in contrast, can capitalize on her body, though she too is confined to roles *as* a Latina, in large part because in Anglo-dominated culture her capacious *culo* marks her as "other." As Frances Negrón-Muntañer brilliantly argues, with no use in reproduction, the butt, and particularly the big butt, carries with it threats of excess of food, excess of shitting, excess of sex, warning of miscegenation, sodomy, and a high fat diet.[46]

Yet, following Rule #2, Lopez' abundant *bunda* simultaneously guarantees her attractiveness to men. "It's all me, and men love it!" she boasts.[47] Her derriere tantalizingly tendered in tight designer suits, playing detective Karen Sisko opposite George Clooney in *Out of Sight*, she recently earned $2 million. Male critics marvelled appreciatively at her heterosexual *chutzpah*: "Just what the doctor ordered!," "[she] makes George Clooney look good in bed – what he's always needed."[48] So successful has Lopez' promotion of her sultry persona been, in fact, that she rates references in movies where she does not even appear: in *The Wood* (Rick Famuyiwa, 1999), for example, four "buppy" studs spin a pizza slice to see who will win a chance at Jennifer Lopez' or Janet Jackson's booty. Small wonder, then, that Lopez recently insured her "body" for $6 million. Her cross-over heterosexual appeal is worth a lot; indeed, in the case of Latinas performing in feature fiction indie and mainstream films directed by Anglos or Latinos, *no importa*, heterosexual appeal seems absolutely essential.

Again Ontiveros demonstrates most clearly just how significant the stamp of heterosexuality is to young and old, men and women. Cast in her most villainous role to date, as Selena's friend, fan club president, and murderer Yolanda Saldivar, Ontiveros is always positioned beside or behind Selena/Lopez. Might she be – oh horror of horrors! – a lesbian? Nothing is said directly, but that Yolanda buys a ring for Selena on behalf of several employees, then presents it as solely her own gift after tenderly massaging Selena's neck and back, is meant to be suggestive. "I'm so proud of you.

. . . You mean so much to me I bought you a little present!" she coos. At the time of the real Selena's death, rumors were rife that a lesbian attraction, not just embezzlement, might be the cause for the killing: in some interviews, Yolanda claimed that she was fighting with Selena over a "secret" she wouldn't reveal.[49] One of the more scandal-mongering biographies, by Univisión talk-show hostess Maria Celeste Arrarás, maintains that Yolanda often massaged Selena's butt to prevent bubbles from forming under the flesh post-liposuction by her lover, Mexican cosmetic surgeon Dr Ricardo Martínez. *People* succinctly and suggestively summarized Arrarás' speculations as follows: "Yolanda was not at all happy that her friend was coming to depend more on Martínez and less on her."[50]

Constraints regarding what constitute marketable looks and permissible sexuality for Latinas thus obviously continue, in most mainstream *and* in many independent, Latino, Anglo, and African American feature films. Yet there *has* been a noticeable widening of roles in response to sociological and demographic shifts. That Lopez' characters are frequently professionals is one example of progress, for, as Carlos Cortés comments, more than other Latinas, Puerto Riqueñas are commonly painted as ghetto dwellers, gang members, drug dealers, and prostitutes.[51] That her spitfires do not die when they plunge into action but get the boy *and* the bucks is awesome. And that some of Lopez' characters, and some of Ontiveros' and Perez' too, live in Miami, Minneapolis, and small towns from Texas to Oregon as well, not just New York or L.A., is momentous.

Meanwhile, moreover, an intriguing development has emerged thanks to current industry formations that promote independents via cross-over niche markets. In several of the post-1994 Latina-directed films, new "Latina" bit players, third wheels, and starlets are surfacing. These "girls" – proudly, loudly dykes and drag queens – playfully imitate, pay homage to, or just plain flout the old rules. In a "bit part" in Lourdes Portillo's *Corpus: A Home Movie for Selena* (1999), for example, a drag queen pads her butt before appearing on stage *as* Selena; as "third wheel" in Rose Troche's *Go Fish*, a young Latina dyke speaks her mind and does her thing in spite of mama; as "starlets" in Ela Troyano's *Latin Boys Go to Hell*, muscular and "pretty" gay men preen and pose before each other; though their fates are generally tragic, to a "man," they look *simply maaavellous*.

And what to predict for the impossible bodies of *my* three Latinas? For me the titles of their films tell all, provided Ontiveros' and Lopez' credits are criss-crossed. Rosie: "it could happen to you." Lupe, your star turns may, alas, be restricted to "U-turns." Jennifer, this is surely not "as good as it gets."

Part III

STARING AT STARS

7

CHANNELING DESIRE,
MAKING WHOOPI

Figure 7.1   Whoopi Goldberg as Oda Mae Brown and Patrick Swayze as Sam
Wheat in *Ghost* (Paramount Pictures, 1990). Courtesy of the Kobal
Collection.

Lost in the Hollywood shuffle

Whoopi. All you need to hear is her first name. Unlike Sly, Arnold, and Clint, rarely do you hear her second. Is this because, like Dolly, she's more familiar, more "family," thanks to her work in so many P.G.-rated, family friendly, films and TV shows? Is the notion of "everyman" changing to include women and non-whites, as is so patently the premise in *Eddie* (Steve Rash, 1996) where Whoopi plays a "Fan," capital F? What does it mean that she has become a box office draw in "shopping mall America?"[1]

Several African American actors came to prominence in 1980s and 1990s films – among them Denzel Washington, Eddie Murphy, Danny Glover, Morgan Freeman, Whitney Houston, Angela Bassett, and Wesley Snipes – but Whoopi is far and away the most successful and prolific African American *female* star. Credits include more than fifty feature and documentary films, nearly twenty made-for-TV movies and documentaries, several television series, a short-lived evening talk show (the only one with a black female host), television guest appearances, roles on and off Broadway, work in radio, a children's book, stage and television benefit performances, and stints as host of the Academy Awards. Add to her popularity with adults the fact that generations of American kids are growing up with her, thanks to *The Rug Rats Movie* (Igor Kovalyov and Norton Virgien, 1998), *Rudolph the Red-Nosed Reindeer: The Movie* (William Kowalchuk, 1998), *Bogus* (Norman Jewison, 1996), *Theodore Rex* (Jonathan Betuel, 1995), *Sister Act* (Emile Ardolino, 1992), *The Lion King* (Rogers Allers and Rob Minkoff, 1984), television roles, cameos, *Sesame Street* guest appearances, and the magnitude of her importance to the contemporary U.S. cultural imaginary is clear.

Granted, Whoopi has acted in many mediocre films; all directed by whites and most featuring predominantly white casts; the majority comedies, family and/or action adventure films, i.e. genres that have historically been white-dominated.[2] At times she has accepted parts some find troublingly reminiscent of mammy and maid roles. Most problematic have been her onscreen involvements with white men and black and white women, and her many real life relationships with white men.

This chapter explores why and how Whoopi has succeeded where other African American women have not, though controversy often surrounds her.

The bulk of the chapter focuses on her interracial relationships in film; the conclusion returns to other factors involved in her notoriety and success. Because both the films and the tabloids show little actual sex, however, I follow their lead and redefine "interracial relationship." A first section discusses actual movie *involvements with* white (and black) men and women; a second evaluates her relationships to, and screen *incarnations of*, white (and black) men; and a third examines her celluloid *embodiments as* white (and black) men and women.

I begin by looking at films like *Made in America* (Richard Benjamin, 1993) and *Boys on the Side* (Herbert Ross, 1995) where Whoopi's characters are literally engaged in relationships with whites, touching on *Moonlight and Valentino* (David Anspaugh, 1995), *Corrina, Corrina* (Jesse Nelson, 1994), *Fatal Beauty* (Tom Holland, 1987), *Jumpin' Jack Flash* (Penny Marshall, 1986), *Sister Act*, and *The Color Purple* (Steven Spielberg, 1985) as well. That Whoopi so often goes after roles written for whites modifies Hollywood stereotypes of black women as tragic mulattos and comic mammies; nonetheless because her characters in this group of films never do more than kiss, if they even do that, hers are at best "(C)overt involvements."

The brief second section, "Celestial incarnations," studies two films, *Bogus* and *Ghost* (Jerry Zucker, 1990), that associate Whoopi's characters with "spooks" who are white and black women and men.[3] Both "legitimate" Whoopi's asexual relationships with dead and living whites by linking her characters to the foreign and/or the bizarre, and again effacing her characters' sexuality. These are among her more popular movies, not only because she is always "friendly," but also because her performances showcase her acting range.

Like many African American actors from the 1920s onwards, Whoopi mocks black clichés and sends up black entertainers. In *Whoopi Goldberg Live* (the video version of the stage act that brought her to Hollywood), and during moments of *Sister Act*, *Sister Act 2: Back in the Habit* (Bill Duke, 1993), *The Player* (Robert Altman, 1992), *Soapdish* (Michael Hoffman, 1991), *Jumpin' Jack Flash*, and *Burglar* (Hugh Wilson, 1987) she also spoofs white stereotypes and performers. "Singular embodiments," the third section, examines these performances. *The Associate* (Donald Petrie, 1996) and *The Telephone* (Rip Torn, 1988) are primary texts because in them Whoopi becomes the first African American *female* to cross-dress as a (white or black) man in mainstream film.

The conclusion compares assessments of her films, her performances, and her life advanced by African American publications, lesbian and gay magazines and newspapers, and mainstream (i.e. straight white) print media. Largely lost in the Hollywood shuffle and publicity hype around Whoopi the star, is Whoopi the actor and the activist, a woman who is expert at channeling desire and capable of helping others, in turn, to "make whoopi."

128

As Audrey Edwards says, "it is a credit to Whoopi's sheer talent and megapower that she has been able (and allowed) to move beyond and between . . . stereotypes to play just about any and everything in Hollywood: a fatal beauty, a computer nerd, a civil-rights heroine, an ex gun moll, a fake nun, a pro basketball coach, a lesbian and, yes, even a hoodoo woman."[4]

(C)overt involvements

Whoopi Goldberg burst into national consciousness in 1985, when she starred as Celie in Steven Spielberg's screen adaptation of *The Color Purple*. The role netted her an Academy Award nomination, but the film was condemned by black audiences and critics because Celie was involved with black men who were wife-beating, child-abusing brutes.[5] More typically, Whoopi's love interests have been white: Jonathan Pryce in *Jumpin' Jack Flash*, Sam Elliott in *Fatal Beauty*, Harvey Keitel in *Sister Act*, Ray Liotta in *Corrina, Corrina*, Ted Danson in *Made in America*, Mary Louise Parker in *Boys on the Side*, and Peter Coyote in *Moonlight and Valentino*. No other African American actress has so frequently been romantically paired with whites. True, 1930s and 1940s melodramas sometimes featured light-skinned actresses like Fredi Washington and Dorothy Dandridge as the unhappy objects of an (often deadly) white male desire. Whoopi's dark-skinned characters, in contrast, are clearly contented subjects who prosper.

Yet the ways Whoopi's romantic involvements are depicted do sometimes continue the simultaneous prohibition and promotion of interracial love characteristic of the Hays Code decades.[6] Although her characters are portrayed as alternately attractive and ugly instead of, as earlier, simply sexy, they too are rarely placed in black familial or community contexts.[7] And much less sex can be seen in Whoopi's films than in other recent romantic comedies. In *Jumpin' Jack Flash*, for example, Terry Doolittle (Whoopi) does not meet her transatlantic dream lover, a British secret agent, until he places a hand on her shoulder and takes her to lunch in the last sequence; her office mates applaud. Though *Fatal Beauty*'s Mike Marshak (Sam Elliott) tells Rita Rizzoli (Whoopi) that he is attracted to her the moment he learns that she is "Italian" and though several overtly sexual scenes were shot at Whoopi's insistence, all save a kiss ended up on the cutting room floor. Sex is largely absent in *Sister Act*, too: mobster Vince LaRocca (Harvey Keitel) presents his mistress, the provocatively sensual singer Deloris Van Cartier (Whoopi), with his wife's purple mink, but Whoopi spends most of the film as a nun, tugging at her habit. *Corrina, Corrina* seems more promising: the educated, articulate, attractive Corrina (Whoopi) is forced to work as a maid because no other work is available in the 1950s, but she ultimately marries the widowed Jewish lawyer whose daughter she tends. Yet here too adult sexual contact amounts to only a

Figure 7.2   Nia Long as Zora Mathews and Whoopi Goldberg as Sarah Mathews in *Made in America* (Warner Bros, 1993). Courtesy of the Kobal Collection.

kiss.[8] And though *Moonlight and Valentino* starts to show Sylvie Morrow (Whoopi) having hot sex with her white husband in a hotel room, most scenes portray her as creative but frigid.

Made in America provides Whoopi with her most "sexually explicit" scene: a long, if passionate, kiss between Sarah Mathews (Whoopi) and Halbert Jackson (Ted Danson) on the steps of Sarah's house. This kiss leads to an excited embrace that sends them careening from room to room. The film as a whole revolves around the traditional screwball gambit: despite their differences, Sarah and Hal are more right for each other than for anyone else, thanks to the peculiar ways they drive, dress, and drink. For much of it, the major obstacle to romance is the possibility that the goofy and irresponsible Hal might be Sarah's daughter's biological father. As the advertising slogan read: "At the sperm bank, she asked for a tall, intelligent, black man. One out of three ain't bad."

Sarah, in particular, rejects the idea of Danson as dad, screaming near the beginning that *she*, Sarah, could not *possibly* have been involved with a *white* man. Of course all opposition melts by the end. Recipient of a science prize at her high school graduation, daughter Zora (Nia Long) introduces Sarah and Hal with, "This is my mom and . . ."; Hal completes, "my dad." An almost entirely African American audience of students, families, and friends applauds and rises to dance along to a Muzak-version of Sly and the Family Stone's 1970s hit "Stand."

The one unhappy ending in this set of films occurs in *Boys on the Side*, where the double taboo of miscegenation and lesbianism seems to necessitate melodramatic "punishment." Here, however, the hesitantly heterosexual Robin (Mary Louise Parker), a.k.a. "the whitest woman on earth," dies after a series of AIDS-related illnesses. Whoopi plays her rough and ready lesbian

Figure 7.3　Mary Louise Parker as Robin and Whoopi Goldberg as Jane in *Boys on the Side* (Canal +/Regency/Alcor, 1995). Courtesy of the Kobal Collection.

friend, Jane. Robin and Jane love each other, but the only sexual initiation Robin enjoys with Jane is verbal: she learns to say "cunt" instead of "hoo hoo," "down there" or "sissy." The two never kiss, and for most of the film the physical distance between them is palpable.

Nothing more could really happen, for, as Jane puts it, Robin "could have been Donna Reed in another life." Like *Made in America* and other films in which Whoopi's character is involved with a European American, however, *Boys on the Side* publicly ratifies her mixed race relationship: in the final scene the wheelchair-bound Robin and the healthy Jane sing of their commitment from across a crowded room of white, black, Latino, and mixed gay and straight couples. The camera pans over smiling faces, then, slowly, moves back around the now empty room to Robin's abandoned wheelchair.

All of the "(c)overt involvement" films confine acceptance of interracial involvement to parties, performances, and/or public spaces, suggesting that social taboos and screen titillations regarding miscegenation are still at work, although parameters have widened. How tenuous acceptance of interracial straight or gay relationships can be is even more apparent in those films where Whoopi is involved with ghostly incarnations. Nonetheless because she shifts performance registers to engage with "other worlds," her acting skills are more visible.

Celestial incarnations

Only two of Whoopi's films, *Bogus* and *Ghost*, fall into the "celestial incarnation" category. Sexual contact between Whoopi and her occult partners is necessarily even more attenuated than when "real life" characters are involved: it is, after all, hard to get physical with non-material beings.

131

Yet like *Made in America* and *Boys on the Side*, respectively, *Bogus* and *Ghost* do intimate that Whoopi's characters are engaged in "heterosexual" (*Bogus* and *Ghost*) and "lesbian" (*Ghost*) relationships. Neither finds it necessary to portray her characters as glamorous or foxy, and each makes a point of contrasting Whoopi's character to another, more attractive, white woman while pairing and comparing her with a white man. Again Whoopi moves primarily in well-to-do white worlds, but now her characters are also placed within grimy, gritty, urban environments.

In *Bogus*, Harriet's (Whoopi) principal interracial involvement is with a little white boy named Albert (Haley Joel Osment). When Albert's beautiful mother, Lorraine (Nancy Travis), is killed in a car crash at the beginning, Harriet finds that, as Lorraine's foster sister, she has been named his guardian. A frumpy workaholic, Harriet lives in a decidedly polluted Newark, her only friend seems to be her white secretary. She refuses the advances of a very attractive black male business acquaintance whom Albert likes.

Harriet tries the best she can to win Albert's love, but she is not used to children and little Albert desperately misses his mother. By the end of the film he has become so unhappy that he is on the verge of suicide. His imaginary friend, Bogus (Gérard Depardieu), comes to the rescue, warning Harriet that something is very wrong. For most of the film, indeed, Bogus serves as Harriet's spiritual advisor; briefly, he is her fantasy romantic partner as well. The epitome of romanticism in his wide-legged pants, embroidered vest, flowing white shirt, and "big brown French coat," he seems the polar opposite of the hard-bitten Harriet, yet midway through the film she dons a big brown French coat like his. Just before the climactic rescue sequence, she dances "Ginger" to his "Fred," wearing a long white ballroom gown and reenacting moves from *Top Hat*'s "Cheek to Cheek" (Mark Sandrich, 1935), on a set evocative of *Gay Divorcée* (Mark Sandrich, 1934). The "amour" she enjoys is marked off as performance, and it disappears at the film's end when Harriet replaces Bogus as Albert's playmate and Lorraine as his "mother."

More emphasis is placed on Whoopi's acting in *Ghost*. As Oda Mae, a crook with a 20-year police record, she pretends to have psychic powers in order to fleece her neighbors. But once Oda Mae meets the ghost of the murdered Sam (Patrick Swayze), her dormant spiritual powers spring to life, enhancing her business. Her cramped consulting room fills with Latino and African American "spooks" and their living loved ones. As Oda Mae's two sisters, several clients, the ghostly Sam, and many other apparitions look on, her cheeks puff out, her eyes roll, and she "becomes" Orlando, a middle-aged, overweight ghost eager to talk with his wife. The pitch of her voice, her diction, and her accent all change markedly.

Her world is very different from that of Sam and Molly (Demi Moore): Oda

Mae lives in a rundown New York neighborhood where danger is literally just around the corner, for the Puerto Rican hitman (Rick Avila) who killed Sam and stalks Molly lives in the next block. Garishly dressed and made up, Oda Mae looks ridiculous when she visits Molly at Sam's urgings. "I don't see what's wrong with what I'm wearing," she complains, voice off over a bird's eye shot of midtown Manhattan. The next shot shows her striding along, resplendent in a badly fitting rose-colored jacket, black flounced skirt, black stockings, white net gloves, bouffant black wig, and rakish hat. Her legs splay apart awkwardly above spike heels. In African leggings she later seems more at ease, but she never looks as deliciously fragile as Molly does in her pixie haircut, baggy sweaters, and spaghetti strap T-shirts.

No wonder, then, that Oda Mae lends her body to the dead Sam when he wants to hold and kiss his wife one last time. "O.K., O.K., you can use me," she says, "You can use my body. Just do it quick before I change my mind." Orlando at least submerged himself in her, before reemerging in ghostly superimposition to hear his wife's response. Sam simply replaces her, obviating the lesbianism implicit in a first, teaser, close-up of Molly's white hands held by Oda Mae's black ones, by suddenly appearing in medium shot to wrap his strong arms protectively around his tremblingly eager widow's torso.

Excised by editing, Whoopi thus literally disappears at the film's climax. Her acquiescence as character/actor was rewarded, of course, by an Oscar for best supporting actress, the second in the entire history of the Academy Awards to go to a black woman. (The first went to Hattie McDaniel 40 years earlier.) Her "embodiments," in contrast, have gone largely unrecognized by either the Academy or critics. Yet since Whoopi here internalizes her "relationships," they showcase her acting range and comedic skill to greater extent, and are in ways key to her stardom.

Singular embodiments

Many white screen actresses (from Katharine Hepburn to Julie Andrews to Lily Tomlin) and many black screen actors (among them Eddie Murphy) have pretended to be white men, but Whoopi is the first, and so far the only, black woman who "becomes" a straight white man in mainstream movies. And her range extends further: at times she embodies black women, black men, white women, children, and men and women of other ethnic backgrounds.

To do so, she draws on years of acting training, calibrating posture, gesture, and voice to explode character and/or cliché for her audiences.[9] Sometimes her irreverent nods to past representations and earlier black and white acting traditions lack narrative motivation. Often, however, they are framed as parodies of a famous individual or figure as send-ups of ethnic and gender types. In most cases they stand out from the main storyline, only occasionally because they are presented to internal audiences.[10]

Like decades of earlier African American performers, Whoopi "acts black" in such a way as to suggest, in Eric Lott's formulation, "a whole social world of irony, violence, negotiation, and learning."[11] Although many of her roles reprise African American female stereotypes, her performances often fuse several together, complicating and diluting the original pejorative references.[12] *Jumpin' Jack Flash* and the *Sister Act* films, for example, feature moments where Whoopi parodies 1960s Motown girl singers who are both decorous and attractive, energetic and powerful. Occasionally, she portrays famous or anonymous historical figures (Myrlie Evers in *Ghosts of Mississippi*,[13] a dignified maid during the Memphis bus boycott in *The Long Walk Home*).

Often she recycles characters from stage to film or from film to film. "Moms Mabley" is her guardian angel, "appearing" first in Whoopi's early, one-woman, stage tribute to the mistress of chitlin' circuit blue humor (a moment is included in *The Telephone*).[14] "Moms" reappears in *Burglar*, though here identifiable only via Whoopi's character's raggedy clothes and outrageous attitude. In *Burglar* Whoopi also reprises the Jamaican cleaning lady she first created on stage for "The Spook Show" and further modified in *Clara's Heart*. A third character first appears in one of the skits in *Whoopi Goldberg Live*. Here Whoopi plays a seven-year-old black girl who wears a white shirt on her head, imagining it is her "beautiful long blonde hair . . . cas..ca..dading down my back." Shyly she tells the audience how she soaked herself in Clorox in order to be white because she saw no characters like her on *The Love Boat* or even on *The Smurfs*. In *Jumpin' Jack Flash* she plays an adult version of this same little "pickaninny," becoming as Albert Johnson says, a "black female rag-doll, comically dressed in oversized garments . . . [someone who] yelled and widened her eyes in precarious situations."[15]

Many performances draw on black and white minstrel traditions where men often pretended to be black women, and sometimes critiqued misogynist and racist stereotypes through their acts.[16] And, like female minstrels previously, Whoopi also cross-dresses as black men. Her take-off of James Brown in *Sister Act 2* is mocking; her portrayal of Fontaine in *Whoopi Goldberg Live*, fiercely satirical: Fontaine has a Ph.D. in philosophy but becomes a junkie because he can't find a job. Again, however, most of the black stereotypes Whoopi sends up are not marked as sexual.

The most decidedly "queer" character in Whoopi's arsenal emerges at the end of *Soapdish*. Chief confidante of a hysterical soap opera heroine (Sally Field), the coolly competent Rose Schwarz (Whoopi), suddenly surfaces on the soap as "Dr Franz Loud," a post-op transsexual surgeon working in a Bethesda sex clinic. As "Dr Loud," Whoopi's delivery changes from the low-pitched, slightly bemused tones she affects as Rose: suddenly she speaks forcefully, with a pronounced German accent. As in *Ghost*, however, Rose/ Dr Loud's primary task is to unite the white hero and heroine. Here, however, Rose's cheerful efficiency underscores the white characters' petulance, ineptness, and self-absorption.

In stark contrast, Whoopi's embodiments of white men and women are often clearly marked as sexual, if not always as sexy, beings. Playing a clueless white valley girl in *Whoopi Goldberg Live*, Whoopi tells of performing an abortion on herself using a coathanger. The itty bitty voice, valley girl vocabulary, and ditsy manner Whoopi affects are entirely at odds with the character's tragic story, making it impossible to overlook how dire the consequences inadequate sex education and lack of access to abortion can be. Her embodiment of Peter Falk's Columbo character in *The Player* also foregrounds gender and sexuality. Although it is obvious that Whoopi is repeating Columbo's offhand manner, flippant asides, and intentionally confusing non-sequiturs, as a black woman detective investigating a Hollywood murder she is literally "in your face" about her womanliness, swinging a super tampon in front of the wanna-be "player" and chief suspect (Tim Robbins) as she interrogates him.

The Associate and *The Telephone* in particular showcase Whoopi playing, respectively, a "man" and "men." Modeled (literally shot for shot in some sequences) on *Some Like It Hot* (Billy Wilder, 1959) and *Nine to Five* (Colin Higgins, 1990), *The Associate* clearly wants to be a popular feminist film. Whoopi plays a black investment consultant named Laurel Ayres who is supplanted by her white rival, Frank (Tim Daley). With the help of an older secretary (Diane Wiest) and an invisible male associate she calls Robert S. Cutty, Laurel launches her own firm. Initially the two women only suggest Cutty's existence via written notes, telegrams, and gifts, but increasingly Laurel is forced to become Cutty, first on the phone, then in person. Thanks to a white drag queen friend who provides her with make-up, white gloves, a white wig, and body padding, she turns herself into a wealthy white man who talks, looks, and acts like a cross between Marlon Brandon in *The Godfather* (Frances Ford Coppola, 1971), George Washington, and Ted Kennedy.[17] For Cutty, as for other influential elderly white men, power and sexuality go hand in hand: again and again, younger men fawn over him and beautiful women try to seduce him as well.

Whoopi's acting range is particularly evident when, as Cutty, she appears as the guest of honor of an elite and exclusionary club of white male brokers. S/he waves to the wealthy guests from the side of the room, then ponderously moves to the podium. With no trace of an ethnic accent, Cutty speaks deliberately of his love for Frank, then grabs Frank and kisses him passionately. Shocked by the overt display of homosexuality, an older man in the audience gasps for air, then grabs his oxygen. Changing pitch, accent, and intonation word by word to add ethnic and geographic shadings, Whoopi as Cutty removes first her gloves, then her wig, then her face mask, and, now as Laurel, scathingly condemns those assembled for refusing membership to women, gays, and black men. The black male waiters in the room applaud; they are joined enthusiastically by women and Laurel's gay friend waiting in the lobby. Finally the white stockbrokers also clap as Laurel, a black woman once again, leaves the dais.

Yet the feminist and anti-racist critiques *The Associate* provides are contained and coopted, because Whoopi is often shown as ugly and consistently portrayed as alone. When an older neighbor asks her, "but when you come home to an empty apartment what do you have?" her proud response, "independence," rings false because we have just seen her listlessly lying on her bed, eating junk food, and watching cartoons on television. And there are homophobic overtones to Cutty's kisses of both a buxom white woman (Bebe Neuwirth) and Frank. As is the case with films like *Tootsie* (Sydney Pollock, 1982) or *Victor/Victoria* (Blake Edwards, 1982), therefore, although *The Associate* tackles social issues and invokes political inequities, the finale's reliance on her black female body as the source of ultimate "truth" reinforces a visual system where women, African Americans, and gays are shown, and seen, as different.[18]

A much earlier film, *The Telephone*, gives Whoopi more opportunities to advance cultural critiques via embodiments of male and female characters. Based on a script by Terry Southern, the film resembles a one-woman stage show. A frame narrative legitimates Whoopi's performances as the impressions and line readings that out-of-work actress Lashti Blue (Whoopi) is practicing in her studio apartment, often but not always over the telephone. Acting everything from a maid to Shakespeare's *Richard II*, Blue is consistently the focus of attention. Not until the conclusion do we learn that she is insane and homicidal: she kills the telephone company representative (John Heard) who comes to remove her already disconnected phone, then calls an imaginary "Sergeant Beckett" to report the death.

Barricaded in her room to avoid bill collectors, Blue is clearly not sexually or romantically involved with anyone. Many of the characters, actors or types she embodies have partners, however: in fact, she often plays both roles, in rapid succession. In the space of just a few minutes, for example, she becomes an upper-class British woman and her husband, squabbling at a high society tea party, then both members of a lower-class African American couple engaged in a knock-down, drag-out fight. The sequence turns on Whoopi's command of accent, pitch, intonation, cadence, and vocabulary. The two impressions that immediately precede this fight – of a Japanese chef and the aging John Wayne as Rooster Cogburn, respectively – additionally demonstrate how adept Whoopi is with props, gestures, movement, and posture. As the chef, her voice is high-pitched, her accent obvious. Skillfully she twirls the "knives" she has invented from salt and pepper shakers before attacking the vegetables she has taken out of her refrigerator and placed on a small butcher block table. Her John Wayne impression is identifiable first via voice: we hear a slow, deep, Texan drawl emanating from behind the swinging half-doors of the cabinet that serves as her bathroom. Then the toilet flushes, and Blue/Wayne hops and stumbles into the room proper as John Wayne, recreating his lurch as an aging drunk via the lowered pants that hobble her ankles.

Most of these impersonations and performances are convincing, but the film's one-woman focus makes it stagey. Not surprisingly, therefore, *The Telephone* did not do very well at the box office. Many of Whoopi's later films, including star vehicles like *The Associate*, *Bogus*, and *Eddie*, have not enjoyed much success in theaters either. And in the final analysis, her most successful and/or notorious films generally uphold the black/white divide that reinforces how we make "sense" of race in the U.S. But "we" are not solely black and white. Assessing how and why different sociological groups in the U.S. appreciate actors like Whoopi is therefore crucial if we are to begin to appreciate what it means that Whoopi alone among the handful of African American actresses regularly working today has become a household name.

Channeling desire, making Whoopi

As a rule, African American publications emphasize Whoopi's performances rather than the stereotyped scripts and predominantly white casts, frequently placing her roles in relation to those of other African American actresses, past and present.[19] The most cheerleading of the three principal publications, *Jet*, promotes all of the film and television appearances Whoopi makes, comments on each of the many celebrity events she attends, and chronicles all of the awards she receives; *Ebony* and *Essence* are by comparison attentive but more reserved.

In all three publications, however, Whoopi "figures as an important touchstone for internal debates about blackness."[20] More than any other African American actor, she has been the subject of criticism and protest by the same organizations who on other occasions applaud her. Various reasons are offered for the rebukes, some having to do with the films, some with her personal life. She is regularly criticized for accepting what are seen as "mammy," "maid," and "hooker" parts. Critiques are made on behalf of the black family, although only black academics signal the lack of black women friends and community.[21] Her on screen interracial relationships are vehemently condemned. Some resent her work with and for whites; others charge that she plays to white sensibilities.[22] The most vituperative attacks are anti-Semitic. Objecting to Whoopi's put-down of Jesse Jackson's boycott of the second Academy Awards show that she hosted, an unidentified woman simply said, "What do you expect? Her last name is Goldberg." Cultural critic Ralph Wiley uses similarly derogatory language: "Caryn [Whoopi's birth name] . . . had a sudden stroke of genius. . . . Here was a performer who openly embraced a name [Goldberg] said to be befitting of the children of Israel. And so Whoopi was 'discovered,' given roles in movies."[23]

Whoopi comes under heavy fire for her "personal" life. Off screen interracial involvements prompt vitriolic outbursts. Countless stories were printed of outraged reactions to then partner Ted Danson's appearance in black face at a Friars Club Roast in her honor: everyone from Carl Rowan to Jesse Jackson to the National Political Congress of Black Women to the black female clientele at a Lexington Avenue hair salon protested.[24] Innumerable objections have been made to Whoopi's appearance: from disgruntlement that for a while she wore colored contact lenses to furor that she rose to receive her Academy Award for *Ghost* wearing yellow leggings and sneakers.[25]

In contrast, lesbian and gay press coverage never speculates about Whoopi's personal life or comments on her acting. Instead, publications like *The Advocate*, *off our backs*, and *Gay Community News* concentrate on Whoopi's "lesbian" roles, a subject about which African American publications have been largely silent. A *Gay Community News'* reviewer complained that *Boys on the Side* was "disappointingly void of overt sexuality, . . . *Philadelphia* all over again."[26] A review in *off our backs* commented approvingly that *Boys* portrayed a "gamut of issues," from AIDS to mother–daughter relationships to domestic violence to women's friendships; another, also in *off our backs*, criticized the film's "racism."[27]

Mainstream white media typically avoid all political issues. Instead, and even more than African American publications, they are fascinated by Whoopi's personal life, especially her interracial involvements. Titillating headlines like "Ted and Whoopi Are Over, Now She's Seeing Her Dentist without an Appointment" are designed to fuel conjecture as to whether or not she was "drilled."[28] Interest extends to what Whoopi wears, when, and where: derogatory comments pepper supermarket bestsellers like *People Weekly*. Film reviews have, however, usually been positive.

Proud of her accomplishments, Whoopi bristles at critiques. She acknowledges that hers has been a bizarre career, but insists it is important she pursue roles written for whites and/or for men (*Jumpin' Jack Flash* was originally destined for Shelley Long, *Fatal Beauty* for Cher, *Burglar* for Bruce Willis, *Sister Act* for Bette Midler, *Made in America* for a white couple, the lead in *The Associate* for a male actor), in part because black independent and Hollywood directors do not respond to her phone calls, in part because she does not like the limitations of labels like "Afro-American" or "woman."[29] Infuriated by charges that she works only for whites in bad mainstream films laden with clichés, she asks scathingly, "Do you think I would sit around and say, 'here's great scripts, here's crappy scripts; I'll do the crappy ones'?"[30]

She thinks of herself as a character actor, a Wallace Beery, a ZaSu Pitts, capable of working in any and all genres, playing any and all roles, from Eleanor of Aquitaine and Joan of Arc to Bernie Coleman and Dinah Washington. She has sought out dramatic and historical scripts; she wants to do Shakespeare and a horror film; she aspires to be *Dame* Whoopi.[31] An oft-stated goal is to blaze a path "for normal looking people," including dark-skinned African American women like herself, who, she points out, are still largely invisible in films made by black male directors.[32] Unlike most actors, she refuses to alter her body to fit standardized codes of beauty, saying bluntly: "I'm really clear about my blackness. Which is why my hair hasn't changed, which is why my nose and my lips are my own. . . . I don't want to look like someone else."[33] She also refuses to conform to what people think she should wear in public, even though fans expect women and/or minority actors, in particular, to dress up when they are not acting.

More than most actors she speaks out on behalf of those who cannot, because she knows from personal experience what it is like to be poor and on welfare.[34] A staunch supporter of Clinton, she nevertheless criticized him sharply for his wimpy stand on gays in the military ("he should have just done it and left Congress to duke it out") and she castigated him for his stand on welfare, too ("you can't reform the welfare system until you fix the fucking economy"). She supports socialized medicine, increased taxes on the rich (including herself), sex education, the right to abortion.[35] Not coincidentally, she views the media's obsession with her interracial relationships as motivated by profit, and frames her response in broader political terms: "Nobody asked about the black men I dated, 'cause they weren't famous and there was no story. There are much more important things to be talking about than who I'm fucking. It's not going to fix the national debt."[36] She makes a point to help other minority actors, as host encouraging Rosie Perez, for example, when she did not win Best Supporting Actress. In Perez' words: "during the commercial break, after my category was announced, Whoopi came down the steps in her Donna Kagan. She kneeled down to me and said, 'It's okay. Walk away from here real proud. They'll come. They're gonna understand what you're doing.' . . . People say she's sold out? She didn't do that for Winona Ryder. She came for me. I love her."[37]

Many share Perez' affection. Grounded as much on appreciation of her activism as of her acting, Whoopi's appeal is basically, broadly, feminist and working class. What she says about Pseudolus – a role in *A Funny Thing Happened on the Way to the Forum* made famous by Zero Mostel, Phil Silvers, and Nathan Lane – describes her own appeal: "it's the character's attitude – not gender – that counts."[38] In Whoopi's case "the sign of *blackness* labors in service of many different interests at once,"[39] but for most audiences and fans more than just "blackness" is usually in play because she so often plays with and against racial stereotypes, gender clichés, and sexual expectations.

In some ways, Andrea Stuart's terse "Whoopi's skin is an *empty* sign," better describes how Whoopi channels not only her own and Hollywood's, but also her audiences' quite diverse desires.[40] Interviewed in *Vogue*, she comments, "I'm like a sponge. I find that I can absorb things and then do them."[41] She thereby becomes, to quote Janet Maslin, "one of the great unclassifiable beings," someone who questions race, unsettles sexuality, and wills herself beyond gender.[42] Audiences can be, and are, attracted for any number of reasons, at any number of moments, to any number of characters, including first and foremost to Whoopi herself, an uppity woman who talks b(l)ack, and makes "making whoopi" look good.

8

THE AGING CLINT

Figure 8.1 Clint Eastwood as Will Munny in *Unforgiven* (Warner Bros, 1992).
Courtesy of the Kobal Collection.

Hi ho, *Silver*!

"[T]he western['s] conventions . . . function precisely to privilege, examine, and celebrate the body of the male," wrote Steve Neale in 1980 in *Genre*.[1] Three years later, in an oft-quoted and reprinted essay entitled "Masculinity as Spectacle," Neale took young, 1960s, western star Clint Eastwood as a prime example of how male heroes engage spectators' "narcissistic phantasies . . . of the 'more perfect, more complete, more powerful ideal ego'."[2]

Following the trails blazed by Neale, many film theorists now stare at the bodies of male stars. Today's hot male box office bodies may not always be as "powerful and omnipotent" as Neale claims the young Eastwood's was, but they are still white, and still heterosexual. Of course fewer westerns are made today. As I argued in "Nouveaux westerns for the 1990s," moreover, no actor really contests Eastwood's title as reigning star in the western firmament; indeed, several younger stars make a point of imitating him.

The western nevertheless continues to be an influential genre; indeed it is widely held to be *the* crucial American genre, albeit now via action and science fiction adaptations. Debates around it persist. Some critics explore the confluence of masculinity and race, noting how thoroughly the genre is imbued by nostalgia for Anglo-American supremacy. Others contemplate sexuality and gender, arguing that a repressed homosexuality underpins the heterosexual display so ritually staged by male gangs wielding guns. Age, however, goes largely unnoticed. I find this oversight intriguing, for two reasons in particular: (1) as Virginia Wexman points out in *Creating the Couple*, the careers of many western stars – Gary Cooper, John Wayne, Jimmy Stewart, and Randolph Scott – "blossomed as their youthful allure faded,"[3] and (2) a number of classic westerns made in the late 1950s to mid-1970s take the aging of these stars as their narrative focus: *Man of the West* (Budd Boetticher, 1958), *The Man Who Shot Liberty Valance* (John Ford, 1962), *Ride the High Country* (Sam Peckinpah, 1962), *The Wild Bunch* (Peckinpah, 1969), *Rio Lobo* (Ford, 1970), and *The Shootist* (Don Siegel, 1976) come instantly to mind.

Recently, film theorists like Linda Dittmar, Vivian Sobchak, E. Ann Kaplan, and Pat Mellancamp have begun to discuss aging in relation to femininity,[4] but to date little attention has been paid to aging and masculinity: that men are "permitted" to age, i.e. to have long careers in film, is taken for granted, dismissed as self-evident, with merely the occasional flip comment offered regarding Walter Matthau and Jack Lemmon's repetitive romps or Sylvester Stallone's latest "come-back."

Why? One reason might be that in our culture, women are aged twice, once at menopause and once in old age, whereas men are only officially aged once, at retirement. A change is, however, in the works: as Margaret Gullette observes, middle-aged and older men, like younger and older women, are increasingly urged by advertising and mass media to stay young.[5] In fact, Gullette maintains, "age, not gender, will identify the system's next market."[6]

In contrast to my earlier focus on relatively *young* bodies in "nouveaux" westerns, therefore, this chapter explores Eastwood's ongoing popularity by looking at gender, genre, and *gerontology*, arguing that (1) certain generic conventions of the western present – and mask – male aging, and that (2) westerns thereby shore up and legitimate perceptions of aging white men as powerful and potent. Since Neale's original example of appealingly powerful masculinity drew on Eastwood's spaghetti western roles, it seems appropriate to hinge observations here around the "aging" Clint, concentrating on the many westerns in which he has starred: *A Fistful of Dollars* (Sergio Leone, 1964), *For a Few Dollars More* (Leone, 1965), *The Good, the Bad, and the Ugly* (Leone, 1966), *Hang 'Em High* (Ted Post, 1967), *Two Mules for Sister Sara* (Siegel, 1969), *Joe Kidd* (John Sturges, 1972), *High Plains Drifter* (Clint Eastwood, 1972), *The Outlaw Josey Wales* (Eastwood, 1976), *Pale Rider* (Eastwood, 1985), *Unforgiven* (Eastwood, 1992) and – Clint's own nouveau western – *Space Cowboys* (Eastwood, 2000). Because the war film *Heartbreak Ridge* (Eastwood, 1986) is the first film where Clint is visibly older and because his last three screen appearances have been in action/adventure films – *Absolute Power* (Eastwood, 1997), *True Crime* (Eastwood, 1999), and *Space Cowboys* – I necessarily also consider other genres, including dramas, romances, and comedies.

I title this introductory section "Hi, ho, *Silver*" to point up how westerns in particular associate masculinity, whiteness, power, and money and to explore why a sizeable subset of films simultaneously integrates aging. Two subsequent sections buttress analyses of Eastwood's aging with biological, sociological and psychoanalytic research. The first scrutinizes how Clint's body and its parts have been presented in nearly three decades of films. In honor of one of his most popular but critically despised movies (James Fargo, 1978) it is called "Of countenance and continence: Every Which Way But Loose."[7] The second, labeled "Figurative families: Clint's bridges and bluffs" per two other Eastwood films, *The Bridges of Madison County* (Eastwood, 1995) and *Coogan's Bluff* (Siegel, 1968), traces the shifts in the Oedipal dyads (father–son, grandfather–father, father–daughter, etc.) featured in Clint's westerns and western offshoots.

The conclusion corrals Eastwood's filmic references to history with an eye to evaluating changes in his narcissistic "draw." Because on the whole he presents an encouragingly active, optimistic model of aging – a kind of older, resolutely heterosexual equivalent of Richard Simmons' bouncy bitchiness – I designate these findings "Aging, ambiguity, and appeal: Any Which Way . . . You *Can*!" This subtitle's optimism must, however, be taken with a grain of salt. For that so many of us find Eastwood's brand of aging attractive does not, alas, mean that we all do or will experience aging as effortlessly as he seems to: masculinity, after all, is neither invariable nor singular, and the political point about theories of dynastic succession and inheritance is that some people do not succeed or inherit. Finally, and as importantly, this chapter's focus on the western and the aging Clint doubly delimits its scope and pertinence to aging in North America. Often imitated, the western is primarily an American genre and, even in 2002, Clint remains one of the most influential American screen heroes.[8]

Of countenance and continence: *Every Which Way But Loose*

As Kathleen Woodward notes, "age is a subtle continuum." Yet contemporary American culture "organize[s] this continuum into 'polar opposites',", with age starkly opposed to youth.[9] Visible changes are key for both sexes, with aging men today constituting the fastest growing market for plastic surgery to remove "love handles" and implant silicone in calves and chests.[10] For both sexes secondary sexual characteristics – facial hair and breasts – that were welcomed in adolescence as markers of a distinctly gendered adulthood become less reliable indicators: in old age, the system of binary sexual difference quite literally sags. Twenty years ago, however, argues William May, things were different: then women "tend[ed] . . . to associate aging and death with the corruption of the bodily form, men with a flagging vitality."[11]

How individual men and women age in the U.S. obviously varies. Some older people gain weight, others lose it; voice caliber, pitch, and sometimes volume modulate; hair color and density change; wrinkles appear; skin tone alters. For many, senility and incontinence occur with increasing frequency. In most cases aging is thus experienced and regarded as deformation, disintegration, and fragmentation rather than, more neutrally, as transformation. As older bodies become less reliable, what is whole is increasingly felt to reside within the individual. As a result, psychoanalyst Charlotte Herfray posits an inverse mirror stage of old age: where Lacan argued that in childhood the mirror image proffers a narcissistic ideal ego as model for the forming ego, Herfray maintains that in old age the mirror represents a narcissistic affront to, even an attack on, the adult ego.[12]

Gender-based differences exist, to be sure: providing they are in good health, older women freed from child-rearing responsibilities become more involved, more extroverted; retired from work, older men become more withdrawn, more introverted; in general they live ten years less than women do. Now that most women work outside as well as inside the home before and after child-bearing, however, such gender-based distinctions may well become less pronounced.

And Clint? At 70, he has passed the age at which most Americans retire, though he has not yet reached "old age," a time now pushed upwards to 75, according to cultural demographer Patrice Bourdelais.[13] Unseen behind the camera, Clint is in good company: there are plenty of precedents for men who direct until they drop, including John Huston, whom Clint plays in *White Hunter Black Heart* (Eastwood, 1990). As actor, however, Clint is also ceaselessly in front of the camera. Not surprisingly, then, journalists have from the mid-1980s onwards commented on the changes in his body, changes which Clint insists he is unconcerned to hide. As performer, the "mirror" he proffers to us is altering, nonetheless it is still vigorous and to all appearances healthy.

Western genre conventions in particular fuel our sense of Clint as elemental patriarch. Especially in long shot, Clint at any age is not just a figure in the landscape, but a figure of the landscape. "Tall, lean, and hard-looking, he should be good for many a year of hero," wrote Archer Winsten prophetically of the then 33-year-old Clint.[14] Watching him as Rowdy Yates in *Rawhide*, Sergio Leone saw "only a physical figure," not a character.[15] Since Western iconography insists on the similarities between objects and bodies, it is indeed easy to view the young, the middle-aged, and even the aging Clint not just as a figure among desert buttes and mountain peaks but as a butte or peak himself.[16] Being part of nature means, moreover, being part of a natural cycle of death and rebirth: that *Unforgiven* begins with Will Munny (Eastwood) first silhouetted beside a tree and his wife's tombstone, then ends with just the tree and the tombstone, legitimates both Eastwood's presence and his absence as natural.

The western hero's loose-fitting clothes – ponchos and long coats, bandanas and buckskins – further disguise aging. Rarely expressive of individual taste, they help establish distinctions between East and West, man and woman, Anglo and Indian, Anglo and Mexican. Age is not among these binaries: old coot and young white wannabe work for and wear the same outfits.[17] In all of Eastwood's films, moreover, no matter what the genre, shadows and backlighting additionally ensure that Clint's age remains unnoticed, unimportant. Following trends established by action films, however, Clint's big guns get ever bigger as he ages. Although he waves large revolvers in the 1976 *The Outlaw Josey Wales*, in the 1988 *The Dead Pool* (Buddy Van Horn), he hefts a harpoon gun. In some of Clint's films, bigger guns serve explicitly as compensation for decreased powers: in one scene in *Unforgiven*, for example, having failed to shoot a can off a fence with a pistol, Will (Clint) brings out a shotgun, making up for his failing aim and eyesight by rougher firepower; in *Space Cowboys* he defuses the biggest of "guns," a.k.a. nuclear missiles.[18]

Nonetheless when you look long and hard for changes in Clint's body, you notice that under the costumes and despite the daily workouts, careful diet, and an array of vitamin and mineral supplements, Clint has, since his twenties, periodically sported a slight gut and love handles.[19] Admittedly, in the vast majority of naked torso shots Clint's well-developed upper body and arm muscles are more than enough to distract attention from his spreading waistline, witness the attention accorded his biceps as he boxes in *Every Which Way But Loose*. Clint's age is quite noticeable, however, in *The Bridges of Madison County*, *True Crime*, and *Space Cowboys*. In the former, Francesca (Meryl Streep) looks down from her window onto Robert (Clint) who is washing up at an outside pump; the reverse shot shows that his breasts are slightly sagging. *True Crime* is more audacious, showing the half-naked Clint in bed with a much younger woman (Laila Robins): the contrasts between his wrinkled and her smooth skin are stark. And *Space Cowboys* tenders not only Clint's but also Donald Sutherland's, Tommy Lee Jones' and James Garner's sagging chests, flaccid tummies, and drooping "cheeks." The only other film where Clint bares his butt is the prison drama *Escape from Alcatraz* (Don Siegel, 1979).

Figure 8.2   Clint Eastwood as The Man With No Name in *For a Few Dollars More* (Prod Eur Assoc/Gonzalez/Constantin, 1965). Courtesy of the Kobal Collection.

Over the decades, and especially in the westerns, little variation can be seen in the omnipresent close-ups of Clint's face and eyes. After all, weather-worn cowboys and gunslingers of all ages grimace and squint, rendering crows feet and wrinkles meaningless as markers of age. Although Clint's youth is undeniable in his early James Dean look-alike studio poses, in most westerns only slightly chubby cheeks or a grizzled beard give his age away. If anything, in the last 15 years, Clint seems more solid, more bulky – about the neck as in *Heartbreak Ridge*; about the midriff in long shots in *A Perfect World* (Eastwood, 1993).

Given Eastwood's comparatively greater bulk in recent pictures, one might expect him to move less, like the aging, beefier John Wayne in *Rio Lobo* whom Glen Ford describes as "poised demurely against newel-posts and porch beams, sprawled in chairs or leaned in doorways, coolly eyeing circum-ambient activity . . . a . . . mammoth shape . . . progress[ing] from spot to spot with the slow forcefulness and sheer inevitability of an iceberg."[20] But even if Clint's movements are not as "catlike" as Leone originally found them,[21] Eastwood still does many of his own stunts, even playing a cat burglar in *Absolute Power*. He slows down only when, as is the case with *In the Line of Fire* (Wolfgang Petersen, 1993) or *A Perfect World*, he plays establishment figures mindful that social conventions demand a certain reserve. Usually, however, as in *In the Line of Fire* or *Space Cowboys*, his 60-something characters demonstrate agility as well as ability, always at some point running through streets or racing around tracks.

As these most recent examples indicate, Clint has to date successfully managed to stay on the edge of the chasm dividing youth from old age. His success depends, however, not only on a body which remains identifi-ably male and for the most part looks every which way but loose, but also on how he is positioned in relation to others.

Figurative families: Clint's bridges and bluffs

The starkest distinctions between youth and old age are made with respect to those who are very old, poor, and/or infirm. In a culture which prizes and rewards mobility and control, truly old people are, in Sally Gadow's words, "doubly 'thinged'," objects in both a physical and a social sense, alienated from their own bodies and segregated from others.[22] Today the very old – i.e. people over 85 – constitute the fastest growing age group in the United States. Too often they are shunted off to nursing homes and hospitals, left to die in the company of others of similar age, mental inca-pacity or physical disability. Those who care for them are frequently so overworked that, in self-defense, they view their charges as genderless bodies to be sedated, silenced, and serviced, rather than as individuals to be looked after, listened to, and loved.[23]

In contrast, older people who are physically mobile and mentally alert are encouraged to continue to function as social subjects. For men of all races and classes, the roles they are expected to play often revolve around fatherhood, and entail both responsibilities and privileges. As fathers, men supposedly have something to teach and bequeath to their children, yet, as Freud maintains in *Totem and Taboo*, "the father holds power through no agency of his own but because of his sons' ambivalence toward him, becoming after his death the powerful and fearsome patriarch." Freud further motivates generational conflict among fathers and sons in terms of "the sons' desire for the father's once exclusive possession of . . . women."[24] Building on Freud, Thomas DiPiero insists that whether or not men are actually fathers, they are always less than patriarchs, for the power they are accorded shifts according to their sexual preference, racial and ethnic affiliations, and class status.

Kathleen Woodward brings additional factors into play, arguing that because the middle-aged Freud was unable to identify with his infirm old father, then profoundly depressed following his father's death, he unconsciously avoided theorizing aging. Woodward stresses, moreover, that in the male networks of *Totem and Taboo* only young, attractive women are desired and fought over, because only they are considered capable of distracting the father's attention from his aging, refuting assumptions that "old age and sexuality are antithetical."[25] From DiPiero's and Woodward's sociologically informed and historically situated psychoanalytic perspectives, therefore, the shape of patriarchy necessarily changes. In today's U.S., for example, only older men in higher income brackets are ever assured access to young women: prompted by business "demands," most middle-aged and aging men find themselves displaced by younger ones.

And the aging Clint? He has certainly had his share of women, divorcing his first wife, Maggie, for Sondra Locke, then leaving Locke for Frances Fisher, and subsequently, at age 66, moving from Fisher to the 32-year-old Dina Ruiz, whom he married in 1996. He has sired children by several women; his youngest daughter, Morgan, was born in 1997. As he put it in a 1998 interview, Morgan is terrific: she gives him the chance "to stay young . . . and tired."[26]

But what of Clint's relationships to men, women, and children in his films? Does it make a difference that in a few he appears as son, in many as father, and in others as grandfather? That he is often a loner, occasionally a lover, rarely a husband? That, in the westerns, a genre traditionally concerned with Oedipal relationships and dynastic succession, only the TV show *Rawhide* positioned Clint as an "initiate hero" with a moral claim to his surrogate father and trail boss Gil Favor's (Eric Fleming) position?

Significantly, in every early western Clint's characters act as equals together with and/or in defiance of other, mostly older, male characters. Many position the young Clint between good and bad fathers, but designate Eastwood and not the older men as all-knowing and all-powerful patriarch. The 1967

Hang 'Em High is a good example: the older Judge Fenton (Pat Hingle) deputizes Jed Cooper (Clint) and tries to "teach" him the moral difference between lynching and hanging. Cooper agrees to become a law man, but only to pursue a gang of three older and three younger men who hung him for a crime he did not commit. In the final shot, he rides out of town having done things *his* way: revenge – and justice – are accomplished without any official assistance, including from the hangman.[27] Though literally childless, several of the young Clint's characters additionally acquire paternal standing by trying to protect younger or smaller characters: a little boy in *Fistful of Dollars*; two teenage brothers in *Hang 'Em High*; a dwarf (Billy Curtis) in *High Plains Drifter*. That these sons are peripheral and/or adopted is classic Clint.[28]

The films where Clint is middle-aged (i.e. those made between 1973 and 1985), foreground the Oedipal aspects of the western with more of a vengeance, for here the dads he plays are usually inept and often deadly. Several take the traditional impulses of the western hero who supports the little and defends the family to extremes. Some are clearly westerns; others might, as Edward Gallafent suggests, more appropriately be termed "road movies"; all are set in the West.[29] In *The Outlaw Josey Wales*, Josey (Clint) has a real son, but he is dead before the film begins. Bent on revenge, Josey does not initially want the second boy, Jamie (Sam Bottoms), who adopts him as "dad" ("I don't want *nobody* belongin' to me!"), though when Jamie is shot, Josey tries – in vain – to nurse him back to health. In the caper film *Thunderbolt and Lightfoot* (Michael Cimino, 1974) Clint's travel companion and adoptive "son" Jeff Bridges also dies, if now at the end of the film, from internal injuries sustained when he is severely beaten because he has playfully kissed one of Thunderbolt's (Clint) homophobic older partners in crime on the lips. In the Depression era drama *Honkytonk Man* (Eastwood, 1982), in contrast, it is exceptionally Red Stovall (Clint) who dies of consumption at the film's end; the only other Clint character to perish is Sergeant John McBurney in the southern gothic, *The Beguiled* (Siegel, 1971). Red takes nephew Whit (real life son Kyle) on the road from dust bowl Oklahoma to Nashville, but he is so drunk and sick that he never manages to teach Whit much of anything, though he does take him to a jazz club and a whorehouse. Clint's most effective middle-aged "parenting" occurs, in fact, not with humans but with orang-utans: in *Every Which Way But Loose* and *Any Which Way You Can* (Buddy Van Horn, 1980) "son" Clyde punches out bad guys and guzzles beer just like his "dad," Philo Beddo (Clint).

Himself frequently a lethal father figure, the middle-aged Clint is nonetheless mockingly deferential yet generous towards adoptive, often Native American or Mexican, elders. Older women are especially well treated: in *Every Which Way But Loose* and *Any Which Way You Can*, "Ma" (Ruth Gordon) is loveable, feisty, and independent. Only older white men come in for attack, usually because they inhibit Clint from protecting his "family." In the two bona fide westerns of this period, *The Outlaw Josey Wales* and

Pale Rider, for example, battles occur between rival patriarchs as Clint pursues his own ends following the anti-Establishment pose made famous in the spaghetti westerns and especially the Dirty Harry series.

The aging Clint patriarchs are, to a man, less glamorous. Clint's latest "true" western, the 1992 *Unforgiven*, portrays Will Munny (Clint) as capable of efficiently killing only after he is thoroughly drunk; more a drama than a western, *A Perfect World* depicts Sheriff Red Garnett (Clint) as an old man who never fires a gun and drinks Geritol instead of whiskey. Clint's characters have, in fact, only "succeeded" as real or surrogate fathers in three recent films featuring "sons," none of which can be called westerns: *Heartbreak Ridge*, *The Rookie* (Eastwood, 1990), and *True Crime*. Significantly, in the bio-pic *White Hunter, Black Heart* and in *Unforgiven* as well, adoptive sons *reject* him as dad; in both films he also proves particularly lethal for black "family" members.

Yet as in the middle-aged films, the aging Clint means to be a good father and/or grandfather. The irony is that he so often fails in spite – or is it because? – of himself. As he ages, in fact, Clint seems more and more often to be watching other male characters die; his last minute resurrection of Frank (Isaiah Washington) in *True Crime* is an exception. In *Space Cowboys*, he instead sends mortally ill best friend and rival Hawk (Tommy Lee Jones) into space and a glamorous death; he ejects two wounded whipper-snapper astronauts over the ocean (predicted to be "20 percent survival rate"), then miraculously manually pilots the disabled space shuttle onto a runway ("0 percent survival rate"). Watching tragedy befall others from the sidelines, does Clint "duck" his own death at the same time as (for example, in *Unforgiven*, *In the Line of Fire* or *Space Cowboys*) he acknowledges his own aging? The most wrenching example of failed fatherhood occurs in *A Perfect World*, where Red watches as surrogate son Butch (Kevin Costner) is gunned down in front of him, a genuinely "nice" guy if a kidnapper and a murderer. Frustrated, remorseful, Red confesses to his adoptive "daughter," criminologist Sally Gerber (Laura Dern): "I don't know nothing, not one damn thing."

In recent "detective" films – notably *Absolute Power* and *True Crime* – daughters replace sons in Oedipal dyads, though Clint still plays inept and/or deadbeat dads. Increasingly, too, Clint casts his real life daughters in supporting roles or bit parts. In *Absolute Power*, estranged daughter Kate (Laura Linney) is in the end happily reunited with her dad; Alison Eastwood and Kimber Eastwood have small parts as an art student and White House guide, respectively. In *True Crime* little Francesca Fisher-Eastwood plays Steve Everett's (Clint) young daughter Kate. Though separated, Steve tries to be a good parent, but work clearly comes first: he is so eager to get back to his job as an investigative reporter that he races around the Oakland Zoo with Kate in a stroller, only to miss a turn, dump her out, and injure her in his haste.

Usually Clint's relationships with adult women are off-handedly romantic. Though his archetypal characters – the Man with No Name, Dirty Harry – are loners, in many early films Clint and Clint alone gets all the girls: in *Hang 'Em High*, first a hotel maid, then Inger Stevens; in *Joe Kidd*, both Stella Garcia and Lynne Marta; in *Coogan's Bluff*, four women, the first in Arizona, three more in New York. In *The Eiger Sanction* (Eastwood, 1975) a busty blonde art student (Candice Rialto) sums up her response to spy/art professor/mountain climber Jonathan Hemlock's (Clint) charm with a succinct "he could climb all over me!"

Sometimes, of course, Clint's seductive powers get him in a heap of trouble: *The Beguiled* and *Play Misty for Me* (Eastwood, 1971) make explicit the masochistic vulnerability that underpins his sadistic virility. Though popular with critics, at the time both were notoriously unsuccessful with audiences, who disliked seeing Eastwood play against tough type. *Two Mules for Sister Sara* more effectively hinted at how erotic pain can prove, and nowhere more so than in the scene where Sister Sara (Shirley Maclaine) removes an arrow from Hogan's (Clint) shoulder by pounding it through to the other side.

In the middle-aged films Clint, coupled with Sondra Locke, becomes more clearly a romantic lead, though their relationships are usually extra-marital: *The Outlaw Josey Wales*, *The Gauntlet* (Eastwood, 1977), *Bronco Billy* (Eastwood, 1980), and *Sudden Impact* (Eastwood, 1983) all provide examples. Much has been written about how feminism tempts and tempers patriarchy in some of the middle-aged films, most notably in cop films like *The Enforcer* (James Fargo, 1976), *Sudden Impact*, and *Tightrope* (Eastwood, 1984).[30] Less has been said about the way generational brakes are applied in Clint's mid-1980s western *Pale Rider*, where the Preacher (Clint) refuses young Megan's (Sydney Penney) advances saying he is too old for her, but adding that someday she will meet the right man, a young man.

The aging Clint's characters are more doubtful whether the right man is a young man: indeed, they usually make it a point to get the girl, if not the girls. The most utopian version of this scenario occurs in *Pink Cadillac* (Buddy Van Horn, 1989). Visually the film underlines Eastwood's age: next to Lou Ann (Bernadette Peters) and her baby he looks more like a grandfather than an adoptive dad. Narratively, however, the film insists that skip tracer Tom Nowack (Clint) is the toughest, smartest, nicest, and funniest guy around: not only a perfect husband and father, but a perfect business partner, too. *In the Line of Fire* and *The Dead Pool* offer other variations on the same theme, each pairing the aging Clint with much younger women (Rene Russo and Patricia Clarkson, respectively). Only *The Rookie* perversely twists this older-man-gets-the-younger-girl formula, as the exotic, erotic, villainous Liesl (Sonia Braga) stands provocatively over Detective Pulovski (Clint), wondering how much of a man he can be without his gun.

More exceptionally in *Heartbreak Ridge*, *The Bridges of Madison County*,

Figure 8.3   Clint Eastwood as The Preacher in *Pale Rider* (Warner Bros, 1985). Courtesy of the Kobal Collection.

and *Space Cowboys*, Clint is matched with middle-aged women. In the former, Sergeant Gunney Highway (Clint) reads women's magazines and tries to get his marriage back together each time he is dismissed as "too old, too stupid, too proud" for the New Marines. At the end of the film, he finally retires and, a hero, is welcomed home from Grenada by his ex-wife (Marsha Mason), propitiously wearing white. *Bridges of Madison County* pairs the aging Eastwood as Robert with Italian farm wife cum fireball Francesca (Meryl Streep, imitating Anna Magnani), positioning Clint as the seductive, worldly stranger who dances and romances, then falls forever in love with her. *Space Cowboys* opens with Clint accidentally locking himself and his wife in their garage. Not one to waste time, he thumps her up on his work bench, and starts to make love.

Clint's romantic appeal and paternal prowess obviously vary from film to film, genre to genre, and decade to decade, but his box office draw is proven and it is ongoing: indeed, over the years he has garnered new audiences. Where many women were enthusiastic Rowdy Yates fans, the spaghetti westerns and Dirty Harry films drew largely young, white, male audiences. In the 1980s, thanks to the "feminist" film noirs and comedies, women began to join men in theaters. Nowadays middle-aged and older audiences of both sexes in particular appreciate Eastwood's acknowledgments of aging and change, his professional and personal dynamism, and his willingness to poke fun at himself.

On the whole, both Clint's characters and Clint himself make aging look more like a good-natured, robust, "ripening" than a despondent, rickety, "rotting." Yet audiences simultaneously realize that Eastwood's wealth makes it easier for him to stay fit, to attract women, even to raise children. Most of us simply cannot afford to say, as he does, "I'm in a stage in life where if it's not enjoyable, I don't want to do it at all."[31] What, then, *does* his very "perfect world" indicate to and for others growing old in the United States today?

Aging, ambiguity, and appeal: Any Which Way . . . You *Can*!

Significantly, gerontology and geriatrics originate as disciplines just as westward expansion ends. Only from the 1890s onwards has old age appeared as a negative frontier and youth a promising one, with adulthood a problematic in-between. In Frederick Jackson Turner's time, in contrast, notes Gerald Gruman, "youth" – which lasted until about age 25 – "was . . . viewed as a clumsy, undesirable time" while middle-age was associated with traits now considered synonymous with youthfulness: "restless, nervous energy, buoyancy, and exuberance, and quick inventiveness."[32]

Only since the 1950s, moreover, have people begun retiring "early enough and in sufficiently good health to enjoy an unprecedented period of . . . creativity and leisure." Only since then, therefore, have social scientists "officially" endowed the category of "old age" with a history, associating it with capitalism and speaking of the elderly as a new minority group.[33] The idea that the elderly are a minority category grew particularly popular in the late 1960s, when psychiatrist Robert Butler coined the word "ageism" in obvious imitation of "sexism" and "racism." For Butler, age, class, and race were connected: he first used the term to describe the angry response of white upper middle-class Maryland suburbanites towards a public housing project that would have placed elderly poor whites and blacks in a "luxury" apartment building, replete with air conditioning, parking, and a swimming pool.[34]

The typical "liberal" counter-response from the 1960s onwards has been to sidestep racial, class and gender differences while insisting that older people, as a group, continue to be active and productive citizens. Unfortunately, this denial of differences – among the elderly, and between younger and older people – reinforces discrimination. Why do we continue to believe in simplistic and rights-based solutions? Psychoanalytic arguments such as those advanced by Woodward and Herfray suggest that unconscious structures shaped by narcissism, denial, and guilt fuel social attitudes and frame scientific approaches; alas, such structures are not easily changed.

That most of Clint's films include only vague references to history underpins the potency of the patriarchal myths they present and occasionally mock. Striking also is the fact that the majority of his films, not just the westerns – which most classically take place post the Civil War and pre the 1890s – are either set in the past or obsessed with the past, and often laud country and small-town values. *Honkytonk Man* takes place on the road during the Depression; *White Hunter, Black Heart* is set in the wilds of 1950s Kenya; *The Bridges of Madison County* primarily occurs in 1950s rural Iowa; *City Heat* (Richard Benjamin, 1984) revisits 1930s Kansas City; *Escape from Alcatraz* returns to a remote prison in 1950s California; *A Perfect World* has as backdrop 1960s Texas and Kennedy's assassination; *Firefox* (Eastwood, 1982) and *Heartbreak Ridge* are preoccupied with Vietnam (in the case of the latter not only by way of photographs "from" the Vietnam war but also by way of documentary film footage "from" the Korean war); *Thunderbolt and Lightfoot* references the Korean war from rural Idaho; *Where Eagles Dare* (Brian G. Hutton, 1968) and *Kelly's Heroes* (Hutton, 1970) restage incidents from World War II; *Space Cowboys* starts in 1958. Tellingly, many of the films set in the "present day" – the Dirty Harry series, *Coogan's Bluff*, *Absolute Power* and more – depict the present as a cesspool, but only *A Perfect World* really gives the lie to nostalgia, suggesting that Texas officialdom, as represented by Clint himself, was as ineptly, fatally paternalist in the 1960s as it is in the 1990s.

Eastwood's fondness for looking backward has often been labeled reactionary, yet nostalgia is not a priori conservative. Rather, it might also – with Clint's films there are no simple answers – be seen as the vision of an aging father for whom what is whole, and good, is felt to reside inside the self, in the past. Certainly the aging Clint in particular no longer solely or simply embodies a more complete, more perfect, ideal ego for the spectator, as Steve Neale originally suggested was the case with his Man with No Name character. Clint's relationship to patriarchy today is more ambivalent, more complicated.

Richard Schickel calls Eastwood's decision "not to hide his age but to play it gracefully . . . the most important factor in perpetuating his career."[35] Makes sense. For if "everyone loves cowboys and clowns," as the opening song of the proudly if cynically American *Bronco Billy* puts it (Billy performs in a tent made of American flags, voluntarily stitched for him by inmates in an insane asylum . . .), it is not only because "you're everybody's hero for just a little while," but also because, many of us, like Billy, participate in the nostalgia for youth expressed in the closing song: "My sequined shirts don't fit as well, but when I see those little buckaroos waiting for me to begin, the years roll back and Bronco Billy becomes just a kid again."

The bottom line of my argument is thus that as soon as we grow older, we all deny age, and especially as it relates to masculinity. After all, that Freud considered disavowal to be "a typically male defense,"[36] does not mean that disavowal is a specifically male defense: hegemonic masculinity is hegemonic because we all participate in the same fears and fantasies. Black and white, female and male, old and young, gay and straight, or from any of the many positions in between and beyond such binaries, we all have a stake, if a different one, in wanting a powerful father to stand behind us at the same time as we sleep in his place. An early Eastwood publicity still captures the concept nicely; a young black boy dozes in the director's chair labeled "Clint Eastwood" as a smiling Clint looms tolerantly, protectively over him.

Maybe, just maybe, we too could be adopted by Clint, be Clint, become Clint? Our desires and fantasies about having and being "dad" – in this case, Clint – are neither ahistorical nor universal. On the contrary, such hopes and dreams constitute a new, as yet poorly explored, frontier, precisely because never before has such a large segment of society grown so old. The roles and relationships we have ringed round aging, moreover, challenge and implicate us all, not just those of us who are elderly. As Simone de Beauvoir puts it in *The Coming of Age*: "If [we] recognize ourselves in this old man or that old woman . . . we will no longer acquiesce in the misery of the last age . . . no longer be indifferent.. . . [W]e shall feel concerned, as indeed we are."[37]

This does not mean that I naively advocate an identity, rights-based politics as *the* answer. Rather I worry, with Paul Higgs, that "the modern citizen is there to be monitored for 'risk', not to be active." He warns: "In the future, . . . [t]hose approaching retirement as well as those experiencing it will be [made] fully aware that its value has steadily been diminishing and any successful old age is fully their responsibility."[38]

Nonetheless as a middle-aged film buff, I cannot help but give the aging Clint the last word – kinda: for in *my* fantasies he snarls encouragingly, "you gotta ask yourself, punk, do you feel lucky, do you? . . . make our future . . . any which way, you can!"

9

MARKETING DOLLY
DIALECTICS

"The Sky is Green, the Grass is Blue"

Figure 9.1   Dolly Parton as Miss Mona Stangley in *Best Little Whorehouse in Texas*
(Universal Pictures, 1982). Courtesy of the Kobal Collection.

"Breasts like impossible ideas"[1]

Fabulously wealthy star of many media, hit of Hollywood and Dollywood, Dolly Parton possesses a truly impossible body, multiply modified over the years. Her persona is more consistent if contradictory, a mishmash of honesty and rehearsal, assertiveness and reserve. Movies are key to her image, because Dolly exceeds her films and always plays a version of herself.[2] Usually seen on television or video, they constitute an easy introduction to, and accessible reminders of, the diminutive (five foot two inch) but expansive (in several senses: "double D," outspoken, generous) celebrity.

In this final chapter, I concentrate on Dolly's screen features in order to signal the region behind the celebrity and the world in love with the star. I am, I confess, something of a fan. As a graduate student at the University of Wisconsin-Madison, I dressed as the down-home Dolly of the 1980 hit cross-over album, "Here You Come Again" – i.e. in tight blue jeans, high heeled boots, high hair wig, and red and white checked shirt straining over (in my case, padded) breasts. Unexpectedly I found myself the belle of a formal attire lesbian ball. For the last 12 years I have taught at the University of Tennessee-Knoxville, right dab smack in the conservative region where Dolly is the foremost living legend and a *big* employer. Here I am constantly reminded of her extraordinarily diverse appeal – to young and old, male chauvinist and feminist, Pentecostal and queer.

What I think of as "Dolly dialectics," i.e. skillful marketing premised on shifting points of reception, ensures that opposites are, if not exactly "transcended," at least shrink-wrapped together and sold. To explore Dolly's popularity, I mine her seven feature length fiction films for the "documentary" proof they offer of 20 years of shape shifts and attitude adjustments. The first film, *Nine to Five* (Colin Higgins, 1980) captures her at age 34, the most recent, *Unlikely Angel* (Michael Switzer, 1997) preserves her at age 51. In between come *Best Little Whorehouse in Texas* (Colin Higgins, 1982), *Rhinestone* (Bob Clark, 1984), *Smoky Mountain Christmas* (Henry Winkler, 1986), *Steel Magnolias* (Herbert Ross, 1989), and *Straight Talk* (Barnet

159

Kellman, 1992).[3] I focus on the films because Hollywood fantasies so inspire Dolly's media personality and business ventures, chief among them Dolly-wood: Dolly is, after all, the only living media star with a successful amusement park. As backdrop, I reference three other sets of "texts": (1) print coverage of Dolly and Dollywood (an average of five in-state articles appear each month); (2) local reception and my impressions of Dollywood; and (3) cultural studies work on obesity, diets, plastic surgery, fundamentalist religion, and Appalachian culture.

The first section, "Peaks and valleys, nips and tucks," concentrates on why Dolly's outré appearance is so strangely familiar and warmly welcomed; the second, "Divine guidance, straight talk," discusses how her star persona reconciles and/or isolates potentially explosive attitudes towards religion, family, feminism, and queers; the third, "Mountain manners, street smarts," surveys Dolly's "doin's" in film narratives and local charitable projects. The conclusion, titled "CEO and Cinderella" in homage to an article by Karen Jaehne, gestures towards Dolly's legacy. Here I explore how audiences around the world transcend what Pam Wilson terms "mountains of contradictions" by, I argue, buying into "Dolly dialectics."[4]

Peaks and valleys, nips and tucks

The first female country singer to expand into film, Dolly always "juts" out as "Dolly," star of impressive proportions who proudly tells folks back home, "I like lookin' like a cartoon. People say less is more, and I say bull. . . . More is more."[5] From the get-go, Dolly presents a paradox: avowedly artificial, she is also the epitome of natural. Breasts and face have changed so much over the years that three things arguably hold together our perception of Dolly as "Dolly": (1) her body's extreme proportions (high hair wigs, huge breasts, tiny feet, and wasp waist); (2) her consistently uppity, up-beat attitude; and (3) her distinctive voice, with its East Tennessee twang, childlike pitch, and infectious giggle.

Within the films, costuming, positioning, and framing emphasize Dolly's more than bountiful measurements; viewed in retrospect, they also reveal the extent of the alterations. In the early films especially, Dolly is huge. In her debut as a secretary in Nine to Five her "headlights" loom large, in one scene profiled front and center in a tight yellow knit dress. As the madame in Best Little Whorehouse she pops in and out of outfits in the opening sequence, the only busty woman in a roomful of flat-chested prostitutes. Later, she and co-star Burt Reynolds lie on a blanket under the stars, talking about their dreams: he wants to run for the state legislature, she wants to be a ballerina but she's "too top heavy" for toe shoes. Proof positive, her "pair" push past Burt to fill the foreground with gathered gingham. In Rhinestone, playing a country singer making her way in New York, she out-swaggers and out-"muscles" cab-driving co-star Sylvester

Stallone, consistently occupying more screen space than he. In most films she does not move much, but in *Rhinestone*, she actually clogs briefly with her "kinfolk" and she twice punches out "bad guys" on Sly's behalf.

In the later films, Dolly's breasts seem to inflate, in part because she loses weight, in part thanks to surgery. The change is obvious in *Steel Magnolias*. As a hairdresser named Truvy, Dolly alone seems normal among a bevy of fake Southern belles: although her border state accent is hardly "deep South" (the film is set in Louisiana), at least it is halfway "genuine." For fans tuned to TV, a "new," more voluptuous Dolly had emerged already in *Smoky Mountain Christmas*. Gone are the deep dimples, full lips, slightly irregular nose, and little double chin of *Nine to Five*, *Best Little Whorehouse*, and *Rhinestone*. In *Unlikely Angel* outfits accent alterations still more strikingly, with the most eye-catching number the blue and white dirndl-esque jumper in which Dolly drops from heaven, bosoms a-bouncing, suitcase and guitar in hand, a penitent sinner who died braking for deer. The film's two children greet her bluntly: "you're a little late for Halloween."

Over the years, most of Dolly's characters can be seen eating, because they are hungry and/or because food is love. Buxom and back home in *Rhinestone* she teaches Sly how to consume biscuits and gravy. Thin, out of work, and penniless in *Straight Talk*, she devours the breakfast food Janice (Teri Hatcher) leaves behind. Sent back to earth in *Unlikely Angel*, she fixes bacon, eggs, waffles, and syrup for the dysfunctional family her task it is to reunite, telling the calorie-conscious teenage girl, "so have a glass of skim milk with it." A bit later she inhales French fries and burgers at a mall, informing the little boy, "where I'm going, I don't need to watch my weight."

Local audiences are keenly aware of these physical changes; some even quote pertinent lines from the films. (Truvy's "There's no such thing as natural beauty" in *Steel Magnolias* is a particular favorite.) Older folks tirelessly but fondly affirm that Dolly was never *that* big in high school, in partial contradiction of Dolly herself, who claims that when she was baptized and her dress became somewhat transparent "the boys on the bank were moved to shout 'hallelujah'."[6] Her running commentary in print and on television about her weight is scrutinized with considerable empathy, for, as Laura Kipnis points out in *Bound and Gagged*, "Fat . . . no other subject can so reliably incite Americans to actually read."[7] According to Roberta Pollock Seid, diet books sell more widely than any other books on the market, except the Bible.[8] All around the U.S. people push, pull, tuck, and tug themselves into (or out of) clothes and shape, although there is a higher concentration of body fat lower down the income scale. Today the average American weighs 15–20 pounds more than at the turn of the twentieth century. Depending on which survey is used, we are told that "34 million of us, or 58 million, or 109 million, are overweight"; that "16 million men are . . . dieting and nearly 30 million women."[9]

Tales like Dolly's of weight gain and loss plug easily into rise and fall narratives of love and loss, sin and redemption, popular with country audiences. Early quips like the 1984 "If I can get my dress on, my weight is under control. My fat never made me less money" strike less responsive chords than post-1986 confessions: "I bought all those videos – Richard Simmons, Jane Fonda, I love to sit and eat cookies and watch 'em. But I just won't do it." That personal heartbreak is occasionally thrown into the mix is a bonus: "It's plain, ain't it? It was a love."[10] Sick and despondent, Dolly plummeted from 165 pounds to 90 in the mid-1980s. Her secret? Tiny, frequent, meals, chewed but then spat out.

Today she is somewhat heavier and probably healthier. Yet her fondness for home-cooked meals, fried food, and junk food continues. Crucially, it is shared by her public, including the millions who dine at Dollywood.[11] "Dollywood's Menu Set Off from Those of Other Parks," promises the head-line of an article in *Amusement Business*.[12] Of the nine full-meal restaurants at Dollywood (among them the Hickory House BBQ, Granny Ogle's Ham 'n' Beans, Aunt Granny's Dixie Fixin's, and Apple Jack's) the only vaguely veggie meal to be found – other than French fries, funnel cakes or ice cream – is cheese pizza. Not for nothing has the *Knoxville News Sentinel* described Dollywood as "the horror of seeing the wrong people in Spandex."[13]

Dolly's openness about the surgical procedures she undergoes might seem more controversial. But she legitimates the interventions by saying, frankly: "At my age, your boobs get saggier." She readily admits to "nips, tucks and several sucks . . . I don't itemize. . . . I don't see the harm in making yourself look better when you're in the public eye. Sometimes I see myself on TV and think, . . . 'I better get my pair off the ground!'"[14]

Her confessions tap contemporary trends. Where in the 1960s breast aug-mentation was mainly for showgirls, today plastic surgeries of all kinds are common.[15] The majority of those who choose plastic surgery are not rich: families with incomes under $25,000 account for 30 percent of patients; those with incomes between $25,000 and $50,000 for another 35 percent."[16]

Dolly's body may thus not represent the norm, but her attitudes towards it are demonstrably normal. Her ability to convince people that "there's a very real person underneath this artificial look" is sheer promotional genius.[17] Who else could so adroitly invoke God, Minnie Pearl, and plastic surgery in virtually the same breath? "People say, ''n' God had wanted you to have this or that, if He'd wanted you to have your hair streaked or bleached' – Well, that's silly. . . . Any old ham looks better with a little red paint, as Minnie Pearl would say." "My spirit is too beautiful and alive to live in some dilapidated old body if it doesn't have to. And I don't."[18] The combination is intriguing, for today's U.S. is often polarized along religious and secular lines. But Dr Dolly specializes in divine guid-ance and straight talk.

Divine guidance, straight talk

Dolly begins her autobiography by reverently telling how a mountain preacher-doctor rode through a snowstorm on horseback to deliver her: "God guided that little horse's steps that day. As he continues to guide every step that I take." She ends by affirming her support for gays and lesbians, and even confesses, that "if I hadn't been a woman, I would have been a drag queen."[19] To those accustomed to thinking of Southern fundamentalism as anti-feminist and homophobic, such juxtapositions are startling. Yet though Dolly was raised Church of God, East Tennessee is home to several mainline and evangelical religious groups, including several indigenous mountain churches with strong independent traditions.[20] Some embrace women as preachers, a practice forbidden since 1984 by the all-male, ultra-conservative leadership of the Southern Baptist Convention, the area's (indeed the nation's) dominant religious force.[21] And of course Dolly now lives part-time in Los Angeles.

As big budget Hollywood films designed to please cross-over audiences, Dolly's pictures contain few direct references to God. Only the made-for-TV *Unlikely Angel* revolves around (non-denominational) salvation, with Ruby (Dolly) cautioned not to engage with sins of the flesh by the angel Peter (Roddy McDowell). *Rhinestone* is more typical: most of the songs performed by Nick (Stallone), an aspiring country crooner, are about lust or drinking; all are written by Dolly. Only the grand finale, belted out by both, is a gospel number whose chorus reiterates, "I'm gonna be there." *Best Little Whorehouse*, *Steel Magnolias*, and *Straight Talk* poke fun in passing at overly religious "Southerners." Each makes Dolly the mouthpiece who "tells it like it is." In *Steel Magnolias* Truvy chides her assistant (Darryl Hannah) for being so insufferably "born-again," reminding her that "God don't care which church you go to, as long as you show up!" And in *Straight Talk* radio psychologist "Dr" Shirlee Kenyon (Dolly) counsels a complaining caller, "Get down off the cross, honey, somebody else needs the wood!"

More frequently, the movies invoke family and/or "family values." Most plots unite heterosexual couples and constitute or reunite nuclear families. *Best Little Whorehouse*, *Rhinestone*, and *Straight Talk* pair off Dolly with Burt Reynolds, Sylvester Stallone, and James Woods, respectively; *Steel Magnolias* reconnects Truvy with her husband Spud (Sam Shepard); *Unlikely Angel* replaces the family's missing mom temporarily with Dolly; *Smoky Mountain Christmas* ends with the local judge (John Ritter) awarding Lorna (Dolly) and Mountain Dan (Bo Hopkins) custody of a troop of little orphans. "She's the best mom in the whole world!" scream the kids. "These little people have changed my whole life for the better," affirms Dolly. The very last we hear of them is the fervent "Thank you God for making us a family again!" No film includes any substantive (hetero)sexual "action." Although

Unlikely Angel features a neck rub and a dream, and *Straight Talk* tantalizes with kisses galore and a tumble on the floor, Dolly appears in "foundations" – ribbons, lace, corset, and garters – solely in *Best Little Whorehouse*.

But at the same time, most of the films are overtly feminist and covertly queer. The most successful – *Nine to Five* and *Steel Magnolias* – demonstrate how much fun Dolly's uppity, independent characters have with other women.[22] *Straight Talk* also includes moments where Shirlee goes out of her way to help other gals. When a middle-aged woman calls to say her husband is cheating on her and a pompous Stanford psychologist (Spalding Gray) warns her she needs to make herself attractive to her man, "Dr" Shirlee defiantly demurs. *She* recommends the woman tell her *husband* "to tinkle or get off the potty!" And "Dr" Shirlee's final advice goes out to a transgendered woman about to have her last operation: "If you're sure, then all I can really say is don't try to perm your own hair and don't wear high heels on a soggy lawn." The line is amply prepared for by the scripts and casts of *Nine to Five*, *Best Little Whorehouse*, and *Steel Magnolias*. Lily Tomlin meets Jane Fonda meets Dolly to revel, revolt, and rule? For some audience members, *queer!* Dom de Luise dons a girdle, stuffs his crotch, knots a red neckerchief, *then* pulls on high-heeled embroidered boots? QUEER! Charles Durning's "little two-step"? Clairee's gay nephew? Ouiser's gay grandson? . . . Queer viewers attuned to nuance miss none of these beats: they savor every last gay character, every single queer moment, and feel welcomed and affirmed in consequence.

The ability to engage audiences interested in "divine guidance" *and* audiences attuned to "queer speak" via "straight talk" entails a balancing act that Dolly manages better than most: few other media personalities can please both right-wing fundamentalists and drag queens. Trust is key, and as with her shape shifts, films and interviews alike foreground her candor. Yet *what* Dolly says in interviews necessarily depends on what she is asked. Local newspapers are interested in her religious beliefs. In a recent *Knoxville News Sentinel* article entitled "The Gospel Side of Dolly," for example, East Tennesseans are assured that she repeats the Lord's Prayer and reads Scripture daily; that her favorite film, *Resurrection*, is about a healer in the Bible belt; that she felt guilty "after agreeing to star as a madame in *Best Little Whorehouse in Texas*" (which she still refers to as "the best little chicken house in Texas").[23]

Partnered with Silver Dollar City, a West Tennessee theme park advertised as "family-friendly," with "a Christian feel to it," Dollywood similarly dedicates itself to singing the Lord's (and of course Dolly's) praises. It houses the Southern Gospel Music Hall of Fame and Museum and the Robert F. Thomas Chapel. Daily stage shows feature gospel tie-ins. For the last two years, a musical bio of Dolly's life called "Paradise Road" has played to packed houses. Early on in the production, a narrator says, "one day, alone as a child, she found God." "God" tells Dolly that her mission is to be a singer, and the seventeen member cast joyously performs "He's Alive," index fingers pointing ecstatically upwards. (Choreography for a later male-only disco number has them point sideways.) The production ends with the narrator intoning "into this world, God sends his poets and troubadours; Dolly is such a poet and troubadour" as the cast sings "I Can See the Light." Housed in the park's largest air-conditioned venue, the production offers material as well as spiritual comfort: during the summer, magnified by acres of blacktop, heat and humidity are hellacious.

(White, overweight) nuclear families are everywhere. Areas like Dreamland Forest cater specifically to young children; rides and reasonably priced season passes appeal to older kids and adults. If you know how to "look," however, gay workers and visitors can occasionally be seen, performing in "Paradise Road," for example, or lounging in and around one specific restaurant. For Dolly has a large gay following, in part because she speaks publicly about her friendships with gays. Her manager, Sandy Gallin, is gay. Rumors have it her constant companion and best and oldest friend, Judy Ogle, is lesbian. Judy says nothing; Dolly volunteers merely that she and Judy "always sleep together in one double bed," and that "I am closer to Judy than I am to Carl [her husband]."[24] Periodically she refutes charges that she herself is gay, but she vehemently opposes conservative religious edicts which hold that homosexuality is a sinful activity: "I believe in . . . the Scripture, 'judge not, lest ye be judged.' I have many gay friends who I love dearly. I have also lost some very special friends to AIDS."[25]

Most Tennesseans do not know that Dolly speaks out on behalf of lesbians and gays. Since no one publicly "asks," no one publicly "tells": Clinton's famous policy on "gays in the military" had decidedly Southern roots. Gossip about heterosexual affairs, in contrast, is commonplace: "running around" is part of country life and lore. Everyone knows that Dolly has a somewhat unusual arrangement with her husband: on several occasions, Dolly has intimated that she and Carl have had extra-marital relationships; she readily admits that they spend little time together.[26] Few care: Dolly the person, character, and star is valued in East Tennessee for maintaining her ties to home, not husband.

Mountain manners, street smarts

Having modeled herself on "trash,"[27] Dolly now makes a point of "recycling," reinvesting a goodly percentage of her profits back home. As she says at the end of *Smoky Mountain Christmas*: "Home. . . . Family. . . . I don't want to be away from that anymore!" Yet the land and the life-style Dolly alludes to are mythical. Most films paint her as Appalachian and/or "cracker," following broad definitions wherein "Appalachia" includes portions of twelve states and all of West Virginia, and "cracker" refers to people living in a back country South that includes parts of Florida, Louisiana, Alabama, Mississippi, and Texas.[28] *Rhinestone* and *Smoky Mountain Christmas* in particular make the country look and sound like Noah's Ark. In the former, sheep, pigs, and cows scatter when Stallone first sings; in the latter, the village doctor has only one human patient; later, his waiting room is filled with sick hogs, dogs, and ducks.

"Hillbilly" movie men are virile, rough, and ready (Mountain Dan in *Smoky Mountain Christmas*; Sheriff Earl in *Best Little Whorehouse*). Often they are shiftless and/or pugnacious (Spud in *Steel Magnolias*, Steve in *Straight Talk*, Barnet in *Rhinestone*). Occasionally they are sleazy (John Sayles' dance school entrepreneur in *Straight Talk*, the sheriff who lusts after Dolly in *Smoky Mountain Christmas*, a bar-owning boyfriend in *Unlikely Angel*). Most sport beards, drink beer, and wave rifles in patent mistrust of big city strangers.[29]

Sets look like postcards; costumes cry "beloved" country. In *Nine to Five* Dolly's fantasy sequence involves roping and branding her boss (Dabney Coleman), clad as a cowgirl; most other characters wear skin tight jeans and high-heeled boots. Often victims of their men and/or the "system," they may be clichés but they always come out on top: Doralee and her friends take over in *Nine to Five*; Miss Mona becomes Texas' First Lady in *Best Little Whorehouse*; Lorna outwits both L.A. paparazzi and mountain magic in *Smoky Mountain Christmas*; married three times to the same ex-con, Shirlee finds true love with a city slicker in *Straight Talk*; Ruby ascends to heaven in *Unlikely Angel*.

And because Dolly's "dolls" are hillbilly trash, not Southern belles, they fit right in with working women and men everywhere. "A sweetly vengeful Democrat," as J. W. Williamson puts it, Dolly always sides with "common folks" because she is, in Shirlee's words, "not a Mercedes, but just a plain old Pontiac, maybe a Chevy."[30] *Nine to Five* and *Straight Talk* both include montage sequences cut to Dolly's hit songs where secretaries and file clerks and construction workers, cops, and kids, respectively, happily work and/or enthusiastically wave. Some films emphasize Dolly's naivete; most insist on her generosity. Shirlee, for example, treats a restaurant full of people to champagne: "Money's meant to be spent. What good is it going to do anybody at the bottom of my panty drawer?"

In a country where one-third of all assets are held by the top 1 percent of households and two-thirds by the richest 10 percent, almost everyone can cheer statements like these.[31] And if tunes like "Tennessee Homesick Blues" (*Rhinestone*) or "Country Memories" (*Smoky Mountain Christmas*) make it seem as if Dolly's desires are retro and rural, that several of her characters prefer living in big cities "up North" permits both country dwellers longing to escape the country *and* urban populations content to be urban to reconcile nostalgia for "home" with life in the fast lane.[32]

Figure 9.2   Dolly Parton as Doralee Rhodes, Lily Tomlin as Violet Newstead, Jane Fonda as Judy Bernly, and Dabney Coleman as Franklin Hart, Jr., in *Nine to Five* (20th Century Fox, 1980). Courtesy of the Kobal Collection.

The national press enthuses over Dolly's provincial ways (example from *People Weekly*: "I still like to pee off the porch every now and then. There's nothing like peeing on those snobs in Beverly Hills").[33] Tennessee papers prefer to cover Dolly's charitable work and business investments. Reports about Dollywood highlight "Craftsmen's Valley," a cluster of shops where local craftspeople blow glass, fashion wagon wheels, string musical instruments, carve rifles, and stitch quilts. Announcements of job openings are common: 2,000 people, largely retirees and high school students, are employed by Dollywood from April to December.[34]

Much is made of the Dollywood Foundation's efforts to "develop and support innovative educational programs in Sevier County." The "Imagination Library" provides preschoolers with a free book every month. Designed for middle-school students, the "Buddy Plan" guarantees $500 to each "buddy" who graduates from high school; if both graduate, they get $1,000.[35] Dolly's interventions are timely: according to the 1990 census, 37 percent of Tennessee adults did not complete high school and 20 percent did not finish ninth grade.[36] Thanks in good part to Dolly, however, by 1995 Sevier

County boasted the second highest (80 plus) percentage of students continuing their education in Tennessee. And regional health care also benefits from Dolly's largesse: the Robert F. Thomas Foundation funds burn and poison centers at the Sevier County Hospital.[37] Such programs make a real difference in a county where one-fifth of all residents are classified as poor and 20 percent of children live below the federal poverty level.[38]

Admittedly, Dolly's philanthropy makes good business sense. According to the *Chattanooga Times/Chattanooga Free Press*, more than 11 million tourists spend $615 million in Pigeon Forge each year; 78 percent are repeat visitors.[39] But add to the tax write-offs and free advertising she receives in exchange for her charitable contributions the ineffable influence of angels: ever since she was little, Dolly has loved angels. She really does want to do well by her neighbors, family, and friends, and she does not mind turning herself into something of a joke to do so. She often quotes her mamma: "angels fly because they take themselves lightly." Not coincidentally, her other pet symbol, the butterfly, is similarly miraculous if not quite so ethereal, a humbler being that nonetheless also transcends its earthbound beginnings for airborne bliss.

CEO and Cinderella

Dolly's own transformations are more material. Hers is the quintessential success saga. She flits from Hollywood to the hills, and plays the parts of CEO and Cinderella with equal brio. "Every day I count my blessings, then I count my money," she happily repeats. Since the 1990s she has become so well known that she even merits mention in films where she does not act: she has a cameo in Penelope Spheeris' 1993 *Beverly Hillbillies*, and she is the subject of endless lesbian gossip when reportedly "sighted" with Fran Leibowitz at a New York lesbian club in Jean Carlomusto's 1991 video, *L Is for the Way You Look*.

The movies in which Dolly stars rehearse the story of her glory. "I'm a chain!" shouts Truvy excitedly at the end of *Steel Magnolias* as Spud drives her past a new "Truvy's West" hair salon. When Lorna takes off for the hills without telling anyone in *Smoky Mountain Christmas*, police ask her butler to describe what she was wearing. He has no idea: "Madame has so many clothes." In *Straight Talk* she rates her own chauffeur and luxury high-rise apartment. But honky tonk angel Ruby reaches the true pinnacle of success: she leads the heavenly choir in Handel's *Messiah* as the final credits roll. Fairy tales, too, play key roles in many of the films, particularly in Dolly's own script, *Smoky Mountain Christmas*, a compendium of Snow White, Santa Claus, and others.

Today Dolly is a millionaire many times over. Dollywood is key to her empire: 2.3 million people visited in 2000 alone; adult tickets cost $31; there are parking fees as well. The Rags to Riches Museum functions as a shrine; there are rides like the "Tennessee Tornado," a roller coaster that boasts a double bosom-shaped loop (Dolly bubbles: "This ride has big features and curves, just like me!").[40] Mounds of "Dolly"-logo merchandise (key chains, T-shirts, baseball hats, magnets, cups, postcards, jewelry and more) are available all around the 118 acres; visitors exit through the giant Dolly Emporium.[41] And she owns other businesses in Pigeon Forge as well, including the 2,000 seat Music Mansion theater and a rodeo show and dinner theater known as the Dixie Stampede. Dixie Stampede branches have also opened in Myrtle Beach, South Carolina, and Branson, Missouri; plans for others in Orlando, Florida, and Queensland, Australia, await approval.

One of the few women in Hollywood with her own production company, Sandollar, she has garnered countless Grammys and Country Music Association awards. She has lent her name to wigs and a line of Revlon cosmetics. In 1990, she accepted an honorary Ph.D. from Carson Newman College, a local Baptist institution, referring to herself as "Dr Double D" and joking, "of course, I'm trying to hide all that under this robe at this fine, Baptist, ceremony."[42] Recently, she received the Association of American Publishers award for promoting literacy. Introduced by Clinton's Education Secretary, Richard Riley, she regaled the National Press Club with her daddy's *Nine to Five*-like take on Riley: "Hell, if he's got that much education, why is he still a secretary? He ought to be the boss!"[43]

What Dolly does not do is get involved in politics. She had no problem lobbying local notables for street, scenic, and sewer improvements in order to develop Dollywood, but she steers clear of national issues, quipping, "I'm not running for office, but I certainly have had a lot of politicians checking out my platform."[44] Asked on a talk show what would change if she ran the world (Gregory Peck would end racism; Jody Foster would stop pollution), Dolly's dreams were elementary: "I'd like to see everybody with a bellyful of food and a houseful of furniture and a car."[45]

Her simplicity is engaging. "Y'all come back now, y'hear?!" she beckons, a welcoming white icon who beams out from within an iris at the end of *Best Little Whorehouse in Texas*; *Unlikely Angel* concludes with her trademark giggle. Audiences can respond to differing pieces of the Parton puzzle. Overwhelmingly from Tennessee, often themselves raised as fundamentalist Christians, many of my students know her films by heart (*Nine to Five*, *Steel Magnolias* are particular favorites). Not all are up on her music, indeed, many do not know her 1999 bluegrass C.D., "The Sky is Green, the Grass is Blue," although everyone can recite older country favorites and cross-over hits. Most are aware of her local charitable work; like their parents, they do not know of her support for lesbians and gays.

The thing is, there is something about Dolly nearly everyone finds sweet, even if you do not like the unsanctioned "Polly Darton" lollipops (high hair and big bosoms on a stick) sold just outside Dollywood. She has a large following in Africa. "Yes, It's True, Zimbabweans Love Dolly Parton," writes Jonathan Zilberg in *The Journal of Popular Culture*.[46] A colleague from Ghana tells me she is equally popular there, he suggests thanks to her more Christian songs and to knowledge that she, too, was raised by poor farmers in a large family.

Whatever the focus, however, the various possibilities within "Dolly dialectics" earn fans. That local old-timers and newcomers should be nostalgic for a simpler past is understandable: when Dolly was young, Sevierville had only 3,000 inhabitants; today the stop-start summer traffic is endless, and the Smokies are smoggy, not smoky.[47] In Dolly's case, however, nostalgia for bygone days and disappearing ways both preserves the past *and* fashions the future. A sign posted three years ago at Dollywood at the entrance to the Fifties section – then under construction – succinctly captured the combination: "Excuse Our Progress: We're Building a Bridge to the Past."

For global audiences, Dolly emerges as the ultimate media model and pomo-retro mix, a down-home sophisticate who is equally comfortable in a shack as in a mansion. At the edge of a new millennium, "her" most momentous transfiguration to date has been the 1997 move out of the manger, into the straw, and back to her Scots-Irish roots as a sheep cloned from a mammary gland in a Scottish lab. With characteristic business acumen and quick wit, the real Dolly responded graciously to the homage tendered her from across the sea: "I'm honored. . . . There's no such thing as baaaaaaaaaaad publicity."

NOTES

INTRODUCTION: IMPOSSIBLE BODIES, COMPROMISED POSITIONS

1 Following Jim Hillier, I use the term "Hollywood" in the broadest sense to designate the U.S. film industry as a whole, not just L.A.-based, studio production. See J. Hillier, *The New Hollywood*, New York, Continuum, 1992, p. 4.

2 T. Levitt, *The Marketing Imagination*, London, Collier-Macmillan, 1993, p. 26, cited in D. Morley and K. Robins, *Spaces of Identity: Global Media, Electronic Landscapes and Cultural Boundaries*, London, Routledge, 1995, p. 15.

3 See, for example, Hillier, *The New Hollywood*; B. Litman, *The Motion Picture Mega-industry*, Boston, Allyn and Bacon, 1998; S. Neale and M. Smith (eds), *Contemporary Hollywood Cinema*, London, Routledge, 1998; and J. Wasko, *Hollywood in the Information Age*, Cambridge, Polity Press, 1994.

4 "The objective for the real global players is to operate across two or even all three of these activities [i.e. production, distribution, and hardware delivery]." Morley and Robins, *Spaces of Identity*, p. 13.

5 See especially J. Wyatt, *High Concept: Movies and Marketing in Hollywood*, Austin, University of Texas Press, 1994, and I. de Silva, "Consumer Selection of Motion Pictures," in Litman, *The Motion Picture Mega-industry*, pp. 144–71.

6 That U.S. military involvements in the 1980s and 1990s took place abroad (in Lebanon, Grenada, Panama, Haiti, Kuwait, Bosnia, and Kosovo) made it easier to concentrate on domestic matters. In addition, the dismantling of "international" Communism (in Reagan's words, "the Evil Empire") with the fall of the Berlin Wall, dissolution of the U.S.S.R., democratization of Eastern Europe, and Sandinista election loss in Nicaragua, made rhetorical and visual representation of *an* enemy difficult. Under Clinton in particular, (New) Cold War strategies were overhauled in consequence. Nonetheless contemporary U.S. foreign policy in many ways continues (New) Cold War precepts: military spending remains high, with technology and hardware buzz words for Republicans and Democrats alike. See N. Chomsky, "Power in the Global Arena," *New Left Review*, July–August 1998, no. 230, pp. 3–27; M. Klare, "Permanent Preeminence: U.S. Strategic Policy for the Twenty-first Century," *NACLA*, November–December 2000, vol. 34, no. 3, pp. 8–15; and J. McSherry, "Preserving Hegemony: National Security Doctrine in the Post-Cold War Era," *NACLA*, November–December 2000, vol. 34, no. 3, pp. 26–7.

7 The extent of domestic focus is further evidenced by the fact that of all the films studied here, only *El Norte* (Gregory Nava, 1983) and *My Family/Mi Familia* (Gregory Nava, 1995) allude to Central American issues, even though U.S. (covert) involvement in Central American Affairs was a comparatively hot

topic in the 1980s. See further S. Prince, *Visions of Empire: Political Imagery in Contemporary American Film*, New York, Praeger, 1992, pp. 81–115.

8 Audiences in Third World countries watching American television series featuring Aryan characters often prefer to identify with the "bad guys" via a process of "reverse identification." A. Mattelart *et al.*, *International Image Markets*, London, Comedia, 1984, cited in Morley and Robins, *Spaces of Identity*, p. 224.

9 The formulation is Chris Straayer's. See C. Straayer, *Deviant Eyes, Deviant Bodies*, New York, Columbia University Press, 1996.

10 Both *Pumping Iron* films are obviously staged and performed for the camera. The second, in particular, is at best a "semi-documentary" since the entire Miss Universe contest was planned and contestants recruited for a one-time event. See A. Kuhn, "The Body and Cinema: Some Problems for Feminism," in S. Sheridan (ed.), *Grafts: Feminist Cultural Criticism*, London, Verso, 1988, pp. 11–23, and D. Aoki, "Posing the Subject: Sex, Illumination, and *Pumping Iron II: The Women*," *Cinema Journal*, Summer 1999, vol. 38, no. 4, pp. 24–44.

11 The spectacular masculinity that Arnold Schwarzenegger and other contestants parade in *Pumping Iron* is not "natural." In contest, muscles and poses are so extreme, so stylized they become costume, even "drag." Where then is masculine "truth"? Women bodybuilders provoke even more consternation, for to many big muscles and femininity seem utterly incompatible. On masculine masquerade see further L. Heywood, "Masculinity Vanishing: Bodybuilding and Contemporary Culture," in P. Moore (ed.), *Building Bodies,* New Brunswick, Rutgers University Press, 1997, pp. 165–83, and C. Holmlund, "Masculinity as Multiple Masquerade," in S. Cohan and I. Hark (eds), *Screening the Male*, New York, Routledge, 1993, pp. 213–29; and on *Pumping Iron II* see further B. Correll, "Notes on the Primary Text: Woman's Body and Representation in *Pumping Iron II: The Women* and 'Breast Giver'," *Genre*, Fall 1989, vol. 23, pp. 287–308, and L. Schulze, "On the Muscle," in J. Gaines and C. Herzog (eds), *Fabrications: Costume and the Female Body*, New York, Routledge, 1990, pp. 59–78, reprinted in P. Moore, *Building Bodies,* New Brunswick, Rutgers University Press, 1997, pp. 9–30.

12 Lesbians and gays are increasingly visible and vital contributors to U.S. society. Latinos are now the largest ethnic group in the U.S. (2000 census figures put Latinos at 12 percent, African Americans at 14 percent, and Asian and Pacific Islanders at 4 percent of the total population). Sixty-one percent of all women work full time, most in low-paying jobs. See T. Caplow *et al.*, "The First Measured Century: An Illustrated Guide to Trends in America, 1900–2000," cited in S. Roberts, "America Then and Now: It's All in the Numbers," *New York Times*, 31 December 2000, section 4, p. 7.

13 Heterosexual audiences often saw the lead characters of these romances as "just friends" thanks to lighting, costuming, casting, and scripting (most characters are involved not only with women but also – initially, sporadically, always or ultimately – with men). Lesbian audiences, in contrast, enthusiastically welcomed the characters as "sisters," showing up in force at screenings, whistling, and applauding. See E. Ellsworth, "Illicit Pleasures: Feminist Spectators and *Personal Best*," *Wide Angle*, 1986, vol. 8, no. 2, pp. 45–56, and C. Straayer, "*Personal Best*: Lesbian Feminist Audience," *Jump Cut*, February 1984, no. 29, pp. 40–4.

Several of the "nouveaux" westerns were also cross-marketed to niche and mainstream (i.e. white, heterosexual) audiences thanks to combinations of "novel" casting and sound tracks with "traditional" western costumes, settings, and scenarios.

A good deal of critical debate surrounds the romances. See further T. de Lauretis, "Film and the Visible," in Bad Object Choices (eds), *How Do I Look?: Queer Film and Video*, Seattle, Bay Press, 1991, pp. 256–7 and 263; J. Halberstam, *Female Masculinity*, Durham, Duke University Press, 1998, pp. 207–22; K. Hollinger, *In the Company of Women*, Minneapolis, University of Minnesota Press, 1998, pp. 139–78; S. Kabir, *Daughters of Desire: Lesbian Representations in Film*, London, Cassell, 1998; M. Merck, "*Lianna* and the Lesbians of Art Cinema," in C. Brunsdon (ed.), *Films for Women*, London, British Film Institute, 1986, pp. 166–75 and "Dessert Heart," in M. Gever *et al.* (eds), *Queer Looks*, New York, Routledge, 1993, pp. 377–82; Jackie Stacey, " 'If You Don't Play, You Can't Win': *Desert Hearts* and the Lesbian Romance Film," in T. Wilton (ed.), *Immortal Invisible: Lesbians and the Moving Image*, London, Routledge, 1995, pp. 92–114; Straayer, *Deviant Eyes, Deviant Bodies*, pp. 9–22; and A. Weiss, *Vampires and Violets*, New York, Penguin Books, 1992, pp. 51–83 and 109–36.

14 Michael Omi and Howard Winant argue convincingly that "race has been a *fundamental* axis of social organization in the U.S." Continuing earlier trends, 1980s and 1990s neo-conservatives and neo-liberals adopted similarly "color-blind" positions, downplaying inequalities in favor of "assimilation." As a result, "far from decreasing, the significance of race in American life has expanded." Consider, for example, the "Reagan Revolution's" invocation of "states' rights" to justify white privilege, deregulate business, and cut federal support for social services. Compare the reduction under Clinton of welfare benefits, a decision primarily affecting blacks, Latinos, and poor whites. M. Omi and H. Winant, *Racial Formation in the United States: From the 1960s to the 1990s*, New York, Routledge, 1994, p. 13, and H. Winant, *Racial Conditions*, Minneapolis, University of Minnesota Press, 1994, p. 68. See further Omi and Winant, *Racial Formation*, especially pp. 145–59.

15 J. Mayne, *Framed: Lesbians, Feminists, and Media Culture*, Minneapolis, University of Minnesota Press, 2000, p. xviii.

16 Because the overwhelming majority of Americans are not wealthy, and women of all racial and ethnic backgrounds, Blacks, and Latinos appear at the bottom of the economic ladder, potential audiences for Whoopi, Clint, and Dolly are large – and diverse. See D. Henwood, "Trash-o-nomics," in M. Wray and A. Newitz (eds), *White Trash: Race and Class in America*, Routledge, New York, 1997, pp. 177–92, and E. Wolff, *Top Heavy: The Increasing Inequality of Wealth in America and What Can Be Done about It*, New York, New Press, 1995.

17 "True Clint," promises the caption accompanying a cover photo of a recent issue of *Modern Maturity*, the A.A.R.P. (American Association of Retired People) bi-monthly magazine addressed, in 10.1 million copies, to people aged 66 and older. See B. Isenberg, "True Clint: The Sweet Side of Dirty Harry," *Modern Maturity*, March–April 2001, pp. 54–9. Thanks to Bonnie Braendlin for bringing this story to my attention.

18 Compare Robyn Wiegman, who asks what it means that today "the visual apparatuses of photography, film, television, and video (as well as the many offshoots of computer technologies) serve as our primary public domain, our main shared context for the contestations of contemporary cultural politics? And perhaps more important, what does it mean that within these technologies, the body is figured as the primary locus of representation, mediation, and/or interpretation?" Though less centrally concerned with film than I am here, Wiegman is also concerned with shifts "from vision to the visual to the visible." R. Wiegman, *American Anatomies: Theorizing Race and Gender*, Durham, Duke University Press, 1995, p. 3.

19 Arnold's heterosexuality is constantly emphasized, but his homoerotic allure is not far off. In his case, a fascist foundation underpins the homoeroticism. Citing an unauthorized biography written by Wendy Leigh, Jonathan Goldberg emphasizes that, as a child, Arnold dreamed of dictators, then underlines Arnold's willingness to be a "boytoy, allowing the look [of other men], if nothing else." J. Goldberg, "Recalling Totalities: The Mirrored Stages of Arnold Schwarzenegger," *Differences*, 1992, vol. 4, no. 1, pp. 177–8.

20 See further R. Dyer, *White*, London, Routledge, 1997, especially pp. 16–17 and 150, and "Swede as 'Other'," here.

21 Earlier – this essay dates from 1989 – I argued that heterosexual male and female spectators reacted, whether to big *bona fide* lesbians or to Bev, primarily through fear of loss of love; today I find my position reductive. I have not changed this particular passage here, however, preferring to leave traces of *when* I wrote. Laurie Schulze worries similarly that she simplified lesbian culture because she earlier posited that big women appeal to lesbians. See Schulze, "On the Muscle," reprinted in Moore, *Building Bodies*, especially pp. 22–3.

22 Writing on *Personal Best* (Robert Towne, 1982) Linda Williams comments that a fit, sporty "look" was popular already in the 1970s and early 1980s. See L. Williams, "*Personal Best*: Women in Love," *Jump Cut*, July 1982, no. 27, p. 1.

23 Y. Tasker, *Spectacular Bodies: Gender, Genre and the Action Cinema*, London, Routledge, 1993, p. 132.

24 See, for example, L. Vickers, "Excuse Me, Did We See the Same Movie?," *Jump Cut*, 1994, no. 39, pp. 25–30.

25 Jeff Berglund has intriguingly extended my original remarks about *Fried Green Tomatoes*. He argues that the film's pernicious association of blackness with cannibalism and lesbianism with protective friendship ("the secret's in the sauce") hides both racism and sexuality. In a world that is normatively white and willfully "feel-good," blackness becomes "a problem that must be overcome." See J. Berglund, " 'The Secret's in the Sauce': Dismembering Normativity in *Fried Green Tomatoes*," *Camera Obscura*, September 1999, no. 42, pp. 125–62.

Of *Basic Instinct* Sharon Willis comments that the narrative urgency around "the mystery of sex and sexuality . . . serves to displace, if not to repress, conflicts around other social differences, even as it may borrow some of its traumatic energy from anxieties that those conflicts generate." Krin and Glen Gabbard unearth the "homoerotically charged relationship between the protagonist and his best buddy on the police force," citing George Dzundza's "rage when he discovers that Michael Douglas is sleeping with a suspect." See S. Willis, *High Contrast: Race and Gender in Contemporary Hollywood Film*, Durham, Duke University Press, 1997, p. 84, and K. and G. Gabbard, "Phallic Women in the Contemporary Cinema," *American Imago*, Winter 1993, vol. 50, no. 4, p. 436.

26 As Winant argues, many white Americans, from the radical left to the fundamentalist right, began to think of "whiteness" as *difference*, as problematic, in the 1980s and 1990s. See H. Winant, "Behind Blue Eyes: Whiteness and Contemporary U.S. Racial Politics," *New Left Review*, September–October 1997, no. 225, pp. 73–88. See further R. Wiegman, "Whiteness Studies and the Paradox of Particularity," *boundary 2*, Fall 1999, vol. 26, no. 3, pp. 115–50.

27 Martial arts sequences constitute a rectification, post-Vietnam, of the U.S. "loss" to a smaller enemy and a negotiation of the "yellow peril" discourse triggered by Japanese financial take-overs of American companies and real estate in the late 1980s. The integration of such sequences into films starring whites additionally indicates Hollywood's recognition of how popular Hong Kong films were with 1970s–1980s inner city and rural audiences. See D. Desser, "The Martial Arts Film in the 1990s," in W. Dixon (ed.), *Film Genre 2000: New*

Critical Essays, Albany, State University of New York Press, 2000, pp. 77–111.
28 W. Sollors, *Beyond Ethnicity: Consent and Descent in American Culture*, New York, Oxford University Press, 1986, pp. 31 and 33.
29 S. Hall, "Notes on Deconstructing 'The Popular'," in R. Samuel (ed.), *People's History and Socialist Theory*, London, Routledge & Kegan Paul, 1981, p. 230.
30 W. Connolly, *Identity\Difference: Negotiations of Political Paradox*, Ithaca, Cornell University Press, p. 32.
31 See A. Doty, *Making Things Perfectly Queer*, Minneapolis, University of Minnesota Press, 1993; and Prince, *Visions of Empire*, p. 6.

1 VISIBLE DIFFERENCE AND FLEX APPEAL

1 This chapter was originally published as an essay in 1989. A few changes have been made here.
2 In the case of the women's movement, organizing around the issues of abortion, rape, physical abuse of women, and pornography is often based as much on the idea that the body should not be violated as on the idea that women have a right to choose for themselves. Unfortunately, organizing predicated on the inviolability of the body frequently overlaps in highly problematic ways with New Right interests.
3 M. Foucault, "The Confession of the Flesh," in *Power/Knowledge: Selected Interviews and Other Writings 1972–1977*, New York, Pantheon Books, 1980, p. 195.
4 M. Foucault, "Body/Power," in *Power/Knowledge*, p. 58.
5 Ibid.
6 No doubt because the *Pumping Iron* films seek to legitimate bodybuilding as "natural" and "healthy," neither film mentions steroids, though male bodybuilders in particular often use them. At one point in *Pumping Iron* Lou Ferrigno takes handfuls of pills, but they are probably vitamins. Except for an oblique – and catty – suggestion by Rachel McLish that Bev Francis may have used steroids ("the question is not how she did it [i.e. how she got so big], but where she's at right now") *Pumping Iron II: The Women* also shies away from the question of drugs. Alteration of the female body through costume (Rachel's bikini top is judged illegal because it is padded) and breast implants (an issue the judges say they ignore because implants are too hard to detect) are the only artificial interventions the film acknowledges.
7 The effacement of production is typical of documentary film and classic narrative cinema. Following Edward Buscombe and Roy Peters, Garry Whannel describes how these cinematic conventions have been adapted to television sports coverage in order to "minimiz[e] audience awareness of the mediating effect of television." The visual style of television sports coverage has in turn influenced the *Pumping Iron* films as sports documentaries. See G. Whannel, "Fields in Vision: Sport and Representation," *Screen*, May–June 1984, vol. 25, no. 3, p. 101. See also E. Buscombe (ed.), *Football on Television*, British Film Institute Television Monograph, London, 1974, and R. Peters, *Television Coverage of Sport,* Stencilled Paper, Centre for Contemporary Cultural Studies, Birmingham, 1976.
8 As Kate Millett points out, however, "the heavier musculature of the male, a secondary sexual characteristic and common among mammals, is biological in origin but is also culturally encouraged through breeding, diet and exercise." Moreover, physical strength has little to do with gender roles and power. On the contrary: "At present, as in the past, physical exertion is very generally a class factor, those at the bottom performing the most strenuous tasks, whether they be strong or not." K. Millett, *Sexual Politics*, Garden City, Doubleday, 1970, p. 27.

9 R. Dyer, "Don't Look Now," *Screen*, September–October 1982, vol. 23, nos. 3–4, pp. 67–8.

10 S. Neale, "Masculinity as Spectacle," *Screen*, November–December 1983, vol. 24, no. 6, pp. 15–16.

11 S. Freud, "The 'Uncanny'," in J. Strachey (ed.), *On Creativity and the Unconscious*, New York, Harper and Row, 1958, pp. 122–61.

12 Freud's analyses encompass both perspectives, but the second is the more basic. Susan Lurie critiques Freud's assumption that men and boys are the norm: "In psychoanalysis the meaning of woman is fixed not as difference, but as 'mutation' in the context of a desired sameness." S. Lurie, "The Construction of the 'Castrated Woman' in Psychoanalysis and Cinema," *Discourse*, Winter 1981–1982, no. 4, p. 54. For similar critiques, see also S. Heath, "Difference," *Screen*, Autumn 1978, vol. 19, no. 3, pp. 51–112, and K. Horney, "The Dread of Woman," in *Feminine Psychology*, New York, W. W. Norton, 1967, pp. 133–46.

13 The first of the three choices Freud discusses is homosexuality. Homosexuals, he argues, openly acknowledge the primacy of the phallus: men are taken as sexual objects because they possess the penis, which the child imagines the mother he loved also had. Yet this solution is unacceptable to society. Fetishism is preferable because "it endow[s] women with the attribute which makes them acceptable as sexual objects." Unlike homosexuality, fetishes are not prohibited by society; on the contrary, as Freud remarks, "they are easily obtainable and sexual gratification by their means is thus very convenient." For these reasons, "the fetishist has no trouble in getting what other men have to woo and exert themselves to obtain." S. Freud, "Fetishism," in J. Strachey (ed.), *Sexuality and the Psychology of Love*, New York, Macmillan, 1963, p. 216.

14 L. Schulze, "*Getting Physical*: Text/Context/Reading and the Made-for-TV Movie," *Cinema Journal*, Winter 1986, vol. 25, no. 2, p. 43.

15 J. Nestle, "The Fem Question," in C. Vance (ed.), *Pleasure and Danger: Exploring Female Sexuality*, London, Routledge and Kegan Paul, 1984, p. 233.

16 S. Freud, "Anxiety and Instinctual Life," in J. Strachey (ed.), *New Introductory Lectures on Psychoanalysis*, New York, W. W. Norton, 1965, pp. 77–8.

17 Ibid., pp. 76–7. Karen Horney would agree, though as usual her evaluation of this phenomenon is critical both of the phenomenon and of Freud's position. See, for example, K. Horney, "The Overvaluation of Love," in *Feminine Psychology*, pp. 182–213 and "The Neurotic Need for Love," in *Feminine Psychology*, pp. 245–58.

18 A. Rich, "Compulsory Heterosexuality and Lesbian Existence," *Signs*, Summer 1980, vol. 5, no. 4, p. 187.

19 No doubt Freud would argue that those women in the film (Bev, Carla) or in the audience (feminists, lesbians) who do not fear the loss of love by men do so only because they covet the phallus/penis directly. They have not made the requisite substitution of baby for penis.

20 See Rich, "Compulsory Heterosexuality and Lesbian Existence," pp. 631–60.

21 M. Pally, "Women of 'Iron'," *Film Comment*, July–August 1985, vol. 21, no. 4, p. 62.

22 Ibid., p. 60.

23 Dyer, "Don't Look Now," p. 71.

24 The confusion of these three categories, as Gayle Rubin convincingly argues, is all the more easily accomplished because in English "sex" refers both to gender and gender identity and to sexual activity. See G. Rubin, "Thinking Sex: Notes for a Radical Theory of the Politics of Sexuality," in Vance, *Pleasure and Danger*, p. 307. In sharp contrast to many feminists, Rubin refuses to see women's experience of sexuality as engendering. For her "sexual oppression cuts

across other modes of social inequality, sorting out individuals and groups according to its own intrinsic dynamics. It is not reducible to, or understandable in terms of, class, race, ethnicity, or gender." Ibid., p. 293.

25 See, for example, H. Bhabha, "The Other Question . . .," *Screen*, November–December 1983, vol. 24, no. 6, pp. 18–36.

26 According to Nik Cohn, Carla's own experiences agree with the film's privileging of sexual difference over racial difference. As an adult, Carla has found sexual discrimination to pose more problems than racial discrimination. As a child, she was sheltered from racial prejudice by class privilege:

> Of all the top women bodybuilders, she was the only black. A lot of brothers and sisters had asked her if that was a dilemma. She always told them No, and that was the truth. She had never been taught that color was a limitation. Those were not the kind of roots she'd grown from.
>
> Her childhood had been wonderful. Her father was a chemist in Newark, and his children were provided with everything they needed. Carla had four sisters and a brother. They lived in a huge house. There were horses and boats, and lots of space to breathe in. *A typical American middle class background*, she called it. They summered on a yacht.
>
> N. Cohn, Women of Iron: The World of Female
> Bodybuilders, n.p., Wideview Books, 1981, p. 59.

27 G. Joseph, "The Media and Blacks – Selling It Like It Isn't," in G. Joseph and J. Lewis (eds), *Common Differences*, Garden City, N.Y., Doubleday, 1981, p. 163.

28 S. Gilman, "Black Bodies, White Bodies," *Critical Inquiry*, Autumn 1985, vol. 12, no. 1, p. 238.

29 See Foucault, "The Confession of the Flesh," pp. 194–5.

30 Bhabha, "The Other Question," p. 27. Bhabha goes on to suggest that Blacks themselves participate in the creation and perpetuation of the stereotype, much as women desire to be seen as different and consent to be fetishized out of a fear of loss of love.

31 E. Said, *Orientalism*, London, Routledge and Kegan Paul, 1978, pp. 58–9.

32 C. Gaines, *Pumping Iron: The Art and Sport of Bodybuilding*, New York, Simon and Schuster, 1981, pp. 220–2.

33 Whannel, "Fields of Vision," p. 99.

34 Pally, "Women of 'Iron'," p. 60.

35 While in the history of Western art men have traditionally been portrayed as muscular, "the shape to which the female body tends to return . . . is one which emphasizes its biological functions . . . most often suggested by a softly curved cello shape." C. Gaines, *Pumping Iron II: The Unprecedented Woman*, New York, Simon and Schuster, 1984, p. 20.

36 There is a clear racial as well as a sexist bias in the advertising business surrounding women's bodybuilding. Gloria Steinem writes: "Though she has great beauty and the speech skills of a first-class actress, Carla Dunlap has been offered no television commercials. Even the dozens of bodybuilding magazines have declined to put this first black woman champion on the cover." G. Steinem, "Coming Up: The Unprecedented Women," *Ms.*, July 1985, vol. 14, no. 1, p. 109.

2 WHEN IS A LESBIAN NOT A LESBIAN?

1 This chapter was originally published as an essay in 1991. Certain footnotes have been abridged or cut in this version.

2 A. Rich, "Compulsory Heterosexuality and the Lesbian Existence," *Signs*, Summer 1980, vol. 5, no. 4, pp. 177–203.

3 See E. Ellsworth, "Illicit Pleasures: Feminist Spectators and *Personal Best*," *Wide Angle*, 1986, vol. 8, no. 2, pp. 45–56; C. Straayer, "*Personal Best*: Lesbian/Feminist Audience," *Jump Cut*, February 1984, no. 29, pp. 40–4; and "The Hypothetical Lesbian Heroine," *Jump Cut*, April 1990, no. 35, pp. 50–8.

4 See, for example, A. Ferguson, "Patriarchy, Sexual Identity, and the Sexual Revolution," *Signs*, Autumn 1981, vol. 7, no. 1, pp. 158–72; J. N. Zita, "Historical Amnesia and the Lesbian Continuum," *Signs*, Autumn 1981, vol. 7, no. 1, pp. 172–87; and C. Golden, "Diversity and Variability in Women's Sexual Identities," Boston Lesbian Psychologies Collective (ed.), *Lesbian Psychologies*, Urbana, University of Illinois Press, 1987, pp. 21–2.

The "we're just like you" politics promoted by the National Gay Task Force incorporated similar contradictions, combining an insistence on coming out with the reassurance that gays were not really different, with – depending on your point of view – a threatening or utopian promise that gay liberation would free the homosexuality in everyone.

There were, of course, many reasons for lesbian feminists to join with heterosexual feminists. Gay historian Barry Adam summarizes some of the reasons for lesbian/gay splits: "Men took for granted many of the social conditions that made it possible for them to be gay. But lesbians needed to address fundamental problems facing all women – such as equal opportunity in employment and violence against women – in order to have sufficient independence to become lesbian." B. Adam, *The Rise of a Gay and Lesbian Movement*, Boston, G. K. Hall & Co., 1987, p. 92.

5 See, for example, C. Holmlund, "Visible Difference and Flex Appeal: The Body, Sex, Sexuality, and Race in the *Pumping Iron* Films," reprinted here; A. Kuhn, "Sexual Disguise and Cinema," *The Power of the Image*, London, Routledge and Kegan Paul, 1985, pp. 48–73 and "The Body and Cinema: Some Problems for Feminism," in S. Sheridan (ed.), *Grafts*, London, Verso, 1988, pp. 11–23; E. Newton, "The Mythic Mannish Lesbian," *Signs*, Summer 1984, vol. 9, no. 4, pp. 557–75; and L. Schulze, "*Getting Physical*: Text/Context/Reading and the Made-for-TV Movie," *Cinema Journal*, Winter 1986, vol. 25, no. 2, pp. 33–50.

6 Punning on "homme" (man), Luce Irigaray's insistence that the lesbian exposes a male hom/m/osexual exchange of women by standing on the margins of such exchange is particularly important here. See L. Irigaray, *Speculum of the Other Woman*, G. C. Gill (trans.), Ithaca, Cornell University Press, 1985.

7 See, for example, J. Butler, *Gender Trouble*, New York, Routledge, 1990 and "Gender Theory, Feminist Theory, and Psychoanalytic Discourse," in L. J. Nicholson (ed.), *Feminism and Postmodernism*, New York, Routledge, 1990, pp. 324–40; J. Nestle, "The Fem Question," in C. Vance (ed.), *Pleasure and Danger*, Boston, Routledge & Kegan Paul, 1984, pp. 232–41 and *A Restricted Country*, Ithaca, Firebrand Press, 1987; E. Newton, *Mother Camp: Female Impersonators in America*, Englewood Cliffs, Prentice Hall, 1972; G. Rubin, "Thinking Sex: Notes for a Radical Theory of the Politics of Sexuality," in C. Vance (ed.), *Pleasure and Danger*, pp. 267–319.

8 J. Riviere, "Womanliness as a Masquerade," in V. Burgin (ed.), *Formations of Fantasy*, London, Routledge & Kegan Paul, 1986, pp. 35–44.

9 J. Nestle, *A Restricted Country*, p. 57. Although I am insisting on the femme's femininity, I do not want to encourage the perceptions common to both gay and straight feminist circles in the 1970s that butch/femme relationships duplicated heterosexual roles. I agree with Nestle that clothing and gestures are less important than erotic attitudes.

10 Nestle, "The Fem Question," p. 233.

11 For discussions of earlier representations of lesbians in film, see Becker *et al.*, "Introduction," *Jump Cut*, March 1981, nos. 24–5, pp. 17–22; C. Charbonneau and L. Winer, "Lesbians in 'Nice' Films," *Jump Cut*, March 1981, nos. 24–5, pp. 25–6; J. Mellon, *Women and Their Sexuality in the New Film*, New York, Horizon Press, 1973, pp. 74–105; V. Russo, *The Celluloid Closet*, New York, Harper & Row, 1987; C. Sheldon, "Lesbians and Film: Some Thoughts," in R. Dyer (ed.), *Gays and Film*, New York, Zoetrope, 1984, pp. 5–26; and B. Zimmerman, "Lesbian Vampires," *Jump Cut*, March 1981, nos. 24–5, pp. 23–5.

12 For a discussion of the promises and limitations of the 1970s women's films, see C. Brunsdon, "A Subject for the Seventies," *Screen*, September–October 1982, vol. 23, nos 3–4, pp. 20–9, and Charbonneau and Winer, "Lesbians in 'Nice' Films."

13 For once, critics in the alternative press provided no gossip about the directors' or stars' sexual preferences, but a few irate comments were made about Mariel Hemingway's and Patricia Charbonneau's insistence on their *heterosexuality*. Hemingway posed nude for *Playboy*, and the same issue included production stills of her and co-star Patrice Donnelly. See "Personal Mariel," *Playboy*, April 1982, no. 29, pp. 104–7.

14 J. Kroll, "Chariots of Desire," *Newsweek*, 8 February 1982, vol. 99, no. 6, p. 60. Stone's attack is biting: "Towne and Hemingway have been telling reporters that *Personal Best* is not about lesbianism, which is rather like saying that *Moby Dick* is about men at sea, nature, and change, but not about whale-hunting." L. Stone, "*Personal Best*: What's New in Towne," *Village Voice*, 16 March 1982, no. 27, p. 23.

15 M. Sragow, "First Time Director Robert Towne Comes Up a Winner," *Rolling Stone*, 15 April 1982, no. 367, p. 94. See also C. Chase, "At the Movies," *New York Times*, 5 February 1982, p. C8; Ellsworth, "Illicit Pleasures"; and "Personal Mariel."

16 C. Rizzo, "John Sayles Interviewed," *Gay Community News*, 1983, vol. 10, no. 30, p. 8.

17 M. Pally, "Come Hither – But Slowly," *Village Voice*, 31 January 1984, no. 29, p. 52. See also A. Insdorf, "Childhood Memories Shape Diane Kurys' *Entre Nous*," *New York Times*, 29 January 1984, no. 133, pp. 13–14, and M. Pally, "World of Our Mothers," *Film Comment*, April 1984, vol. 20, no. 2, p. 15.

18 E. Gordon, "Deitch Makes Feature Debut with Drama of Self-Discovery," *Film Journal*, February 1986, vol. 90, no. 2, p. 56.

19 Patricia Charbonneau made a point of saying her character was *not* bisexual. K. Garfield, "A Lesbian Love Story Heats Up the Screen," *The Advocate*, 18 February 1986, p. 46.

20 See S. Baaron, "Voyeur Pleasure," *Stills*, April 1986, no. 27, p. 156.

21 P. Kael, "The Current Cinema: The Women," *New Yorker*, 5 March 1984, no. 60, p. 133.

22 J. Coleman, "Chic to Chic," *New Statesman*, 21 October 1983, vol. 106, no. 2744, p. 28.

23 Mandy Merck argues that in *Entre Nous* and *Lianna* "the sexual curiosity incited by both is rendered innocent by their use of children as both fascinated onlookers and auditors." M. Merck, "*Lianna* and the Lesbians of Art Cinema," in C. Brunsdon (ed.), *Films for Women*, London, British Film Institute, 1986, pp. 172–3.

24 J. Huston, "Trading Phone Numbers in the Theater: Fans Make *Desert Hearts* a Cult Classic," *Gay Community News*, 25 January 1987, vol. 14, no. 27, p. 8.

25 M. Nichols, "Doing Sex Therapy with Lesbians: Bending a Heterosexual

179

Paradigm to Fit Gay Life," in Boston Lesbian Psychologies Collective, *Lesbian Psychologies*, pp. 242–60.

26 J. Bristow, "Being Gay: Politics, Identity, Pleasure," *New Formations*, Winter 1989, no. 9, p. 71.

27 Straayer, "The Hypothetical Lesbian Heroine," p. 51.

28 P. White, "*Madame X on the China Seas*," *Screen*, Autumn 1987, vol. 28, no. 4, p. 82.

29 Some of the women Ellsworth interviewed saw Tory, not Chris, as the main character because she sent more signals that she "was" a lesbian through body language, speech, and facial gestures. Ellsworth, "Illicit Pleasures," pp. 53–5.

30 See P. Kael, "The Man Who Understands Women," *The New Yorker*, 22 February 1982, vol. 58, no. 1, p. 112. See also Denby, "*Personal Best*," p. 87: "sex is no big deal, it just happens."

31 T. Catalano, "*Personal Best*: A Critique of the Movie," *Women and Therapy*, Winter 1982, vol. 2, no. 4, p. 87.

32 See Ellsworth, "Illicit Pleasures," p. 54; Stone, "*Personal Best*: What's New in Towne," pp. 52–3; and Straayer, "*Personal Best*: Lesbian/Feminist Audience," p. 44.

33 V. Canby, "*Personal Best*, Olympic Love," *New York Times*, 5 February 1982, no. 131, p. C8.

34 Lucy Fischer noted that Sayles' use of "visual strategy generally reserved for heterosexual love . . . at least conveys a stylistic sense of equality." L. Fischer, *Shot/Countershot: Film Tradition and Women's Cinema*, Princeton, Princeton University Press, 1990, p. 266.

35 L. di Caprio, "Liberal Lesbianism," *Jump Cut*, February 1984, no. 29, p. 45; J. Coleman, "Click, Click," *New Statesman*, 10 February 1984, vol. 107, no. 2760, p. 31; and C. Rizzo, "Love and Learn," *Gay Community News*, 19 February 1983, vol. 10, no. 3, p. 7.

36 M. Bishop, "*Lianna*," *Spare Rib*, 1984, no. 111, p. 44, and A. Marney, "*Lianna*: A Move Toward Better Things," *off our backs*, April 1983, vol. 13, no. 4.

37 See Merck, "*Lianna* and the Lesbians of Art Cinema."

38 Straayer, "The Hypothetical Lesbian Heroine," p. 52.

39 Fischer, *Shot/Countershot*, p. 67. Writing for *In These Times* Barbara Presley Noble agreed, describing the street scenes as "15 or 20 seconds of self-discovery that utterly captures the transformative nature of [Lianna's] decision about her sexuality." B. Noble, "John, Maggie, and *Lianna*," *In These Times*, 9–22 March 1983, vol. 7, no. 15, p. 13.

40 See Straayer, "The Hypothetical Lesbian Heroine," pp. 53–4.

41 Nestle, *A Restricted Country*, pp. 106–7.

42 According to Straayer, the exchanges of looks between Lena and Madeleine facilitate "lesbian reading" because the two are framed as a couple, positioned next to each other and shown in medium two-shots. See Straayer, "The Hypothetical Lesbian Heroine," p. 52.

43 E. Jackson, "Dude Ranch Romance Fifties Style," *Body Politic*, November 1985, no. 120, p. 34.

44 Garfield, "A Lesbian Love Story Heats Up the Screen," p. 45 and Huston, "Trading Phone Numbers in the Movie Theater," p. 8.

45 See, for example, Nichols' discussion of sexual avoidance by long-term lesbian couples. Nichols, "Doing Sex Therapy with Lesbians," p. 104.

46 E. Rapping, "Where the Lesbians Roam," *The Guardian*, 11 June 1986, vol. 38, no. 36, p. 20.

47 Pornography and sado-masochist lesbian sex were particularly controversial. See, for example, S. Duggan *et al.*, "False Promises: Feminist Antipornography

Legislation in the U.S.," in V. Burstyn (ed.), *Women Against Censorship*, Vancouver, Douglas & McIntyre, 1985, pp. 130–51; Nestle, *A Restricted Country*, p. 123; A. Snitow, "Retrenchment versus Transformation: The Politics of the Antipornography Movement," in Burstyn, *Women Against Censorship*, pp. 107–20; A. Snitow *et al.*, "Introduction," in Vance, *Powers of Desire*, pp. 9–50; C. Vance, "Pleasure and Danger: Toward a Politics of Sexuality," in Vance, *Pleasure and Danger*, pp. 1–28; L. Williams, *Hard Core: Power, Pleasure, and the "Frenzy of the Visible,"* Berkeley, University of California Press, 1989; and E. Willis, "Feminism, Moralism, and Pornography," in *Powers of Desire*, pp. 460–7.

48 D. Waldman, "Film Theory and the Gendered Spectator: The Female or the Feminist Reader?," *Camera Obscura*, September 1988, no. 18, p. 88.

49 Linda Williams characterized the combination of sports and sex in *Personal Best* as a box office "stroke of genius," noting that "[t]hose who would normally be shocked or at least irritated by a lesbian relationship in any other context find it quite 'natural' among female athletes who, it is presumed, are simply more physical than other people." L. Williams, *"Personal Best*: Women in Love," *Jump Cut*, July 1982, no. 27, p. 11.

50 Straayer, *"Personal Best*: Lesbian/Feminist Audience," pp. 41–2.

51 No one noticed that this is the one lesbian film that refers, however obliquely, to class: the woman who Lianna has her casual affair with is the only lesbian in all the films who breaks the narrow range of tolerated femininity. Her manner, diction, and job (she's in the Air Force) suggest that she is probably working class.

52 Marney, *"Lianna*: A Move Toward Better Things," p. 18.

53 Jackson, "Dude Ranch Romance Fifties Style," p. 34.

54 M. Colbert, "Impair et passe," *Cinema Papers*, November 1986, no. 60, p. 44.

55 D. Ansen, "When Being Gay Is a Fact of Life," *Newsweek*, 9 January 1986, no. 107, p. 23 and Huston, "Trading Phone Numbers in the Movie Theater," p. 8.

56 Kael, "The Man Who Understands Women," p. 112. As Angela Marney said in her critique of *Lianna's* "common ground formula": "the result for heterosexuals is that they are free (i.e., less defensive) to accept the premise of lesbianism (and by implication homosexuality in general) because the film isn't asking them to question their heterosexuality, only to accept homosexuality." Marney, *"Lianna*: A Move Toward Better Things," p. 18.

57 G. Forshey, "Romancing the Stone," *Christian Century*, 18–25 July 1984, vol. 101, no. 23, p. 723. See also Jack Kroll's review of *Personal Best*: "[it] dares ... to show a loving sexual relationship between women ... not as a statement about homosexuality but as a paradigm of authentic human intimacy." Kroll, "Chariots of Desire," p. 60.

58 B. Rich, "Desert Heat," *Village Voice*, 8 April 1986, no. 31, p. 72. Aufderheide's comments echoed Rich's: "What's unusual about *Desert Hearts* is that the lovers are both women. ... Even more unusual, the film is not 'a lesbian love story.' It's a love story whose protagonists happen to be women." P. Aufderheide, *"Desert Hearts*: Interview with Donna Deitch," *Cineaste*, 1986, vol. 15, no. 1, p. 18.

59 See Ellsworth, "Illicit Pleasures," pp. 54–5, and Huston, "Trading Phone Numbers in the Theater," p. 8.

60 Dyer, "Stereotyping," in Dyer, *Gays and Film*, p. 32.

61 Butler, "Gender Trouble, Feminist Theory and Psychoanalytic Discourse," p. 325.

62 J. Minson, "The Assertion of Homosexuality," *m/f*, 1981, nos 5–6, p. 21.

63 A. Britton, "For Interpretation: Notes Against Camp," *Gay Left*, 1978, no. 7, p. 12.

64 A. Partington, "Feminist Art and Avant-Gardism," in H. Robinson (ed.), *Visibly Female: Feminism and Art Today*, New York, Universe Books, 1988, p. 234.

65 J. Scott, "Deconstructing Equality-Versus-Difference: Or, the Uses of Post-structuralist Theory for Feminism," *Feminist Studies*, Spring 1988, vol. 14, no. 1, p. 47.

3 NOUVEAUX WESTERNS FOR THE 1990S

1 As Richard Slotkin notes, an average of only four westerns a year were released from 1977 to 1982, and no new western television series appeared between 1972 and 1975. R. Slotkin, *Gunfighter Nation: The Myth of the Frontier in Twentieth-Century America*, New York, Harper Collins, 1992, pp. 627–8.

2 Ibid., pp. 627 and 630.

3 A. Thompson, "Beyond the Pale Riders," *Film Comment*, July–August 1992, vol. 28, no. 4, p. 54.

4 W. Wright, *Sixguns and Society*, Berkeley, University of California Press, 1975, p. 5.

5 See G. Custen, *Hollywood Bio/Pics: How Hollywood Constructed Public History*, New Brunswick, Rutgers University Press, 1992.

6 For brevity, I subsequently refer to *John Carpenter's Escape from L.A.* as *Escape from L.A.*

7 Walter Hill is the exception. Credits include scripts for Sam Peckinpah and John Huston, *The Long Riders* (1980) and *Geronimo: An American Legend* (1993).

8 *Desperado* and *Escape from L.A.* are made by major studios (Columbia and Paramount, respectively); Rodríguez is listed as writer, producer, and director; Carpenter as director, writer, and composer. *The Quick and the Dead* is produced by Tri-Star with Japan Satellite Broadcasting. Stone is star and co-producer. *Last Man Standing* is a New Line/Lone Wolf production released by New Line; Hill is credited as director, writer, and producer. *Posse* is a Working Title Production released by Grammercy/Polygram (U.S./England). Mario van Peebles is both director and star; credits also list him as executive sound track producer and composer.

9 *Tombstone* (George Cosmatos, 1993) features a voice over by Kirk Douglas; *Dead Man* (Jim Jarmusch, 1996) casts Douglas as "Dickinson"; *The Ballad of Little Jo* (Maggie Greenwald, 1995) enlists Bo Hopkins, a Peckinpah regular, to play "Frank Badger."

10 Strode's better-known roles include *Once upon a Time in the West* (Sergio Leone, 1968), *The Professionals* (Richard Brooks, 1966), *The Man Who Shot Liberty Valance* (John Ford, 1962), and *Sergeant Rutledge* (John Ford, 1960).

11 Compare Antonio Banderas as Zorro in *The Mask of Zorro* (Martin Campbell, 1998).

12 J. Hoberman snidely notes: "The director-star keeps sneaking up on his stylish self in fractured 360-degree pans (a reminder that the anagram of Posse is Poses)." J. Hoberman, "New Jack Prairie," *Village Voice*, n.p.

13 We learn that Jesse Lee deserted in Manila and assaulted an officer in Nicaragua.

14 Beginning with Strode's opening speech, audiences are encouraged to think about *why* white historians propagate lies like "Columbus discovered America" when, Strode insists, "That's like me tellin' you and you're sittin' in your car, that I discovered your car! Then they want to call 'em the evil red savages, because they didn't give up the car soon enough!" *Dead Man* also condemns capitalists and deconstructs frontier myths. See G. Rickman, "The Western under Erasure: *Dead Man*," in J. Kitses and G. Rickmann (eds), *The Western Reader*, New York, Limelight, 1998, pp. 381–404.

15 Jesse Lee's father teaches him using the Biblical story of Nicodemus; Jesse Lee passes the story on to a boy he saves; that boy turns out to be the narrator (Strode); Strode tells the story to black journalists (the Hudlins). The credits offer final proof of cultural transmission: the film is dedicated to two historical figures, one the grandfather of co-screenwriter Sy Richardson, who helped found an all-black township. *Posse* production materials, Grammercy/Polygram Pictures, p. 1.

16 A sequel, *Los Locos* (Mario van Peebles, 1998), received little attention and less promotion.

17 Van Peebles dubbed the film "edu-tainment." See T. Christie, "Posse-Footing," *Buzz*, October 1993, p. 58. Strode's closing inditement continues the film's critique of Hollywood and mainstream history: "African Americans are 12 percent of Americans, but own less than ½ of 1 percent of America's wealth. Although ignored by Hollywood and most history books, the memory of the more than 8000 black cowboys that roamed the early West lives on."

18 See further Y. Tasker, *Working Girls: Gender and Sexuality in Popular Cinema*, London, Routledge, 1998, p. 58.

19 Interviewed on set, Raimi's friend Bruce Campbell insisted, however, that Stone was "allowing herself to look like a rough, haggard cowgirl." See J. Clark, "Some of Sam," *Premiere*, March 1995, no. 8, p. 76.

20 Tasker notes that posters read "you can't resist her." Tasker, *Working Girls*, p. 58.

21 Compare *Posse* where, Pat Dowell charges, "women are featured the way rock videos show them, in close-ups of bumps and grinds and body parts." P. Dowell, "The Mythology of the Western: Hollywood Perspectives on Race and Gender in the Nineties," *Cineaste*, 1995, vol. 21, nos. 1–2, p. 8.

22 Of the three "girl" nouveaux westerns released in theaters – *Bad Girls* (Jonathan Kaplan, 1994), *The Ballad of Little Jo*, and *The Quick and the Dead* – only *Ballad* was ever reviewed by feminist critics or covered by the feminist alternative press. See further J. Kitses, "An Exemplary Post-modern Western: *The Ballad of Little Jo*, in Kitses and Rickmann (eds), *The Western Reader*, pp. 367–80.

23 Dern's western credits include *Waterhole #3* (William Graham, 1967), *Will Penny* (Tom Gries, 1967), *Support Your Local Sheriff* (Burt Kennedy, 1969), *The Cowboys* (Mark Rydell, 1972), *Posse* (Kirk Douglas, 1975), and *Wild Bill* (Walter Hill, 1995).

24 L. Jung, "*Desperado* Background: But Don't Stop the Story," *Creative Screenwriting*, Winter 1995, vol. 2, no. 4, p. 16.

25 A. Taubin, "Men on the Verge," *Village Voice*, 29 August 1995, p. 56.

26 Ibid., p. 56. Promotional tag lines for print advertising included, "When the smoke clears, it just means he's reloading" and "He came back to settle the score with someone. Anyone. Everyone."

27 Many of the same characters, actors, and events reappear. The chief villain from the first film, Moco (Peter Marquardt), shows up in a club where Banderas is singing and playing. As in the first film, the Mariachi (now Banderas) is forced to watch as his girlfriend is killed. Gallardo plays a band member and brother in arms.

28 In Hollywood to sell his first film, Rodríguez was constantly asked whether he liked Leone and whether he knew Woo's work. See R. Rodríguez, *Rebel without a Crew*, New York, Penguin, 1995, pp. 84–5, 97, and 160.

29 Rodríguez' first film made "stars" of a turtle found on the side of the roadside and a friend's pit bull, included garish objets d'art, and featured in passing a humble fruit stand and vendor. See C. Ramírez Berg, "Ethnic Ingenuity and Mainstream Cinema: Robert Rodríguez's *Bedhead* (1990) and *El Mariachi* (1993)," in C. Noriega and A. López (eds), *The Ethnic Eye: Latino Media Arts*,

Minneapolis and London, University of Minnesota Press, 1996, pp. 107–28, and C. List, *Chicano Images: Refiguring Ethnicity in Mainstream Film*, New York and London, Garland Publishing, 1996, pp. 154–60.

30 Rodríguez felt the lack of explosions lessened the "production value" and marketing appeal of his first film. Rodríguez, *Rebel without a Crew*, pp. 277–8. See also K. Turan, "*Desperado*: Loud, Familiar Echoes of the 'Mariachi' Tune," *L.A. Times*, 25 August 1995, pp. F1 and F8.

31 Rodríguez, *Rebel without a Crew*, pp. 20–1. See also Ramirez Berg, "Ethnic Ingenuity and Mainstream Cinema," p. 123.

32 G. Andrew, "*Desperado*," *Time Out*, 7 February 1996, n.p.

33 Robert Cumbow says of *Escape from New York*: "[the film] owes much to Leone: ... the elemental, violent confrontation, the simplified universe, the strong motivation of revenge, the cryptic dialog, the episodic structure, the quest-narrative." R. Cumbow, *Order in the Universe: The Films of John Carpenter*, Metuchen, Scarecrow Press, 1990, p. 107.

34 Ibid., p. 191. Rodríguez credits Carpenter as key to his filmmaking. As a teenager he watched *Escape from New York* (Carpenter, 1981) repeatedly, and he returned to it again while shooting *El Mariachi*. Rodríguez, *Rebel without a Crew*, pp. vii and 44.

35 Other collaborations include *Elvis* (1979), *Escape from New York* (1981), *The Thing* (1982), and *Big Trouble in Little China* (1986).

36 *The Wizard of Oz* (Victor Fleming, 1939), *Night of the Living Dead* (George Romero, 1968), *Batman* (Tim Burton, 1989), *Dr. Strangelove* (Stanley Kubrick, 1964), *Endless Summer* (Bruce Brown, 1966), *Easy Rider* (Dennis Hopper, 1969), *Spartacus* (Stanley Kubrick, 1960), *Rocky* (John Avildsen, 1982), *First Blood* (Ted Kotcheff, 1982), *Them* (Howard Hawks, 1954), *Soylent Green* (Richard Fleischer, 1973), *Bring Me the Head of Alfredo Garcia* (Sam Peckinpah, 1974), *Star Wars* (George Lucas, 1977), *Blade Runner* (Ridley Scott, 1982), and *Jaws* (Steven Spielberg, 1975) are all mentioned.

37 T. Engelhardt, *The End of Victory Culture: Cold War America and the Disillusioning of a Generation*, New York, Harper Collins, 1995, p. 301.

38 See Engelhardt, *The End of Victory Culture*, p. 277.

39 See S. Neale, "Masculinity as Spectacle," *Screen*, 1983, vol. 24, no. 6, pp. 2–16, and P. Willemen, "Anthony Mann: Looking at the Male," *Framework*, 1981, nos. 15–17, pp. 16–20.

40 J. Kitses, "Introduction: Post-modernism and the Western," in Kitses and Rickman (eds), *The Western Reader*, p. 19.

My sample includes *Ravenous* (Antonia Bird, 1999), *The Mask of Zorro, Dead Man, Buffalo Girls* (TV, Rod Hardy, 1995), *Wild Bill, Maverick* (Richard Donner, 1994), *Wyatt Earp* (Lawrence Kasdan, 1994), *Bad Girls, Unforgiven, City Slickers: The Legend of Curly's Gold* (Paul Weiland, 1994), *The Desperate Trail* (P. J. Pesce, 1994), *Legends of the Fall* (Edward Zwick, 1994), *Geronimo: An American Legend, Tombstone, The Ballad of Little Jo, Geronimo* (TV, Roger Young, 1993), *Broken Chain* (TV, Lamont Johnson, 1993), *Last of the Mohicans, City Slickers* (Ron Underwood, 1991), *Dances with Wolves, Young Guns II, Back to the Future: Part III* (Robert Zemeckis, 1990). I also looked at late 1980s movies like *Lonesome Dove* (TV, Simon Wincer, 1989), *Young Guns, Silverado*, and *Pale Rider*.

41 Walter Nugent draws a distinction between Type I (farming) and Type II (prospecting, ranching) frontiers. See W. Nugent, "Frontiers and Empires in the Late Nineteenth Century," in P. Limerick *et al.* (eds), *Trails: Toward a New Western History*, Lawrence, University Press of Kansas, pp. 161–81.

4 CRUISIN' FOR A BRUISIN'

1 This chapter was originally published as an essay in 1994. Some notes have been abridged or cut in this version.

2 I mention *Aliens* twice because it contains two deadly dolls: one, Vasquez (Jenette Goldstein), is killed leading the fight against the aliens; the other, the heroine Ripley (Sigourney Weaver), escapes and, at the end of the film, plans to return to earth. For a more complete discussion of deadly doll films made between 1981 and 1991, see C. Holmlund, "A Decade of Deadly Dolls," in H. Birch (ed.), *Moving Targets: Women, Murder, and Representation*, Berkeley, University of California Press, 1994, and London, Virago Press, 1992, pp. 127–51.

3 For Carol Clover, the generic precedents of rape-revenge films are wide-ranging: "vengeance may very well be the mainspring of American popular culture, from westerns and *Dirty Harry* to teen comedies and courtroom dramas. Nor is the rape-revenge drama exclusive to 'low' genres; the success of such mainstream films as *Lipstick*, *The Accused*, *Straw Dogs*, *Extremities*, *Sudden Impact*, and *Deliverance* (a male-only version) suggests that the appeal of rape-revenge stories is in fact broadly based." C. Clover, *Men, Women, and Chain Saws*, Princeton, Princeton University Press, 1992, p. 115.

4 On these female characters' motives for murder, see Holmlund, "A Decade of Deadly Dolls," especially pp. 127–9.

5 See my discussion of shifts in how sociologists, criminologists, and psychologists view battered women and rape-survivors. Ibid., pp. 131–4.

6 Clover, *Men, Women, and Chain Saws*, p. 223. In a footnote, Clover suggests that this response subtends both male and female genres: "in the same way horror exploits male masochistic fantasies, 'weepies' exploit female ones." Ibid. See also Peter Lehman's insightful analysis of the contradictory ways rape-revenge films address and appeal to men. P. Lehman, " 'Don't Blame This on a Girl': Female Rape-Revenge Films," in S. Cohan and I. Hark (eds), *Screening the Male*, London, Routledge, 1993, pp. 103–17.

7 Today the most common murder weapon used by both sexes is a gun. See, for example, A. Browne, *When Battered Women Kill*, New York, Free Press, 1987; A. Goetting, "Homicidal Wives," *Journal of Family Issues*, September 1987, vol. 8, no. 3, pp. 332–41; and R. Weisheit, "Female Homicide Offenders: Trends over Time in an Institutionalized Population," *Justice Quarterly*, 1984, vol. 1, no. 4, pp. 471–89.

8 Clover also notes how important "pretechnological" weapons like "knives, hammers, axes, ice picks . . . and the like" are in slasher films. Clover, *Men, Women, and Chain Saws*, p. 32. She further argues that while rape-revenge films may reference feminism by "holding men at least theoretically culpable for such acts as rape, wife-beating and child abuse, . . . [they] also wor[k] to naturalize sadistic violence as a fixture of masculinity – one of the few fixtures remaining in a world that has seen the steady erosion of such." She concludes that such films thereby "en[d] up confirming what [they] deplor[e]," an important twist on the typical feminist trashing of such films. Ibid., p. 226.

9 Deadly doll films where one woman attacks another (e.g., *Single White Female* and *Hand that Rocks the Cradle*) are but variations on the same pro-patriarchal, anti-lesbian theme. The women who are attacked are invariably coded as heterosexual. Often they are also portrayed as mothers, and their child-bearing and -rearing functions are stressed.

10 Elsewhere I have suggested the following explanation for the obligatory "whiteness" of deadly dolls:

Most of the model male murderers today – Sylvester Stallone and Arnold Schwarzenegger, Jean-Claude Van Damme, even Mel Gibson – are ethnic or foreign. Virility, once home-grown and Anglo-American, is now imported. Deadly doll films, which overtly acknowledge that white American men are weaklings and/or nincompoops while at the same time insisting that heterosexual passion is still possible, will not – cannot – simultaneously acknowledge cross-racial alliances and relationships. In the USA today, so many people still find miscegenation unacceptable and unsuitable that miscegenation plus emasculation is, quite literally, unthinkable.

Holmlund, "A Decade of Deadly Dolls," p. 151.

11 I. Julien and K. Mercer, "Introduction: De Margin and De Centre," *Screen*, Autumn 1988, vol. 29, no. 4, pp. 2–11.

12 M. Gever, "The Names We Give Ourselves," in R. Ferguson *et al.* (eds), *Out There: Marginalization and Contemporary Cultures*, New York, New Museum of Contemporary Art, 1990, p. 194.

13 "Ice Pick Envy" is taken from A. Taubin and C. Carr's reviews of *Basic Instinct*. See *Village Voice*, 28 April 1992, pp. 35–6.

14 Holmlund, "A Decade of Deadly Dolls," pp. 144–51.

15 Because, as Tony Bennett and Janet Woollacott argue, secondary print texts participate in the "socially predominant forms of . . . distribution and circulation," they can be useful indicators of where the boundaries of social imaginaries lie at a given moment. T. Bennett and J. Woollacott, *Bond and Beyond*, New York, Methuen, 1987, p. 77.

16 That *Basic Instinct* was a "big" film (it cost a whopping $49 million to make) and *Fried Green Tomatoes* a "little" one (with a mere $3 million price tag) is reflected in the number of written commentaries listed for each in the indexes I consulted (the *National Newspaper Index,* the *General Periodicals Index*, the *Film Literature Index*, and the *Alternative Press Index*): by spring 1993 there were 52 entries for *Basic Instinct* but only 20 for *Fried Green Tomatoes*. Significantly, no reviews or articles are indexed for either film in journals or newspapers with largely African American readerships.

17 J. Simon, "Tenors, Tomatoes, and a Turkey," *National Review*, 30 March 1992, p. 44.

18 Those who did mention race did so very briefly. See, for example, R. Brown, "Why Audiences Hunger for *Fried Green Tomatoes*," *New York Times*, 19 April 1992, p. H22. Only Janet Maslin pointed out that African American actors who play "the film's principal black characters . . . are given little to say." J. Maslin, "Finding Strength in Women," *New York Times*, 27 December 1991, p. C3.

19 Occasionally interviews stressed how healthy Jessica Tandy was after chemotherapy treatments for cancer.

20 Print and television ads originally focused on Jessica Tandy's character, Ninny. See T. King, "Little Film Shifts Its Aim to Big Audience," *Wall Street Journal*, 31 January 1992, p. B1. When the advertising focus shifted to the younger stars, the Mary Kay cosmetics company jumped on the *Fried Green Tomatoes* bandwagon, offering a free make-over and cosmetics with the purchase of a used video. See M. Berman, "Mary Kay Cosmetics Joins *Tomatoes* Promotion Team," *Variety*, 22 June 1992, p. 18.

21 Richard Schickel's capsule review is the only exception. See R. Schickel, "A Home-Cooked Tale," *Time*, 27 January 1992, p. 67. Admittedly, the attachment between Idgie and Ruth is more prominent – and more accepted by other

characters – in the original book by Fannie Flagg. See F. Flagg, *Fried Green Tomatoes at the Whistle Stop Cafe*, New York, McGraw-Hill, 1987.

22 See Brown, "Why Audiences Hunger," and D. Ehrenstein, "Homophobia in Hollywood II," *Advocate*, 7 April 1992, pp. 37–43. Elsewhere Ehrenstein vehemently critiques the "delesbianization" of Idgie and Ruth in the film and the accompanying press kit. As described by Universal Pictures, for example, the story is about "the deepest bond of friendship" between a "young maverick unrefined by etiquette and untamed by men" and a "God-fearing woman." "So much for 'butch' and 'femme'," Ehrenstein concludes. D. Ehrenstein, *"Fried Green Tomatoes* Caps a Banner Year for Delesbianization," *Advocate*, 11 February 1992, p. 67.

23 See, for example, J. Gallagher, "Hollywood under Fire," *Advocate*, 4 June 1991, pp. 46–7, and L. Kauffman, "Queer Guerrillas in Tinseltown," *Progressive*, July 1992, vol. 56, no. 7, pp. 36–7. One lesbian from GLAAD made a point of saying, "Most lesbians I know focus on long relationships. I don't know any ice pick-wielding lesbians." Cited in J. Simpson, "Out of the Celluloid Closet," *Time*, 6 April 1992, p. 65.

24 See "Censors on the Street," *Time,* 13 May 1991, p. 70; D. Ehrenstein, "Joe Eszterhas and His *Basic Instinct*," *Advocate*, 16 July 1991, p. 70; D. Fox, "S. F. Gays Defy Court, March on Movie Location," *Los Angeles Times*, 25 April 1991, p. A28; S. Harris and M. Corwin, "Opposition to Film *Basic Instinct* Rises," *Los Angeles Times*, 21 March 1992, p. B3; and J. Lew, "Gay Groups Protest a Film Script," *New York Times* (Local), 4 May 1991, p. 11.

25 Simpson, "Out of the Celluloid Closet."

26 See Gallagher, "Hollywood under Fire," p. 47, and Simpson, "Out of the Celluloid Closet." Charges that pejorative portrayals of lesbians and gays fueled "gay bashing" were also leveled during the 1980s protests of *Cruising*, *Dressed to Kill*, and *Windows*. See, for example, S. Tucker, "Sex, Death, and Free Speech: The Fight to Stop Friedkin's *Cruising*," in E. Jackson and S. Persky (eds), *Flaunting It*, Vancouver, New Star Press and Toronto, Pink Triangle Press, 1982, pp. 197–206.

27 Harris and Corwin, "Opposition to Film *Basic Instinct* Rises." See further N. Brozan, "Protestors Try to Crash 'Saturday Night Live' Monologue," *New York Times* (Evening Edition), 13 April 1992, p. B8, and Lew, "Gay Groups Protest a Film Script."

28 Friedkin's refusal triggered on-location protests. See Tucker, "Sex, Death, and Free Speech," pp. 200–3.

29 See Ehrenstein, "Eszterhas and His *Basic Instinct*," and B. Johnson, "Killer Movies," *Maclean's*, 30 March 1992, p. 50.

30 Carolco's later willingness to cut sexually explicit scenes to avoid the financially disastrous NC-17 rating exposed its motives as far more pecuniary than artistic. As it was, *Basic Instinct* did poorly only in Scandinavia, where the representation of violence is more taboo than the representation of sex. See D. Groves, "Killer *Instinct, Wayne* Wows," *Variety*, 8 June 1992, p. 32.

31 Reviews in the *Christian Science Monitor, Newsweek*, the *New Yorker* and the *Wall Street Journal* echoed activist accusations that *Basic Instinct* was homophobic and/or misogynist, as did those of leftist and feminist publications like *In These Times, The Nation*, and *Spare Rib*.

32 See J. Maslin, "Sure, She May Be Mean, But Is She a Killer?," *New York Times*, 20 March 1992, p. C8, and T. McCarthy, *"Basic Instinct,"* *Variety*, 16 March 1992, p. 58.

33 Peter Travers' review in *Rolling Stone* is typical: "protests from the gay community about the film's negative treatment of lesbians are . . . pointless, since no

one in this kinky sex fantasy demonstrates anything resembling recognizable human behavior." P. Travers, "*Jagged Edge* Meets *Fatal Attraction*," *Rolling Stone,* 16 April 1992, p. 90. John Simon also chided the protestors, stating, "the treatment of heterosexuals is ultimately every bit as insulting." J. Simon, "More Basic than *Basic*," *National Review*, 27 April 1992, p. 52.

34 As Brian Johnson put it, *Basic Instinct* is "a male fantasy land of beautiful, bisexual, bloodthirsty vixens." B. Johnson, "Killer Movies," *Maclean's*, 30 March 1992, p. 50.

35 Amy Taubin objected to Ehrenstein's attacks on Sharon Stone in the gay monthly the *Advocate*: "If Ehrenstein wanted a small production story to cut his teeth on, he should have let [on] . . . the clause in Douglas's contract specifying that his penis could never be shown on screen." A. Taubin, "The Boys Who Cried Misogyny," *Village Voice*, 28 April 1992, p. 36.

   John Simon engages in the most virulent Michael Douglas bashing: "Michael Douglas, women tell me, has a sexy mouth. Here, unfortunately, you can see the rest of him, too." J. Simon, "More Basic than *Basic*," *National Review*, 27 April 1992, pp. 52.

36 Taubin, "The Boys Who Cried Misogyny," p. 35.

37 R. Picardie, "Mad, Bad, and Dangerous," *New Statesman and Society*, 1 May 1992, p. 36.

38 L. Gaist, "Two Girls and an Ice Pick," *Gay Community News*, 19 April–8 May 1992, p. 7.

39 Ibid., emphasis mine.

40 As Stone put it in an interview in *Playboy*, "I'm enormously sympathetic with the fact that it's always the blonde people in the movies. Where are the inter-racial relationships? Where are the Puerto Rican men and women? If there weren't these incredible racial issues, Billy Dee Williams would have been one of our biggest movie stars – a fine, talented, gorgeous, charismatic actor. Why is that? It's not right. It's not fair." "*Playboy* Interview: Sharon Stone," *Playboy*, December 1992, vol. 39, no. 12, p. 73.

41 Julien and Mercer, "Introduction," p. 8.

42 Such recoding is typical of the portrayals of lesbians in mainstream and independent films alike. See, for example, C. Holmlund, "When Is a Lesbian Not a Lesbian?: The Lesbian Continuum and the Mainstream Femme Film," reprinted here, and C. Straayer, "The Hypothetical Lesbian Heroine," *Jump Cut*, April 1990, no. 35, pp. 50–8.

43 For nuanced analyses of the contradictions and complexities of lesbian reading formations, see D. Clark, "Commodity Lesbianism," *Camera Obscura*, January/May 1991, nos. 25–6, pp. 181–202, and J. Mayne, *Cinema and Spectatorship*, London and New York, Routledge, 1993, especially Chapter 8. See also my discussion of mixed straight and lesbian responses to lesbian experimental film. C. Holmlund, "Fractured Fairytales and Experimental Identities: Looking for Lesbians in and around the Films of Su Friedrich," *Discourse*, Fall 1994, vol. 17, no. 1, pp. 16–46.

   Clark's explanation of why advertising agencies never market products directly to lesbians applies also to Hollywood films. She argues that, historically, lesbians have been neither an economically powerful social group nor an easily identifiable one since lesbians are a part of all race, income, and age groups and many prefer not to be identified as lesbian. In addition, advertising agencies, producers, and directors often "fear that by openly appealing to a homosexual market their products will be negatively associated with homosexuality and will be avoided by heterosexual consumers." Clark, "Commodity Lesbianism," p. 182.

44 Screenwriter Joseph Eszterhas saw Hazel as a heterosexual, not a lesbian, however. See Ehrenstein, "Joe Eszterhas and His *Basic Instinct*," p. 72.

45 K. Weston, *Families We Choose*, New York, Columbia University Press, 1991, p. 154.

46 Ibid., p. 147.

47 Ehrenstein, "*Fried Green Tomatoes* Caps a Banner Year for Delesbianization."

48 Scott Tucker's objections to *Cruising*, a decade earlier, hold for queer protests against *Basic Instinct* as well: "in gay S/M interactions, the 'S' may signify either Sadist or Slave, the 'M' either Masochist or Master. A reduction of S/M to the give-and-take of pain – or to murder, as in *Cruising* – ignores the permutations of power which it may involve: masochists may be masterful and sadists slavish." Tucker, "Sex, Death, and Free Speech," p. 204.

49 R. Dyer, "White," *Screen*, Autumn 1988, vol. 29, no. 4, p. 47. Cornel West notes similarly, " 'Whiteness' is a politically constructed category parasitic on 'Blackness'." C. West, "The New Cultural Politics of Difference," in Ferguson, *Out There: Marginalization and Contemporary Cultures*, p. 29.

50 This suggestion was made by the anonymous reader of an earlier version of this essay.

51 Dyer, "White," p. 46.

52 Here the film differs substantially from the book. In the book there are two women characters, Sipsey and Onzell; Naughty Bird is not Sipsey's younger sister; Big George has a family; there are many minor African American characters; and the connections and disjunctures between black life in the city and the country are the focus of several chapters. Yet the book, too, stereotypes African Americans; Ninny frequently says things like "you never know where colored people come from" and "you can never tell how old colored people are." Flagg, *Fried Green Tomatoes at the Whistle Stop Cafe*, pp. 47, 50.

53 B. Christian, *Black Feminist Criticism: Perspectives on Black Women Writers*, New York, Teachers College Press, 1985, p. 2.

54 Mayne, *Cinema and Spectatorship*, p. 143.

55 M. Diawara, "Black Spectatorship: Problems of Identification and Resistance," *Screen*, Autumn 1988, vol. 29, no. 4, p. 71.

56 The only other African American female lead who kills does so in the independent spoof *Surf Nazis Must Die*. She too is portrayed as a "mammy," but unlike Sipsey she kills to avenge the death of her son, not to protect a white baby. The rape-revenge films Lehman studies differ sharply on this point. See Lehman, " 'Don't Blame This on a Girl'."

57 M. Wallace, "Negative Images: Towards a Black Feminist Cultural Criticism," in L. Grossberg *et al.* (eds), *Cultural Studies*, New York, Routledge, 1992, p. 662.

58 Maslin, "Finding Strength in Women."

59 Display of a limp penis is a Verhoeven trademark. See P. Lehman, *Running Scared: Masculinity and the Representation of the Male Body*, Philadelphia, Temple University Press, 1993.

60 K. Woodward, *Aging and Its Discontents*, Bloomington, Indiana University Press, 1991, pp. 47, 9 and 30.

61 In contrast to frontal male nudity, which is virtually taboo in Hollywood movies, rear nudity has been a staple of action adventure films since the 1970s. A number of male stars, including Sylvester Stallone, Clint Eastwood, Mel Gibson, and Kurt Russell, have bared their buns for "art." In each case, of course, the homoerotic overtones which accompany images of rear male nudity are contained within predominantly heterosexual narratives. For an analysis of the limits placed around homoeroticism in Stallone's *Lock Up* (John Flynn, 1989) and *Tango and Cash* (Andrei Konchalevsky, 1989), see C. Holmlund,

"Masculinity as Multiple Masquerade: The 'Mature' Stallone Loves the Stallone Clone," in Cohan and Hark, *Screening the Male*, pp. 213–29.

62 Woodward, *Aging and Its Discontents*, p. 155. Woodward speaks of old age as a "masquerade" because, she says, "if we are old we carry youth with us; we identify in part with the young." Ibid., p. 156.

63 By adding the second mystery of identity to the first murder mystery, the film version of *Fried Green Tomatoes* deviates substantially from the book. In Flagg's novel, Idgie and Ninny are two *different* characters. Ninny dies but Idgie lives. In contrast, the film's final shots reveal that the two characters are one, called "Ninny" when she is old and "Idgie" when she is young.

64 D. Crimp, "Portraits of People with AIDS," in D. Stanton (ed.), *Discourses of Sexuality*, Ann Arbor, University of Michigan Press, 1992, pp. 379–80.

65 Kauffman, "Queer Guerrillas in Tinseltown," p. 37. Tom Waugh sounds yet another warning: "while the positive-image gay critic has usually been dead-on in his targeting of the *Cruisings* of the (hetero) patriarchal entertainment industry and has effectively revolutionized the reception of mainstream media within gay culture, he has too often gunned for the . . . gay . . . art cinema as well, and with counter-productive effect." T. Waugh, "The Third Body," in M. Gever *et al.* (eds), *Queer Looks*, New York, Routledge, 1993, p. 155.

66 Kauffman, "Queer Guerrillas in Tinsel Town," p. 37. Stone and Douglas themselves recognized as much. As Stone put it, *Basic Instinct* provided "a unique opportunity for the gay community to use a big media event as a way to be heard." "*Playboy* Interview: Sharon Stone," p. 73. Douglas concurred: "I appreciate their [the protestors'] savvy political abilities and I think that they hooked on to a big Hollywood-type film to get a lot of publicity." He then added: "I resent people constantly trying to impose their own values on somebody else." B. Johnson, "Steaming Up the Screen," *Maclean's*, 30 March 1992, p. 54. Stone, too, insisted, "I don't think films are responsible for political issues unless they're being made specifically about a political issue. Films are there to inspire your fantasy. . . . Journalism is responsible for telling the truth about the world." "*Playboy* Interview: Sharon Stone," p. 73.

67 West, "The New Cultural Politics of Difference," p. 28.

68 Clover, *Men, Women and Chain Saws*, p. 227.

69 A. Lorde, *Sister Outsider*, New York, Crossing Press, 1984, p. 111.

70 Woodward, *Aging and Its Discontents*, p. 159.

71 Class is a glaring omission in my analysis here but, as feminist analyses of housework have taught us, must obviously be considered not just in terms of production. How, for example, are people in nursing homes to be "classed"?

5 SWEDE AS "OTHER"

1 E. Buscombe (ed.), *The BFI Companion to the Western*, London, British Film Institute, 1988, p. 226.

2 R. Dyer, *White*, London, Routledge, 1997, pp. 20 and 13.

3 See J. Higham, *Strangers in the Land: Patterns of American Nativism 1860–1925*, New Brunswick, Rutgers University Press, 1988, pp. 9 and 132; see also R. Daniels, *Coming to America: A History of Immigration and Ethnicity in American Life*, New York, Harper Collins, 1990.

4 See K. Martin, "Diversity Orientations: Culture, Ethnicity, and Race," in L. Naylor (ed.), *Cultural Diversity in the United States*, Westport, Bergin and Garvey, 1997, p. 83.

5 Nearly two million Scandinavians came to the U.S. between 1866 and World War I. "Swedes and Norwegians comprised nearly 90 percent of the total

Scandinavian migration, with the former outnumbering the latter by a ratio of approximately two to one." L. Dinnerstein *et al.*, *Natives and Strangers: A Multi-cultural History of Americans*, New York, Oxford University Press, 1996, p. 102. See also L. Ljungmark, *Swedish Exodus*, K. Westerberg (trans.), Carbondale, Southern Illinois University Press, 1979.

6 I use the terms "non-white" and "Other" to point up power imbalances. Both are problematic, "non-white" because it is too general and takes "white" as a norm, "Other" because it too often becomes a "convenient, catchall category when the delineation of ethnic, class, and gender relations requires greater historical specificity." S. Higashi, "Ethnicity, Class, and Gender in Film: DeMille's *The Cheat*," in L. Friedman (ed.), *Unspeakable Images: Ethnicity and the American Cinema*, Urbana, University of Illinois Press, p. 115.

7 N. Asther, *Narrens Väg: Ingen Gudasaga*, Stockholm, Carlssons, 1988, p. 46. My translation.

8 Ibid., pp. 214–18.

9 See I. Jarvie, "Stars and Ethnicity: Hollywood and the U.S., 1932–51," in Friedman, *Unspeakable Images*, pp. 82–111.

10 By 1920 fully one-third of the U.S. population was either foreign born or had at least one foreign-born parent. Daniels, *Coming to America*, pp. 274–5.

11 At most 140,000 Japanese immigrants and their descendants lived in the contiguous U.S. Statistics include both first and second generations: earlier, "Japanese" was a racial category on census forms. See Daniels, *Coming to America*, p. 250.

12 See further N. Browne, "The Undoing of the *Other* Woman: Madame Butterfly in the Discourse of American Orientalism," in D. Bernardi (ed.), *The Birth of Whiteness: Race and the Emergence of U.S. Cinema*, New Brunswick, Rutgers University Press, 1996, pp. 227–9; Higashi, "Ethnicity, Class, and Gender in Film," pp. 124–5; G. Marchetti, *Romance and the "Yellow Peril": Race, Sex, and Discursive Strategies in Hollywood Fiction*, Berkeley, University of California Press, 1993; and R. Oehling, "The Yellow Menace: Asian Images in American Film," in R. Miller (ed.), *The Kaleidoscopic Lens: How Hollywood Views Ethnic Groups*, Jerome S. Ozer, 1980, p. 187.

13 That a Scandinavian actor played Yen made *Bitter Tea* possible, argues Gina Marchetti, since the Hays Code rendered the representation of miscegenation taboo. Marchetti, *Romance and the "Yellow Peril,"* p. 50. *Bitter Tea* was banned in the British Empire for miscegenation, and as a result lost money. See F. Capra, *The Name Above the Title*, New York, Macmillan, 1971, pp. 141–2. Both films did well in the U.S.: *Bitter Tea* was the first film to be shown at Radio City Music Hall, then the world's largest theater; *Wild Orchids* was applauded around the world. Asther, *Narrens Väg*, p. 150.

14 Asther and Garbo were good friends and probably lovers; they took shared vacations. Asther maintains that Garbo was the only woman he ever loved: he proposed three times. Asther, *Narrens Väg*, pp. 115–41.

15 Capra studied "Oriental" eyes, ordering Asther's upper lids immobilized and his eyelashes clipped to make him look "Chinese." Capra, *The Name Above the Title*, p. 142. Asther studied Chinese "manners": "I am . . . fascinated by [the Chinese], so it was with pleasure that I made new acquaintances in the small picturesque Chinese neighborhoods. I spoke with learned old men, looked slit-eyed men of my own age in the eye and drank tea together with doll-like Chinese beauties. Soon I felt that I knew the yellow race better." Asther, *Narrens Väg*, pp. 134–5. My translation.

16 See further Marchetti, *Romance and the "Yellow Peril,"* pp. 53–5. Dream sequences are rare in Capra's films, although it is common for one character "first to spurn

another and then gradually to convert to that person's perspective." C. Maland, *Frank Capra*, Boston, Twayne, 1980, p. 75.

17 Marchetti, *Romance and the "Yellow Peril,"* p. 49. Compare Miriam Hansen on Rudolph Valentino: "The nativist crusade against interethnic romance was already a displacement, a defense against the threat of female sexuality. The project of the ethnic and racially male other as sexually potent, uncontrollable, and predatory no doubt reflected anxieties related to the ongoing crisis of WASP masculinity. The source of these anxieties, however, was more likely the New Woman." M. Hansen, *Babel and Babylon: Spectatorship in American Silent Film*, Cambridge, Harvard University Press, 1991, p. 255.

18 Although he does not speak with an accent, the dour Joshua Knudsen (R. G. Armstrong) in *Ride the High Country* (Sam Peckinpah, 1962) is also Scandinavian, possibly Swedish.

19 P. Limerick, *The Legacy of Conquest*, New York, W. W. Norton, 1987, pp. 280 and 260.

20 Daniels maintains that by 1870, 48 percent of Swedes were landless. Daniels, *Coming to America*, p. 168. A low death rate, high birth rate, laws of partible inheritance, crop failures, and church tensions all triggered emigration. See Ljungmark, *A Swedish Exodus*, especially pp. 6, 8, 10–12, 29–30.

21 F. Turner, *The Frontier in American History*, New York, 1920, p. 23, cited in Higham, *Strangers in the Land*, p. 22.

22 Limerick, *The Legacy of Conquest*, p. 260.

23 See R. Slotkin, *Gunfighter Nation: The Myth of the Frontier in Twentieth-Century America*, New York, Harper Collins, 1992, especially pp. 29–59.

24 Dyer, *White*, p. 35.

25 According to Tom Gunning, few Swedish characters can be found in American films before *The Big Trail* (Raoul Walsh, 1930). Private conversation of 5 July 1998.

26 See B. Henderson, *"The Searchers*: An American Dilemma," *Film Quarterly*, 1980–1, vol. 32, no. 2, pp. 9–23. Slotkin reads the film in terms of Cold War foreign policy. See Slotkin, *Gunfighter Nation*, pp. 461–73.

27 On "ethnicity theory," see M. Omi and H. Winant, *Racial Formation in the United States from the 1960s to the 1990s*, New York, Routledge, 1994, especially pp. 14–23.

28 Jones cited by J. Clark, "Filmographies: Dolph Lundgren," *Premiere*, July 1992, vol. 5, p. 103.

29 See G. Fuller, "Dolph Lundgren," *Interview*, July 1992, vol. 22, pp. 84–7; M. Gray, "Universal Men," *Film Monthly*, August 1992, no. 4, pp. 32–3; S. Saban, "The Action Man Who Fell to Earth," *Movieline*, July 1995, vol. 6, pp. 46–51; and M. Schulze, "Beyond Body and Mind," *Utne Reader*, July–August 1996, pp. 28–30.

30 "Of the approximately 20 million foreign-born in our population today . . . over 40 percent are of Hispanic background, mostly Mexicans, whereas perhaps 25 percent are Asians." Dinnerstein, *Natives and Strangers*, p. 272. Winant argues that right-wing sympathies among suburban and rural whites "reflec[t] racial fears . . . [and] expres[s] the anxieties of a working class whose economic security is now in greater jeopardy than at any time since the 1930s." H. Winant, *Racial Conditions: Politics, Theory, Comparisons*, Minneapolis, University of Minnesota Press, 1994, p. 45.

31 On transnational communities, see N. Rodríguez, "The Real 'New World Order': The Globalization of Racial and Ethnic Relations in the Late Twentieth Century," in M. Smith and J. Feagin (eds), *The Bubbling Cauldron: Race, Ethnicity, and the Urban Crisis*, Minneapolis, University of Minnesota Press, 1995,

pp. 211–25. As Daniels points out, Cold War rhetoric about "the free world" also made immigration policies which excluded and restricted immigration from Asia, Latin America, and Africa embarrassing. See Daniels, *Coming to America*, p. 329.

32 H. Winant, "Dictatorship, Democracy, and Difference: The Historical Construction of Racial Identity," in Smith and Feagin, *The Bubbling Cauldron*, pp. 31–49.

33 Omi and Winant argue that neo-conservative defenses of "group rights" under Reagan-Bush were proposed in the name of "egalitarianism"; neo-liberal avoidance of race under Clinton was made possible by proposing "universal reforms" and rejecting "group-specific demands." The effect is similar: race is downplayed, but rules. Omi and Winant, *Racial Formation*, pp. 20 and 151. See also pp. 139–42 and 147–52.

34 See H. Gans, "Symbolic Ethnicity: The Future of Ethnic Groups and Cultures in America," *Ethnic and Racial Studies*, January 1979, no. 2, pp. 1–20; Winant, *Racial Conditions*, especially pp. 44–7; and R. Alba, *Ethnic Identity: The Transformation of White America*, New Haven, Yale University Press, pp. 291–319.

35 An ideology of "individualism" was also key to Republican interpretations of "the world events of 1989 and 1990. . . . The 'collapse of Communism' simply reinforced the 'triumph of capitalism.' Complex events in Eastern Europe and the Soviet Union were treated as simple and homogeneous." M. Delli Carpini, "The Making of a Consensual Majority: Political Discourse and Electoral Politics in the 1980s," in M. Klein (ed.), *An American Half Century*, London, Pluto Press, 1994, p. 251.

36 The character Lundgren plays in *Masters of the Universe* does look amazingly like the cartoons of huge blond musclemen in Viking outfits featured in pamphlets distributed by White Aryan Resistance (WAR). See J. Ridgeway, *Blood in the Face: The Ku Klux Klan, Aryan Nations, Nazi Skinheads, and the Rise of a New White Culture*, New York, Thunder's Mouth Press, 1995, p. 184. Dyer indites the "crypto-fascist" casting behind Lundgren's "Californian" characters as well. Dyer, *White*, p. 150.

37 Compare George Bush's (*père*) framing of Manuel Noriega as a ruthless, drug-dealing, dictator to replace Reagan's anti-Communist "evil empire" rhetoric as motivation for military intervention abroad. See Delli Carpini, "The Making of a Consensual Majority," p. 255.

38 In *Silent Trigger* Lundgren has an English female partner (Gina Bellman). Together they repulse a crazy Irish American and his even more threatening white boss; occasionally they make lyrical low-lit love.

39 Dyer, *White*, p. 21.

40 The Street Preacher sells salvation to mutants on stretchers in the heart of the Free City of Newark's hospital. Lundgren carefully modeled his character on American televangelists: "I studied lots of tapes of tapes . . . to learn the way they speak and gesture, the way they manipulate their audiences. I looked at biblical books to see how people dressed and wore their hair." Saban, "The Action Man Who Fell to Earth," p. 47.

41 On the ambivalent attitudes towards technology manifest in late 1980s films, see S. Jeffords, *Hard Bodies: Hollywood Masculinity in the Reagan Era*, New Brunswick, Rutgers University Press, 1994, pp. 104–18, and M. Ryan and D. Kellner (eds), *Camera Politica: The Politics and Ideology of Contemporary Hollywood Film*, Bloomington, Indiana University Press, 1988, pp. 245–53.

42 See Gray, "Universal Men," p. 32, and Saban, "The Action Man Who Fell to Earth," p. 51.

43 J. MacTrevor, "Dolph Lundgren: Je ne suis pas une tête vide . . .," *Ciné Télé Revue*, 14 July 1988, no. 14, p. 21. My translation.

44 J. L. Anderson, *Scandinavian Humor and Other Myths*, Minneapolis, Nordbook, 1986, p. 24.
45 E. Shohat, "Ethnicities in Relation: Toward a Multicultural Reading of American Cinema," in Friedman, *Unspeakable Images*, pp. 244–5.
46 Alba, *Ethnic Identity*, p. xiv.
47 Winant, *Racial Conditions*, p. 68.
48 Dyer, *White*, p. 31.
49 Winant, "Dictatorship, Democracy, and Difference," p. 45.
50 Dyer, *White*, pp. 19–20.

6 LATINAS IN LA-LA LAND

1 The first Hollywood feature film about Chicanos was Universal's *Walk Proud* (Robert Collins, 1979). It sparked protests because it starred white actor Robby Benson (replete with brown contact lenses!) as a Chicano gang member who falls in love with a white woman.
2 In 1992, for example, Latino film and television directors worked only 1.3 percent of total membership time. Director's Guild statistics, cited in C. List, *Chicano Images: Refiguring Ethnicity in Mainstream Film*, New York, Garland, 1996, p. 11.
3 In 1999, publicity and costume design helped shift attention to Lopez' breasts and face.
4 A. Avila, "The 25 Most Powerful Hispanics in Hollywood," *Hispanic*, April 1996, p. 26, cited in C. Rodríguez, "Introduction," in C. Rodríguez (ed.), *Latin Looks: Images of Latinas and Latinos in the U.S. Media*, Boulder, Westview Press, 1997, p. 1.
5 *The Goonies* was written and produced by Spielberg and distributed by Warner Brothers. *My Family/Mi Familia* is a 1995 New Line release of an American Zoetrope production. *As Good As It Gets* is a Sony release of a Tri-Star presentation of a Gracie Films production.
6 The child of prosperous Mexican parents who owned tortilla factories in El Paso, Ontiveros grew up on both sides of the U.S.-Mexican border. Her first job was as an L.A. social worker. She stumbled on acting when she netted a role in a 1973 made-for-television movie. Though a woman agent asked her to Anglicize her name because it was "too ethnic," she refused. See V. Escalante, "Social Work More than Role for Actress," *L.A. Times,* 9 June 1985, p. 14.
7 See V. Fuentes, "Chicano Cinema; A Dialectic between Voices and Images of the Autonomous Discourse Versus Those of the Dominant," in C. Noriega (ed.), *Chicanos and Film: Representation and Resistance*, Minneapolis, University of Minnesota Press, 1992, p. 209, and D. Rosen, "Crossover: Hispanic Specialty Films in the U.S. Movie Marketplace," also in Noriega, *Chicanos and Film*, p. 242, and D. Rosen, *Off-Hollywood: The Making and Marketing of Independent Films*, New York, Grove Weidenfeld, 1987, pp. 56–77. List mentions that when *El Norte* was aired on PBS, it was presented as an "immigration parable." List, *Chicano Images*, p. 112.
8 See ibid., pp. 106–7; R. Fregoso, *The Bronze Screen: Chicana and Chicano Film Culture*, Minneapolis, University of Minnesota Press, 1993, pp. 108–10; and D. West, "Filming the Chicano Family Saga," *Cineaste*, 1995, vol. 21, no. 4, pp. 26–9.
9 Buena Vista was generally at a loss as to how to market the picture, switching strategy mid-way through its promotional campaign to change the title and bill the movie as a family drama rather than a gang epic. During its relatively short 1991 run, however, *Bound by Honor* performed best in Latino and action

markets. See K. Honeycutt, *"Bound by Honor* Gets L.A. Date," *Hollywood Reporter*, 6 May 1993, pp. 15–16, and T. Pristin, "A Matter of 'Honor'," *L.A. Times*, 21 May 1993, p. F14.

10 Casting and shooting were plagued by charges, ultimately traced to Universal Pictures' *American Me* project (Edward James Olmos, 1992), that the film would be "derogatory to Hispanics" because it centers on gangs, drugs, and crime. Yet the narrative was based on Baca's prison experiences; many scenes were shot on location in San Quentin; and several former gang members, Community Gang Youth Services, and the United Neighborhoods Association were enlisted to help with shooting. In addition, tatoo artist Freddy Negrete was enlisted to create designs for tatoos using images from Aztec mythology and Christian symbolism, and Consuela Norte, an artist and curator from Chicano Arts Community in L.A, was tapped to design the Day of the Dead sequences. *Bound by Honor*, production materials, pp. 12–22.

11 See O. Blackburn, *"Blood In, Blood Out," Sight and Sound*, 1993, vol. 3, no. 10, p. 40.

12 Directed and scripted by Pérez, . . . *And the Earth Did Not Swallow Him* is distributed by American Playhouse Theatrical Productions.

13 Ontiveros' appearance as "bad" mother contrasts with her roles in *Zoot Suit* and *Born in East L.A.* In the latter, her costume provides a colorful contrast to Rudy's (Cheech Marin) white T-shirt, jeans, and blue flannel shirt: she first appears wearing a blue, pink, and red flowered dress and a differently flowered apron. Her yard is carefully kept, her house a monument to Catholicism and kitsch: a dual-perspective picture of Christ hangs over the telephone and *velas* are everywhere. She bustles about; Rudy lounges in a chair, swilling beer and watching porn on TV. See further C. Noriega, " 'Waas Sappening?': Narrative Structure and Iconography in *Born in East L.A.," Studies in Latin American Popular Culture*, 1995, vol. 14, pp. 14, 21–2.

14 Perez was "discovered" by Spike Lee dancing in a club on his birthday. High energy dance performances are key to her performances in *Do the Right Thing*, *Untamed Heart*, and *Somebody to Love*. Other dance credits include being dance coordinator on *Soul Train*, choreographing videos for Bobby Brown, Diana Ross and others, and working with the Fly Girls as a choreographer. Perez' political activism, too, often involves dance: she organized AIDS fundraisers for 7,000 people at a time as dance-a-thons in the L.A. Coliseum. See J. Zaslow, "Rosie Perez: Learn to Be Fearless," *USA Weekend*, 14–16 June 1997, p. 18, and G. Buchalter, " 'The World Doesn't Owe Me a Thing'." *Parade Magazine*, 19 September 1993, pp. 12–13.

15 Perez beat out Rosanna Arquette and Holly Hunter for the role of Gloria in *White Men Can't Jump*, and Madonna for the role of Carla in *Fearless*. See D. Smith, "Rosie Perez," *The US Interview*, July 1994, p. 91.

16. See Zaslow, "Rosie Perez: Learn to Be Fearless," p. 18; T. Carson, *"White Men Can't Jump," L.A. Weekly*, 3 April 1992, p. 33; K. Turan, "Rosie Perez," *L.A. Times*, 27 March 1992, pp. F1, F16. As a child Rosie couldn't pronounce her own name except as "Wosie" until she received speech therapy in 5th grade. See G. Hershey, "Queen of the Fly Girls," *G.Q.*, August 1992, pp. 52–8.

17 Perez was strongly criticized by the L.A.-based Mexicanos Unidos en Norteamericana for describing ethnic divisions among Latinos as follows: "Cubans look down on everybody; Mexicans hate Puerto Ricans. Brazilians are above Mexicans." "Morning Report", *L.A. Times*, 26 November 1993, F2. See further Rodríguez, "Introduction," p. 1.

18 Financed and distributed by Universal, the $6.5 million *Do the Right Thing* was produced by Spike Lee's Forty Acres and a Mule production company. Lee

not only acted in, but also produced, wrote, and directed it (keeping the right to final cut). The film was a cross-over hit, grossing three times the production costs in the first 12 weeks of release alone, and ranking 45th of 124 titles on *Variety's* "big rental films of 1989" list. See E. Guerrero, *Framing Blackness: The African American Image in Film*, Philadelphia, Temple University Press, 1993, p. 146.

19 Casting agents have skillfully coordinated Perez' personal experiences – she was a child born out of wedlock, growing up on welfare, with ten other siblings – with those of her characters. See Zaslow, "Rosie Perez: Learn to Be Fearless," p. 18, and Buchalter, " 'The World Doesn't Owe Me a Thing'," p. 12. She has never played an upper class character.

20 Perez received no screen-writing credit. See G. Trebay, "Rosie the Riveting," *Village Voice*, 20 June 1989, n.p.

21 C. Cortés, "Chicanas in Film: History of an Image," in Rodríguez (ed.), *Latin Looks*, p. 135.

22 See D. Kellner, "Aesthetics, Ethics, and Politics in the Films of Spike Lee," in M. Reid (ed.), *Spike Lee's "Do the Right Thing,"* Cambridge, Cambridge University Press, 1997, pp. 92–7, and 105, notes 34–7 for a summary of bell hooks' and Michele Wallace's critiques. In contrast, Victoria Johnson defends the "alliance between visual image and musical sound track" begun in this opening sequence, while Kellner suggests that "Lee possibly intends [the sequence] to be a powerful image of a woman of color." V. Johnson, "Polyphony and Cultural Expression: Interpreting Musical Traditions in *Do the Right Thing*," *Film Quarterly*, Winter 1993–4, vol. 47, no. 2, p. 25, and Kellner, "Aesthetics, Ethics, and Politics in the Films of Spike Lee," p. 105, n. 37.

23 See b. hooks, *Yearning, Race, Gender and Cultural Politics*, Boston, South End Press, 1990, p. 173. J. Hoberman, for example, lauded the picture as "a performer's movie" with a "splendidly eccentric cast." J. Hoberman, "*Night on Earth*," *Sight and Sound*, 1994, vol. 2, no. 4, p. 6.

24 The film was made with French financing by Lumiere Pictures.

25 See photos accompanying K. Sessums, "Jennifer Lopez," *Vanity Fair*, July 1998, n.p.; D. Handelman, "A Diva Is Born," *Mirabella*, July–August 1998, no. 7/8, pp. 82, 84, 124; J. Brodie, "Jennifer Lopez Gets Cheeky," *G.Q.*, September 1996, pp. 280–1. For distinctions between English- and Spanish-language coverage, see M. Beltrán, "The Hollywood Latina Body as Site of Social Struggle: Jennifer Lopez's Celebrity Construction and 'Cross-Over Butt'," unpublished conference paper, presented at Society for Cinema Studies Conference, March 2000.

26 As Selena Lopez garnered both a "Diversity Award" and a "Lasting Image Award." For coverage of her casting, see D. Elmer, "Tex-Mex Appeal," *Time Out*, 7–14 May 1997, p. 13. Like Perez, Lopez has at times netted roles originally written for white characters: her role in *U-Turn* was destined for Sharon Stone, for example, and she beat out Sandra Bullock and several others for the part in *Out of Sight*. She originally rose to fame in television (starring in *Second Chances* in 1993–1994, in *Hotel Malibu* in 1994, in *South Central* in 1994, and as one of the original Fly Girls on *In Living Color*).

27 Lopez commented: "They wanted a Latina . . . somebody who could be with Wesley, and with Woody. Apparently in Hollywood, brown is some kind of mediating color between black and white." Y. Murray, "Jennifer Lopez," *Buzz*, April 1997, no. 69, p. 72.

28 Both films were big budget ventures: *Money Train* is a Columbia TriStar release of Columbia Pictures Corporation, Peter Entertainment Corporation production; *Anaconda* is a Sony Pictures Entertainment/Columbia TriStar release of a

Columbia Pictures, ACL Cinema Line Films Corporation, Skylight Cinema Euro Art Ltd. production.

29 Nava spent five years pitching the story for *Mi Familia* before Coppola's American Zoetrope Productions (together with Anna Thomas, New Line, Cinema Newcom, Majestic Films and American Playhouse) agreed to fund the project. As in Coppola's more expensive 1996 project, *Jack*, Lopez does not receive much screen time, perhaps because here too she manifests few personal "resources."

30 Great concern was taken with locations, sets, and art design. See *Mi Familia*, production materials, p. 22.

31 *Mi Familia*, production materials, p. 18.

32 That Lopez has one of the major female roles substantiates List's and others' comments that for Latinas, the family generally represents a "constraining social formation." See List, *Chicano Cinema*, p. 126.

33 A British-American co-production, *Blood and Wine* was released through Twentieth Century Fox.

34 D. Rooney, "*Blood and Wine*," *Variety*, 20 September–6 October 1996, p. 8.

35 Warner Brothers assiduously promoted the film via print, network, and spot ads in both Spanish and English and multiple promotion tie-ins (with Budweiser, Coca Cola, an EMI album, and so on). In markets with large Hispanic populations, *Selena* was distributed in both Spanish and English versions. See A. Hindes, "Warner Brothers Betting on Appeal of *Selena*," *Variety*, 17 March 1997, p. 42.

36 A. Weir, "It's Out and I'm Proud," *Sunday Times*, 20 September 1998, p. 6, and C. Goodwin, "Bum's the Word," *Sunday Times*, 20 September 1998, p. 7.

37 See J. Leydon, "Keeping Her Dreams Alive," *L.A. Times*, 8 December 1996, p. 77, and D. Elmer, "Tex-Mex Appeal," *Time Out*, 7–14 May 1997, pp. 12–13.

38 C. Kleinhans, "Siempre Selena!," *Jump Cut*, December 1998, no. 42, p. 28. Like Nava, the actors, foremost among them Edward James Olmos as papa Abraham, touted the film as being "about the love of a family and how that helped them reach such a success." *Selena*, production materials, p. 6. Coverage of the filming noted his suspicious interest in young Becky Lee Meza as the child Selena; at the time Olmos was accused of child sexual abuse and under court order prohibiting him from being left alone with his 11-year-old daughter. At the custody trial he admitted to regularly watching videos alone in his bedroom with a teenage girl. See G. Fitzgerald, "*Selena*," *Premiere*, March 1997, vol. 10, no. 5, p. 78.

39 Kleinhans maintains that Selena's "feminism" (she becomes a career woman in spite of her father and Tejano agents; she initiates her romance and marriage; ultimately *she* decides she wants to have both a career and a family) is also used as a cross-over marketing ploy. Kleinhans, "Siempre Selena!," p. 28.

40 Bio-pics traditionally promote a code of suffering for women, and 29 percent include a death scene. See G. Custen, *Bio/Pics: How Hollywood Constructed Public History*, New Brunswick, Rutgers University Press, 1992, pp. 22–3, 75, and 153.

41 D. McLane, "*Selena*," *Village Voice*, 1 April 1997, p. 70, and B. Goodwin, "Under All that Sparkle? Victoria's Secret Bras," *L.A. Times*, 20 March 1997, p. E2.

42 Two monologs in particular reveal where Nava's *corazón* lies. In the first, Selena's father, Abraham (Edward James Olmos), teaches the young Selena to sing in Spanish phonetically because: "you're also Mexican, deep inside. . . . You can't be anything if you don't know who you are." In the second he complains to the 20-something Selena and her brother Abie (Jacob Vargas) that "being Mexican American is tough. . . . We gotta know about John Wayne AND Pedro Infante. Frank Sinatra AND Agustín Lara. Oprah AND Christina. It's exhausting!"

43 Yet cinematographer Ed Lachman eagerly worked with Tejano artist Carmen Lomen Garza to learn how she saw and painted her culture, and readily acknowledged a debt to Gabriel Figueroa as well. See D. Williams, "A Life of Color and Light," *American Cinematographer*, May 1997, vol. 78, no. 5, pp. 53–9.

44 K. Newman, "Latino Sacrifice in the Discourse of Citizenship: Acting against the 'Mainstream,' 1985–1988," in Noriega, *Chicanos and Film*, p. 62.

45 Smith, "Rosie Perez," p. 91.

46 F. Negrón-Muntañer, "Jennifer's Butt," *Aztlán: A Journal of Chicano Studies*, Fall 1997, vol. 22, no. 2, p. 189.

47 Goodwin, "Bum's the Word," p. 7.

48 G. Pearce, "Just What the Doctor Ordered," *London Sunday Times*, 16 August 1998, p. 6.

49 See, for example, R. Corliss, "Viva Selena!," *Time*, 42 March 1997, p. 89. Citing *Univisión* talk-show hostess, María Celeste Arrarás, Corliss suggests, however, that Selena's "secret" might have been a love affair with the married Mexican plastic surgeon who performed liposuction on her.

50 B. Kantrowitz, "Memories of Selena," *People*, 1 April 1996, p. 112.

51 In many of her bigger budget films, Lopez' characters are professionals, not workers: in *Money Train* she plays an undercover transit cop; in *Anaconda*, a documentary filmmaker; in *Jack*, an elementary school teacher; in *Selena*, a singer; in *Out of Sight*, a detective. This is unusual, as Carlos Cortés notes, because even more than other Latina characters, Puerto Riqueñas are typically portrayed as ghetto dwellers, gang members, drug dealers, and prostitutes. Cortés, "Chicanas in Film," pp. 75 and 76.

7 CHANNELING DESIRE, MAKING WHOOPI

1 A. Stuart, "Making Whoopi," *Sight and Sound*, February 1993, vol. 3, no. 2, p. 13.

2 As Mark Reid notes, however, independent black producers and directors have also worked in these genres. M. Reid, *Redefining Black Film*, Berkeley, University of California Press, 1993.

3 Other films connect her in passing to otherworldly beings: in *Moonlight and Valentino* her character consults the Tarot; in *Boys on the Side*, she visits a reader/advisor to learn what the future holds in store; in *Clara's Heart* (Robert Mulligan, 1988) she is haunted by the memory of her demented, dead son. And of course as *Star Trek* character Guynan, Whoopi has repeatedly been involved with intergalactic explorations on television. She appears as Guynan in the film, *Star Trek: Generations* (David Carson, 1994) as well.

4 A. Edwards, "Why Whoopi: An Appreciation," *Essence*, January 1997, vol. 27, no. 9, p. 58.

5 See C. Butler, "*The Color Purple* Controversy: Black Woman Spectatorship," *Wide Angle*, July–October 1991, vol. 13, nos. 3–4, pp. 62–9. See also J. Bobo, "Black Women in Fiction and Nonfiction: Images of Power and Powerlessness," *Wide Angle*, July–October 1991, vol. 13, nos. 3–4, pp. 72–81; "*The Color Purple*: Black Women as Cultural Readers," in D. Pribram (ed.), *Female Spectators*, London, Verso, 1988, pp. 90–109; "Reading through the Text: The Black Woman as Audience," in M. Diawara (ed.), *Black American Cinema*, New York, Routledge, 1993, pp. 272–86; and "Sifting through the Controversy: Reading *The Color Purple*," *Callaloo*, Spring 1989, vol. 12, no. 2, pp. 232–42. See further L. Norment, "*The Color Purple*: Controversial Book Becomes an Equally Controversial Movie," *Ebony*, February 1986, vol. 41, no. 4, pp. 146, 148, 150, 155.

6 See C. Cortés, "Hollywood Interracial Love: Social Taboo as Screen Titillation,"

in P. Loukides and L. K. Fuller (eds), *Beyond the Stars: Plot Conventions in American Popular Film*, vol. 2, Bowling Green, Bowling Green State University Press, 1991, pp. 21–35.

7 Very occasionally, Whoopi has had kind black husbands – most notably in *Ghosts of Mississippi* (Rob Reiner, 1996), *Sarafina!* (Darrell James Roodt, 1992), and *The Long Walk Home* (Richard Pearce, 1990). *Kingdom Come* (Doug McHenry, 2001) places her in an all-black cast film for the first time, in a supporting role.

8 In interviews Whoopi insists that the role was intended to showcase the class, style, brains, and courage of educated African American women in the 1950s. See "Whoopi Goldberg and Ray Liotta Go for Laughs and Love in *Corrina, Corrina*," *Jet*, 29 August 1994, vol. 886, no. 17, pp. 32–5. In *Playboy*, she maintained: "I never said I wouldn't play a maid. I said that I wouldn't *just* play maids. But in the words of Hattie McDaniel, 'Better to play one than to be one.' She used to get a lot of shit for the roles she was playing, too, but people don't realize that she wasn't turning down Scarlett O'Hara. . . . In my case, I've never played a maid who wasn't a lead in the movie. And the story of these women, who clean other people's houses and take care of their children, is a worthy one to tell." "*Playboy* Interview: Whoopi Goldberg," *Playboy*, January 1997, p. 54.

9 Whoopi began taking acting classes at age 8. Over the years she has carefully studied other actors' performances and other acting traditions, including the "Method." (For a time she worked with Lee Strasberg at the Actor's Studio.) She speaks of wanting to draw on Marlon Brando, Bette Davis, and Robert de Niro: "I want the essence of what they do to be the foundation for what is a jumping-off point for me." See J. Skow, "The Joy of Being Whoopi," *Time*, 21 September 1992, vol. 140, no. 12, pp. 58 and 60. See also P. Noe, "Who Is Whoopi Goldberg and What Is She Doing on Broadway???" *Ebony*, March 1985, no. 40, pp. 27–34, and L. DeLaria, "Whoopi Goldberg: Lesbian at Work," *The Advocate*, 7 February 1995, no. 674, pp. 50–1.

10 At times, Whoopi's embodiments thus demonstrate what James Naremore terms "opposing attitudes toward the self" while providing an "illusion of unified, individualized personality"; at other times, and often within the same film, they become comic personae who "threate[n] to disrupt coherence at every level . . ., deriving laughter not only from the foolish inconsistency of the characters but from a split between actor and role." J. Naremore, *Acting in the Cinema*, Berkeley, University of California Press, 1988, pp. 72 and 77.

11 E. Lott, *Love and Theft*, New York, Oxford University Press, 1993, p. 29.

12 Whoopi's melding of two or more stereotypical representations constitutes a variation on the trends K. Sue Jewell detects in 1980s African American representations: "On the one hand, the media would introduce more positive and representative images of African American women yet, simultaneously, include one of the old stereotypical images of African American women. The other practice was to introduce an image reflecting the strengths and positive qualities of African American women and then, later, seek to invalidate the positive attributes of this image." K. Jewell, *From Mammy to Miss America and Beyond: Cultural Images and the Shaping of U.S. Social Policy*, London, Routledge, 1993, p. 36.

13 To play Myrlie Evers, Whoopi even learned a different cadence and manner. See "*Ghosts of Mississippi*," *Jet*, 30 December–6 January 1997, vol. 91, no. 7, pp. 56–61.

14 According to Whoopi, "Moms Mabley is with me all the time. A great much of her [sic] is on my shoulder. Periodically I feel wafts of Dorothy Dandridge."

"*Playboy* Interview, Whoopi Goldberg," p. 56. Moms became a cultural heroine in the 1960s because she was tough, resilient, and feisty. In the 1970s she regularly poked fun on TV at political figures. See D. Bogle, *Brown Sugar*, New York, Da Capo, 1980, p. 158.

15 A. Johnson, "Moods Indigo: A Long View, Part 2," *Film Quarterly*, Spring 1991, vol. 44, no. 3, p. 21. Johnson generally likes Whoopi's performance.

16 See Lott, *Love and Death*, p. 9.

17 Eight prosthetic pieces were designed to redefine the shape, size, and skin tone of Whoopi's face. She wore "seven layers of make-up, a fat suit designed to proportion her body, a bald cap to cover her hair, and a man's suit." Buena Vista Press Kit, 25 September 1996, pp. 24–5.

18 On the reliance on body as "truth" in mainstream cross-dressing films, see further A. Kuhn, *The Power of the Image*, London, Routledge and Kegan Paul, 1985, pp. 48–73, and Straayer, *Deviant Eyes, Deviant Bodies*, pp. 42–78.

19 As Bogle argues, black film history is "found in . . . what certain talented actors have done with the stereotype." D. Bogle, *Toms, Coons, Mulattoes, Mammies, and Bucks*, New York, Viking Press, 1973. On differences between black and white audience responses, see J. Mayne, *Cinema and Spectatorship*, London, Routledge, 1993, pp. 146–53.

20 H. Gray, *Watching Race*, Minneapolis, University of Minnesota Press, 1995, p. 52.

21 *The Color Purple* in particular was the target of pickets and demonstrations, condemned by the Coalition against Black Exploitation for its "negative and unrealistic story about the Black family" and sanctioned by the NAACP for its "misrepresentation" of black people. See "Actor Danny Glover Answers Critics about Black Men," *Jet*, 13 January 1986, no. 69, p. 61. See also Butler, "*The Color Purple* Controversy"; Bobo, "Black Women in Fiction and Nonfiction," "*The Color Purple*: Black Women as Cultural Readers," "Reading through the Text," and "Sifting through the Controversy"; E. Guerrero, *Framing Blackness*, Philadelphia, Temple University Press, 1993, pp. 50–6; and A. Stuart, "*The Color Purple*: In Defense of Happy Endings," in L. Gamman and M. Marshment (eds), *The Female Gaze*, Seattle, The Real Comet Press, 1989, pp. 60–75.

22 See, for example, Guerrero, *Framing Blackness*, pp. 237–8, and O. Idowu, "Black Like Me," *Vibe*, February 1997, vol. 5, no. 1, pp. 80–2.

23 The woman is cited in M. Rosenfeld, "Enough Already!," *Washington Post*, 14 April 1996, no. 119, p. G5. See also R. Wiley, *Dark Witness: Why Blacks Should Be Sacrificed Again*, New York, One World, Ballentine, 1996, p. 252.

24 See "After the Friar's Roast, Fire and Smoke" and "Blacks Fail to See Humor in Ted Danson's Blackface Tribute to Whoopi Goldberg," *Jet*, 1 November 1993, vol. 85, no. 1, pp. 56–9; see also K. G. Bates, "Whoopi, Ted: We Are Not Amused," *Los Angeles Times*, 13 October 1993, no. 112, p. B7.

25 See J. Wenner, "This Sister's Act," *Us*, 7 April 1985, no. 195, pp. 58–74 and 88.

26 E. Pincus, "Side Dish," *Gay Community News*, Winter 1995, vol. 20, no. 4, p. 26.

27 L. Butterbaugh, "Girls on Our Side," *off our backs*, April 1995, vol. 25, no. 4, p. 16, and C. Gage, "*Boys on the Side*," *off our backs*, April 1995, vol. 25, no. 4, p. 17.

28 S. Levitt and K. Johnson, "Changing Partners," *People Weekly*, 22 November 1993, vol. 40, no. 21, p. 48.

29 See D. Meeley, "Whoopi Goldberg," *Screen Actor*, Fall 1988, p. 19; "Whoopi Goldberg," *People Weekly*, 28 December 1992, vol. 38, no. 26, p. 97; and

"Whoopi: I Am No Saint," *Jet*, 25 October, 1993, vol. 84, no. 7, pp. 14 and 60.
30 Skow, "The Joy of Being Whoopi," p. 60.
31 See J. Kearney, "Color Her Anything," *American Film*, December 1985, vol. 11, no. 3, p. 27; "Remaking Whoopi," *Vogue*, January 1991, p. 219; "Whoopi Goldberg and Ray Liotta Go for Laughs and Love," p. 34; and "Whoopi Goldberg Talks about Her Role in 'Ghost' and Blasts Critics Over Her Film Choices," *Jet*, 13 August 1990, vol. 78, no. 18, p. 60.
32 See Kearney, "Color Her Anything," p. 28, and Idowu, "Black Like Me," p. 82.
33 Idowu, "Black Like Me," p. 82.
34 Her street credentials are "impeccable": she dropped out of school at age 14, turned to drugs, got married at age 17 to her drug counselor, had one daughter with him, left him to pursue an acting career, lived on welfare, worked a variety of odd jobs (from cosmetician in a mortuary to brick layer) to support herself and her daughter, and now has a granddaughter, born out of wedlock to her daughter. See DeLaria, "Whoopi Goldberg"; Stuart, "Making Whoopi"; Wenner, "This Sister's Act"; L. Randolph, "The Whoopi Goldberg Nobody Knows," *Ebony*, March 1991, vol. 46, no. 5, pp. 110–12; and "Whoopi Sounds Off on Sex, Drugs, Race," *Jet*, 15 June 1987, vol. 72, no. 12, p. 24.
35 One of the first calls that Clinton took on election night was from Whoopi. "Whoopi Goldberg," *People Weekly*, 97.
36 Idowu, "Black Like Me," p. 82.
37 Ibid.
38 H. Haun, "The Big Whoopi To-Do," *Playbill*, 31 March 1997, vol. 15, no. 6, p. 14.
39 Gray, *Watching Race*, p. 84. Emphasis added.
40 Stuart, *"The Color Purple,"* p. 66.
41 "Remaking Whoopi," *Vogue*, p. 178.
42 Janet Maslin, cited in "Remaking Whoopi," p. 219.

8 THE AGING CLINT

1 S. Neale, *Genre*, London, BFI, 1980, p. 57.
2 S. Neale, "Masculinity as Spectacle," *Screen*, 1983, vol. 24, no. 6, p. 12.
3 V. Wexman, *Creating the Couple: Love, Marriage and Hollywood Performance*, Princeton, Princeton University Press, 1993, p. 69.
4 See L. Dittmar, "Of Hags and Crones: Reclaiming Lesbian Desire for the Trouble Zone of Aging," in C. Holmlund and C. Fuchs (eds), *Between the Sheets, In the Streets: Queer, Lesbian, Gay Documentary*, Minneapolis, University of Minnesota Press, 1997, pp. 71–90. See also E. A. Kaplan, "Trauma and Aging: Marlene Dietrich, Melanie Klein, and Marguerite Duras," V. Sobchak, "Scary Women: Cinema, Surgery, and Special Effects," and P. Mellancamp, "From Anxiety to Equanimity: Crisis and Generational Continuity on TV, at the Movies, in Life, in Death," in K. Woodward (ed.), *Figuring Age: Women, Bodies, Generations*, Bloomington, Indiana University Press, 1999, pp. 171–94, 200–11, 310–28, respectively.
5 Such shifts in the ways middle-aged and older men were treated started earlier in the century, but were not noticed because women were so obviously targets of age-based oppression. M. Gullette, "All Together Now: The New Sexual Politics of Midlife Bodies," *Michigan Quarterly Review*, Fall 1993, vol. 32, no. 4, p. 687.
6 Ibid., p. 675.
7 Only *Superman* outgrossed *Every Which Way But Loose* in 1979, despite the fact that *Newsweek*'s pan ("One can forgive the orang-utan's participation – he couldn't

read the script – but where is Eastwood's excuse?") was typical of critical response. I. Johnstone, *The Man with No Name*, New York, Morrow Quill, 1981, p. 120. Richard Schickel maintains the film was Eastwood's most profitable ever, returning more than ten times its cost in domestic theatrical rentals alone, thanks to its novel release pattern of simultaneous openings in small towns and cities. R. Schickel, *Clint Eastwood*, New York, Knopf, 1996, pp. 353–6.

8 In part, argues Edward Gallafent, this is because in the 30 plus years of his acting career he has "never play[ed] anything but an unmistakable American except for a brief period in disguise in *Firefox*" (Eastwood, 1982). E. Gallafent, *Clint Eastwood, Filmmaker and Star*, New York, Continuum, 1994, p. 8.

9 K. Woodward, *Aging and Its Discontents: Freud and Other Fictions*, Bloomington, Indiana University Press, 1991, p. 6.

10 Gullette, "All Together Now," p. 675.

11 W. May, "The Virtues and Vices of the Elderly," in T. Cole and S. Gadow (eds), *What Does It Mean to Grow Old?*, Durham, Duke University Press, 1986, p. 56.

12 See C. Herfray, *La Vieillesse: Une interprétation psychanalytique*, Paris, Desclée de Brouwer, EPI, 1988.

13 P. Bordelaise, "Death and Dying in Two Cultures," lecture delivered at "A French-American Dialogue on Care Near the End of Life," Reid Hall, Paris, France. 25–7 June 1997. Cited in K. Woodward, "Introduction," in Woodward, *Figuring Age*, p. xv.

14 Cited in B. Zmijewsky and L. Pfeiffer, *The Films of Clint Eastwood*, New York, Citadel, 1994, p. 8.

15 See Johnstone, *The Man with No Name*, p. 36.

16 Jane Tompkins argues similarly that in westerns "to be a man is not only to be monolithic, silent, mysterious, impenetrable as a desert butte, it is to be the desert butte." J. Tompkins, *West of Everything: The Inner Life of Westerns*, New York, Oxford University Press, 1992, p. 56.

17 Costume designer Glenn Wright worked with Clint on *Rawhide* and many films; cinematographers Jack Green and Bruce Surtees, composer Lennie Niehaus, editor Joel Cox, have also collaborated on multiple movies.

18 In *The Outlaw Josey Wales*, the guns' size is accentuated by lack of depth cues and foreground placement. See further P. Lehman, "In an Imperfect World, Men with Small Penises Are Unforgiven: The Representation of the Penis/Phallus in American Films of the 1990s," *Men and Masculinities*, October 1998, vol. 1, no. 2, pp. 123–37; see also D. Bingham, *Acting Male: Masculinities in the Films of James Stewart, Jack Nicholson, and Clint Eastwood*, New Brunswick, Rutgers University Press, 1994, p. 236.

19 See, for example, the publicity photos and stills of the young Clint and the middle-aged Clint in J. Ryder, *Clint Eastwood*, New York, Dell, 1987, between pp. 96 and 97.

20 G. Ford, "Mostly on *Rio Lobo*," in B. Nichols (ed.), *Movies and Methods*, Berkeley, University of California Press, 1976, pp. 347–8.

21 See Johnstone, *The Man with No Name*, p. 35.

22 S. Gadow, "Subjectivity: Literature, Imagination and Frailty," in Cole and Gadow, *What Does It Mean to Grow Old?*, p. 134.

23 Woodward notes that in the U.S. in 1995: "there were some 250 women for every 100 men in the age group of 85 and older. Three-quarters of the residents in nursing homes are women." Woodward, "Introduction," in Woodward, *Figuring Age*, p. xxvi.

24 Paraphrased in T. DiPiero, "White Men Aren't," *Camera Obscura*, May 1992, vol. 30, pp. 121, 119.

25 Woodward, *Aging and Its Discontents*, p. 47.
26 P. Merigeau, "Eastwood in His Carmel," in R. Kapsis and K. Coblentz (eds), *Clint Eastwood Interviews*, Jackson, University Press of Mississippi, 1999, p. 237.
27 See also Dennis Bingham's chapter on the early westerns. Bingham, *Acting Male*, pp. 163–79.
28 On adoptive sons, see further P. Smith, *Clint Eastwood: A Cultural Production*, Minneapolis, University of Minnesota Press, 1993, p. 40.
29 See E. Gallafent, *Clint Eastwood: Filmmaker and Star*, pp. 156–98.
30 See, for example, Bingham, *Acting Male*, especially pp. 195–218; C. Holmlund, "Sexuality and Power in Male Doppelgänger Cinema: the Case of Clint Eastwood's *Tightrope*," *Cinema Journal*, Fall 1986, vol. 26, no. 1, pp. 31–41; and J. Mayne, "Walking the *Tightrope* of Feminism and Male Desire," in A. Jardine and P. Smith (eds), *Men in Feminism*, New York, Methuen, 1987, pp. 62–70.
31 J. Tibbetts, "Clint Eastwood and the Machinery of Violence," *Literature/Film Quarterly*, January 1993, vol. 21, no. 1, p. 14.
32 G. Gruman, "Cultural Origins of Present-day 'Age-ism': The Modernization of the Life Cycle," in S. Spicker *et al.* (eds), *Aging and the Elderly: Humanistic Perspectives in Gerontology*, Atlantic Highlands, Humanities Press, 1978, pp. 364–5.
33 P. Laslett, *A Fresh Map of Life: The Emergence of the Third Age*, cited in D. Troyansky, "Historical Research into Aging, Old Age and Older People," in A. Jamieson *et al.* (eds), *Critical Approaches to Aging and Later Life*, Buckingham, Open University Press, 1997, p. 50.
34 See further Gruman, "Cultural Origins of Present-day 'Age-ism'," pp. 360–4.
35 Schickel, *Clint Eastwood*, p. 422.
36 K. Silverman, *Male Subjectivity at the Margins*, New York, Routledge, 1992, p. 45.
37 S. de Beauvoir, *The Coming of Age*, Patrick O'Brien (trans.), New York, Warner, 1978, pp. 4–5.
38 P. Higgs, "Citizenship Theory and Old Age: From Social Rights to Surveillance," in Jamieson *et al.*, *Critical Approaches to Aging and Later Life*, p. 129.

9 MARKETING DOLLY DIALECTICS

1 C. Buchanan, *Maiden*, New York, William Morrow, 1999 (1972), p. 41.
2 Dolly confesses: "I'm not a technical actress . . . I only do projects that are close enough to my personality to where I can do a good job." See B. Pickle, "It's Already a Hit with Me," *Knoxville News Sentinel*, 3 April 1992, p. 6.
3 Seven of Dolly's films are available on video. Two – *Smoky Mountain Christmas* and *Unlikely Angel* – were made for television; two others – *The Best Little Whorehouse* and *Steel Magnolias* – were adapted from the stage. Dolly's second film, *Best Little Whorehouse in Texas*, was one of the top-grossing films that year. The $28 million *Rhinestone* was a huge failure. Studio heads rolled at Fox when domestic rentals totaled only $12.2 million. See further M. Litwak, *Reel Power: The Struggle for Influence and Success in the New Hollywood*, New York, New American Library, 1987, pp. 21–31.
    Four made-for-TV movies have not been released on video and so are not discussed here.
4 See K. Jaehne, "CEO and Cinderella: An Interview with Dolly Parton," *Cineaste*, 1990, vol. 17, no. 4, pp. 16–20 and P. Wilson, "Mountains of Contradictions: Gender, Class, and Region in the Star Image of Dolly Parton," *South Atlantic Quarterly*, Winter 1995, vol. 94, no. 1, pp. 109–34.
5 G. Plaskin, "Hello, Dolly! East Tennessee's Daughter Speaks Her Mind," *Knoxville News Sentinel*, 2 December 1990, p. A1.

6 D. Parton, *My Life and Other Unfinished Business*, New York, Harper Collins, 1994, p. 79.

7 L. Kipnis, *Bound and Gagged: Pornography and the Politics of Fantasy in America*, New York, Grove Press, 1996, p. 93.

8 R. Seid, *Never Too Thin: Why Women Are at War with Their Bodies*, New York, Prentice Hall, 1989, p. 4.

9 G. Gaesser, *Big Fat Lies: The Truth about Your Weight and Your Health*, New York, Fawcett Columbine, 1996, pp. 3, 20, 22–3. Peter Stearns cites a 1995 study that finds 71 percent of all Americans over 25 are overweight. See P. Stearns, *Fat History: Bodies and Beauty in the Modern West*, New York, New York University Press, 1997, p. 133. Seid maintains that 90 percent of us think we weigh too much. Seid, *Never Too Thin*, p. 3.

10 See N. Hellmich, "A New Dolly," *Knoxville Journal*, 8 April 1986, p. A1; G. Plaskin, "Hello, Dolly!," p. A4; and K. Sessums, "Good Golly, Miss Dolly!," *Vanity Fair*, June 1991, p. 165.

11 During the filming of *Rhinestone*, Stallone reportedly opened her refrigerator and was shocked to find "things . . . that had no connection with life as we know it. . . . I said, 'Seriously, you can't be alive. Either that or you're totally preserved because they are all preservatives'." S. Haller, "The Lady or the Tiger?," *People Weekly*, 9 July 1984, vol. 22, p. 89.

12 T. O'Brien, "Dollywood's Menu Set Off from Those of Other Parks," *Amusement Business*, 7 May 1990, vol. 102, no. 18, p. 45.

13 T. Morrow, "Doing Dollywood the Right Way," *Knoxville News Sentinel*, 5 June 1998, p. B1.

14 G. Plaskin, "Hello, Dolly!," p. A4, and S. Kahn, "Planet Dollywood," *McCall's*, January 1996, vol. 123, no. 4, p. 43.

15 According to Sander L. Gilman, in 1992 alone, 30,000 women had their breasts enlarged, 8,000 had them lifted, and 4,000 had them reduced; 16,000 people had tummy tucks, 20,000 had chemical peels, 40,000 had collagen injections to fill out wrinkles, 50,000 had nose jobs, 50,000 had liposuction to remove fat, and 60,000 had eyelid corrections. S. Gilman, *Creating Beauty to Cure the Soul: Race and Psychology in the Shaping of Aesthetic Surgery*, Durham, Duke University Press, 1998, p. ix.

16 1994 statistics cited in E. Haiken, *Venus Envy: A History of Cosmetic Surgery*, Baltimore, Johns Hopkins University Press, 1997, p. 161. Gilman adds that although neither state nor private health insurance covers aesthetic surgery, in 1996 there was one procedure for every 150 people. S. Gilman, *Making the Body Beautiful: A Cultural History of Aesthetic Surgery*, Princeton, Princeton University Press, 1999, pp. 4 and 6.

17 Sessums, "Good Golly, Miss Dolly!," p. 10.

18 C. Chase, "Sassy, Unsinkable Dolly," *Cosmopolitan*, October 1989, vol. 207, no. 4, p. 198, and Parton, *My Life and Other Unfinished Business*, p. 278.

19 Parton, *My Life and Other Unfinished Business*, pp. 2 and 309. See also S. Haller, "Come on Down to Dollywood," *People*, 5 May 1986, p. 139.

20 Evangelical churches include the various Baptist congregations, Nazarenes, Churches of Christ, Bible churches, independent and non-denominational, non-Pentecostal groups. There are several Churches of God, including some autonomous groups. See B. Leonard, "Introduction: The Faith and the Faiths," in B. Leonard (ed.), *Christianity in Appalachia: Profiles in Regional Pluralism*, Knoxville, University of Tennessee Press, 1999, especially pp. xv–xxi. See further L. Jones, "Mountain Religion: An Overview," M. Daugherty, "Serpent Handlers: When the Sacrament Comes Alive," and D. Bowdle, "Holiness in

the Highlands: A Profile of the Church of God," all in Leonard, *Christianity in Appalachia*, pp. 91–102, 138–52, and 243–56, respectively.

21 A third of the region, moreover, either does not share fundamentalist beliefs or is wholly indifferent. See J. Welch, "Uneven Ground: Cultural Values, Moral Standards, and Religiosity in the Heart of Appalachia," in Leonard, *Christianity in Appalachia*, pp. 59–60. Southern Baptist seminaries encouraged diversity until 1979, when conservative fundamentalists gained control of the Southern Baptist Convention. Since then a rhetoric of inerrancy has allowed pastors to exclude people or groups (foremost among them masons, liberals, and homosexuals). Women cannot be ordained as pastors but are included in everyday church affairs. See C. Kell and L. Camp, *In the Name of the Father: The Rhetoric of the New Southern Baptist Convention*, Carbondale, Southern Illinois University Press, 1999, pp. xv, 32–3, 122.

22 For further analysis of Dolly's "populist" feminism, see Wilson, "Mountains of Contradictions."

23 See T. Morrow, "The Gospel Side of Dolly," *Knoxville News Sentinel*, 16 April 1999, p. E17.

24 Ibid., p. 198; Haller, "The Lady or the Tiger?," p. 86L; Sessums, "Good Golly, Miss Dolly!" p. 162.

25 Parton, *My Life and Other Unfinished Business*, p. 309.

26 See, for example, Plaskin, "Hello, Dolly!" p. A4.

27 Dolly says that as a child she was impressed with "trash" with "blond hair and . . . nail polish and tight clothes. I thought they were beautiful." See J. Williamson, *Hillbillyland: what the Movies Did to the Mountains and What the Mountains Did to the Movies*," Chapel Hill, University of North Carolina Press, 1995, p. 258.

28 See Leonard, "Introduction," in Leonard, *Christianity in Appalachia*, p. xvi, and G. McWhiney, *Cracker Culture: Celtic Ways in the Old South*, Tuscaloosa, University of Alabama Press, 1988, p. 8. Most "crackers," McWhiney points out, are of Scots-Irish descent; Dolly is no exception.

29 For analyses of Hollywood's portrayals of hillbillies, see Williamson, *Hillbillyland*, and C. Ward, "The Southern Landscape in Contemporary Films," in P. Loukides and L. Fuller (eds), *Beyond the Stars: Locales in American Popular Film*, vol. 4, Bowling Green, Bowling Green State University Popular Press, pp. 103–18.

30 Williamson, *Hillbillyland*, p. 259.

31 See D. Henwood, "Trash-o-nomics," in M. Wray and A. Newitz (eds), *White Trash: Race and Class in America*, New York, Routledge, 1997, p. 183.

32 Most Americans now live in cities. See R. Farley, *The New American Reality*, New York, Russell Sage Foundation, 1996, pp. 282, 298–9.

33 Haller, "Come on Down to Dollywood," p. 139.

34 Wages are low, but typical of the region: in 1999, 15 year olds averaged $5.50 an hour, those 16 and above, $6.00 an hour. A. McRary, "Step Right Up," *Knoxville News Sentinel*, 8 July 1999, p. B1. The average wage in Sevier County was $8.30 in 1996; the figure encompasses judges to sales clerks. A single parent with one child and a seasonal job paying $7.50 per hour lives under the federal poverty level. S. Henighan, "Making Enough to Live On," *Mountain Press*, 24 August 1998, p. A3.

35 To date 100,000 books have been donated to preschoolers. See, for example, L. Martin, "Dolly Wants Kids to Read," *Mountain Press*, 6 February 2000, p. A21, and "Pop Quiz with Dolly Parton," *People Weekly*, 10 April 2000, vol. 53, no. 14, p. 22.

36 See S. Henighan, "Education Boosts Financial Health," *Mountain Press*, 26 August 1998, p. A1.

37 See Jaehne, "CEO and Cinderella," p. 18, and H. Gleason, "Dolly Parton: Here I Come Again," *Saturday Evening Post*, October 1989, vol. 261, no. 7, p. 47.
38 See S. Henighan, "A Have and Have Not Society," *Mountain Press*, 23 August 1998, p. A2.
39 See M. Longina, "48 Hours in Pigeon Forge," *Chattanooga Times/Chattanooga Free Press*, 13 June 1999, p. H3.
40 T. Allen-Mills, "Parton Goes from Bust to Boom at Dollywood," *London Sunday Times,* 12 July 1998, p. 21.
41 See "Dolly Parton's Pigeon Forge, Tennessee," *People Weekly*, 21 April 1997, vol. 47, no. 15, p. 111; Kahn, "Planet Dollywood," p. 43; T. Morrow, "Make Way for Dolly!," *Knoxville News Sentinel*, 15 April 2000, p. A1; and "Up, Up, Up! Park Prices Get Scarier than Rides," *The Tennessean*, 28 April 2000, p. 1E.
42 T. Morrow, "She's Dr. Parton Now," *Mountain Press*, 22 October 1990, p. A1.
43 R. Powelson, "Parton's a Smash at National Press Club," *Knoxville News Sentinel*, 24 March 2000, p. A6.
44 Ibid.
45 C. Chase, "Sassy, Unsinkable Dolly," *Cosmopolitan*, October 1989, vol. 207, no. 4, p. 202.
46 Zilberg attributes Dolly's phenomenal appeal to her emphasis on love, invocation of family values, recognition of exploitation, and pride in (past) poverty; he finds it significant that she invokes a working-class identity without calling for revolutionary consciousness. J. Zilberg, "Yes It's True: Zimbabweans Love Dolly Parton," *Journal of Popular Culture*, Summer 1995, vol. 29, no. 1, pp. 111–14.
47 Longina, "48 Hours in Pigeon Forge," p. H3.

FILMOGRAPHY

Absolute Power, U.S., Clint Eastwood, 1997
Accused, The, U.S., Jonathan Kaplan, 1988
Aliens, U.S., James Cameron, 1986
Anaconda, U.S., Luis Llosa, 1997
. . . And the Earth Did Not Swallow Him, U.S., Severo Pérez, 1994
Any Which Way You Can, U.S., Buddy Van Horn, 1980
As Good As It Gets, James Brooks, 1997
Associate, The, U.S., Donald Petrie, 1996
Ballad of Little Jo, The, U.S., Maggie Greenwald, 1995
Basic Instinct, U.S., Paul Verhoeven, 1992
Beguiled, The, U.S., Don Siegel, 1971
Best Little Whorehouse in Texas, The, U.S., Colin Higgins, 1982
Beverly Hillbillies, The, U.S., Penelope Spheeris, 1993
Bitter Tea of General Yen, The, U.S., Frank Capra, 1934
Black Widow, U.S., Bob Rafelson, 1986
Blazing Saddles, U.S., Mel Brooks, 1973
Blood and Wine, U.S., Bob Rafelson, 1997
Blue Steel, U.S., Kathryn Bigelow, 1990
Bogus, U.S., Norman Jewison, 1996
Born in East L.A., U.S., Cheech Marin, 1985
Bound by Honor, U.S., Taylor Hackford, 1993
Boys Don't Cry, U.S., Kimberly Pierce, 1999
Boys on the Side, U.S., Herbert Ross, 1995
Bridges of Madison County, The, U.S., Clint Eastwood, 1995
Bronco Billy, U.S., Clint Eastwood, 1980
Buck and the Preacher, U.S., Sidney Poitier, 1970
Buffy the Vampire Slayer, U.S., Fran Rubel Kuzui, 1992
Bullets for Breakfast, U.S., Holly Fisher, 1992
Burglar, U.S., Hugh Wilson, 1989
Cell, The, U.S., Tarsem Singh, 2000
Chuck and Buck, U.S., Miguel Arteta, 2000
City Heat, U.S., Richard Benjamin, 1984

Clara's Heart, U.S., Robert Mulligan, 1988

Color Purple, The, U.S., Steven Spielberg, 1985

Coogan's Bluff, U.S., Don Siegel, 1968

Corpus: A Home Movie for Selena, U.S., Lourdes Portillo, 1999

Corrina, Corrina, U.S., Jesse Nelson, 1994

Crouching Tiger, Hidden Dragon, China/Hong Kong/Taiwan/U.S., Ang Lee, 2000

Cruising, U.S., William Friedkin, 1980

Dances with Wolves, U.S., Kevin Costner, 1990

Days of Heaven, U.S., Terence Malick, 1978

Dead Man, U.S., Jim Jarmusch, 1996

Dead Pool, The, U.S., Buddy Van Horn, 1988

Desert Hearts, U.S., Donna Deitch, 1986

Desperado, U.S., Robert Rodríguez, 1995

Do the Right Thing, U.S., Spike Lee, 1989

Dressed to Kill, U.S., Brian de Palma, 1980

Eating Raoul, U.S., Paul Bartel, 1982

Eddie, U.S., Steve Rash, 1996

Eiger Sanction, The, U.S., Clint Eastwood, 1975

El Mariachi, U.S., Robert Rodríguez, 1993

El Norte, U.S., Gregory Nava, 1983

Emigrants, The, Sweden, Jan Troell, 1971

Enforcer, The, U.S., James Fargo, 1976

Entre Nous (French title *Coup de foudre*), France, Diane Kurys, 1983

Escape from Alcatraz, U.S., Don Siegel, 1979

Every Which Way But Loose, U.S., James Fargo, 1978

Fatal Attraction, U.S., Adrien Lyne, 1987

Fatal Beauty, U.S., Tom Holland, 1987

Fearless, U.S., Peter Weir, 1993

Firefox, U.S., Clint Eastwood, 1982

Fistful of Dollars, Italy, Sergio Leone, 1974

For a Few Dollars More, Italy, Sergio Leone, 1965

Fried Green Tomatoes, U.S., John Avnet, 1992

Gauntlet, The, U.S., Clint Eastwood, 1977

Ghost, U.S., Jerry Zucker, 1990

Ghosts of Mississippi, U.S., Rob Reiner, 1996

Girlfriends, U.S., Claudia Weill, 1978

Go Fish, U.S., Rose Troche, 1994

Good, the Bad, and the Ugly, The, Italy, Sergio Leone, 1966

Goonies, The, U.S., Richard Donner, 1985

Grifters, The, U.S., Stephen Frears, 1990

Handmaid's Tale, The, U.S., Volker Schlondorff, 1990

Hand that Rocks the Cradle, The, U.S., Curtis Hanson, 1992

Hang 'Em High, U.S., Ted Post, 1967

Heartbreak Ridge, U.S., Clint Eastwood, 1986
Heartland, U.S., Richard Pearce, 1979
Heathers, U.S., Michael Lehman, 1989
High Noon, U.S., Fred Zinnemann, 1952
High Plains Drifter, U.S., Clint Eastwood, 1972
Hiroshima, mon amour, France, Alain Resnais, 1959
Honkytonk Man, U.S., Clint Eastwood, 1982
Hunger, The, U.S., Tony Scott, 1983
In the Line of Fire, U.S., Wolfgang Petersen, 1993
It Could Happen to You, U.S., Andrew Bergman, 1994
Jagged Edge, U.S., Richard Marquand, 1985
Jennifer 8, U.S., Bruce Robinson, 1992
Joe Kidd, U.S., John Sturges, 1972
John Carpenter's Escape from L.A., U.S., John Carpenter, 1996
John Carpenter's Escape from New York, U.S., John Carpenter, 1981
Johnny Mnemonic, U.S., Robert Longo, 1995
Julia, U.S., Fred Zinnemann, 1977
Jumpin' Jack Flash, U.S., Penny Marshall, 1986
Kelly's Heroes, U.S., Brian Hutton, 1970
Last Man Standing, U.S., Walter Hill, 1996
Last of the Mohicans, U.S., Michael Mann, 1992
Latin Boys Go to Hell, U.S., Ela Troyano, 1997
Lianna, U.S., John Sayles, 1983
Lion King, The, U.S. Roger Allers and Rob Minkoff, 1984
L Is for the Way You Look, U.S., Jean Carlomusto, 1991
Long Walk Home, The, U.S., Richard Pearce 1990
Made in America, U.S., Richard Benjamin, 1993
Magnificent Seven, The, U.S., John Sturges, 1960
Man of the West, U.S., Budd Boetticher, 1958
Man Who Shot Liberty Valance, The, U.S., John Ford, 1962
Matrix, The, U.S., Andy and Larry Wachowski, 1999
Money Train, U.S., Joseph Rubin, 1995
Moonlight and Valentino, U.S., David Anspaugh, 1995
Mortal Thoughts, U.S., Alan Rudolph, 1991
New Jack City, U.S., Mario van Peebles, 1991
New Land, The, Sweden, Jan Troell, 1972
Nine to Five, U.S., Colin Higgins, 1980
Northern Lights, U.S., John Hanson, 1979
Nuts, U.S., Martin Ritt, 1987
Once Upon a Time in the West, U.S./Italy, Sergio Leone, 1968
Outlaw, The, U.S., Howard Hughes, 1943
Outlaw Josey Wales, The, U.S., Clint Eastwood, 1976
Out of Sight, U.S., Steven Soderbergh, 1998
Pale Rider, U.S., Clint Eastwood, 1985

Parents, U.S., Bob Balaban, 1989
Pentathalon, U.S., Bruce Malmuth, 1994
Perfect World, A, U.S., Clint Eastwood, 1993
Personal Best, U.S., Robert Towne, 1982
Pink Cadillac, U.S., Buddy Van Horn, 1989
Player, The, U.S., Robert Altman, 1992
Play Misty for Me, U.S., Clint Eastwood, 1971
Posse, U.S., Mario van Peebles, 1993
Pumping Iron, U.S., George Butler and Robert Flore, 1979
Pumping Iron II: The Women, U.S., George Butler, 1984
Punisher, The, U.S., Mark Goldblatt, 1989
Quick and the Dead, The, U.S., Sam Raimi, 1995
Red Scorpion, U.S., Joseph Zito, 1989
Red Shift, U.S., Gunvor Nelson, 1984
Rhinestone, U.S., Bob Clark, 1984
Ride the High Country, U.S., Sam Peckinpah, 1962
Rio Lobo, U.S., John Ford, 1970
Road Warrior, Australia, George Miller, 1981
Rocky IV, U.S., John Avila, 1986
Rudolph the Red-Nosed Reindeer: The Movie, U.S., William Kowalchuk, 1998
Rug Rats Movie, The, U.S., Igor Kovalyov and Norton Virgien, 1998
Searchers, The, U.S., John Ford, 1956
Shane, U.S., George Stevens, 1952
Shootist, The, U.S., Don Siegel, 1976
Showdown in Little Tokyo, U.S., Mark Lester, 1991
Silence of the Lambs, The, U.S., Jonathan Demme, 1981
Silent Trigger, U.S., Russell Mulcahy, 1997
Silverado, U.S., Lawrence Kasdan, 1985
Single White Female, U.S., Barbet Schroeder, 1992
Sister Act, U.S., Emile Ardolino, 1992
Sister Act II: Back in the Habit, U.S., Bill Duke, 1993
Sixth Day, The, U.S., Roger Spottiswoode, 2000
Smoky Mountain Christmas, U.S., Henry Winkler, 1986
Soapdish, U.S., Michael Hoffman, 1991
Some Like It Hot, U.S., Billy Wilder, 1959
Space Cowboys, U.S., Clint Eastwood, 2000
Steel Magnolias, U.S., Herbert Ross, 1989
Straight Talk, U.S., Barnet Kellman, 1992
Sudden Impact, U.S., Clint Eastwood, 1983
Surf Nazis Must Die, U.S., Peter George, 1987
Telephone, The, U.S., Rip Torn, 1988
Terror in a Texas Town, U.S., Joseph Lewis, 1958
Thelma and Louise, U.S., Ridley Scott, 1991
Theodore Rex, U.S., Jonathan Betuel, 1995

Thunderbolt and Lightfoot, U.S., Michael Cimino, 1974
Tightrope, U.S., Clint Eastwood, 1984
Time for Drunken Horses, A, France/Iran, Bahman Ghobadi, 2000
Tootsie, U.S., Sydney Pollack, 1982
True Crime, U.S., Clint Eastwood, 1999
Turning Point, U.S., Herbert Ross, 1977
Two Mules for Sister Sara, U.S., Don Siegel, 1969
Unforgiven, U.S., Clint Eastwood, 1992
Universal Soldier, U.S., Roland Emmerich, 1992
Unlikely Angel, U.S., Michael Switzer, 1997
Untamed Heart, U.S., Tony Bill, 1993
Victor/Victoria, U.S., Blake Edwards, 1982
Where Eagles Dare, U.S., Brian Hutton, 1968
White Hunter, Black Heart, U.S., Clint Eastwood, 1990
White Men Can't Jump, U.S., Ron Shelton, 1992
Whoopi Goldberg Live, U.S., Thomas Schlamme, 1985
Wild Bunch, The, U.S., Sam Peckinpah, 1969
Wild Orchids, U.S., Sydney Franklin, 1928
Windows, U.S., Gordon Willis, 1980
Wood, The, U.S., Rick Famuyiwa, 1999
X-Men, U.S., Bryan Singer, 2000
Young Guns, U.S., Christopher Cain, 1988
Young Guns II, U.S., Geoff Murphy, 1990
Zoot Suit, U.S., Luis Valdez, 1981

SELECTED BIBLIOGRAPHY

Adam, B., *The Rise of a Gay and Lesbian Movement*, Boston, G. K. Hall, 1987.

Alba, R., *Ethnic Identity: The Transformation of White America*, New Haven, Yale University Press, 1990.

Anderson, J., *Scandinavian Humor and Other Myths*, Minneapolis, Nordbook, 1986.

Aoki, D., "Posing the Subject: Sex, Illumination, and *Pumping Iron II: The Women*," *Cinema Journal*, Summer 1999, vol. 38, no. 4, pp. 24–44.

Asther, N., *Narrens Väg: Ingen Gudasaga*, Stockholm, Carlssons, 1988.

Becker, E. *et al.*, "Introduction," *Jump Cut*, March 1981, nos. 24–5, pp. 17–22.

Beltrán, M., "The Hollywood Latina Body as Site of Social Struggle: Jennifer Lopez's Celebrity Construction and 'Cross-Over Butt'," unpublished conference paper, Society for Cinema Studies Conference, March 2000.

Bennett, T. and J. Woollacott, *Bond and Beyond*, New York, Methuen, 1987.

Berg, C. R. "Ethnic Ingenuity and Mainstream Cinema: Robert Rodriguez' *Bedhead* (1990) and *El Mariachi* (1993)," in C. Noriega and A. López (eds), *The Ethnic Eye: Latino Media Arts*, Minneapolis, University of Minnesota Press, 1996, pp. 107–28.

Berglund, J., "'The Secret's In the Sauce': Dismembering Normativity in *Fried Green Tomatoes*," *Camera Obscura*, September 1999, no. 42, pp. 125–62.

Bernardi, D. (ed.), *The Birth of Whiteness: Race and the Emergence of U.S. Cinema*, New Brunswick, Rutgers University Press, 1996.

Bhabha, H., "The Other Question," *Screen*, 1983, vol. 24, no. 6, pp. 18–36.

Bingham, D., *Acting Male: Masculinities in the Films of James Stewart, Jack Nicholson, and Clint Eastwood*, New Brunswick, Rutgers University Press, 1994.

Bobo, J., "*The Color Purple*: Black Women as Cultural Readers," in D. Pribram (ed.), *Female Spectators*, London, Verso, 1988, pp. 90–109.

—— "Sifting through the Controversy: Reading *The Color Purple*," *Callaloo*, Spring 1989, vol. 12, no. 2, pp. 332–42.

—— "Black Women in Fiction and Nonfiction: Images of Power and Powerlessness," *Wide Angle*, July–October 1991, vol. 13, nos. 3–4, pp. 72–81.

—— "Reading through the Text: The Black Woman as Audience," in M. Diawara (ed.), *Black American Cinema*, New York, Routledge, 1993.

Bogle, D., *Toms, Coons, Mulattoes, Mammies, and Bucks*, New York, Viking Press, 1973.

—— *Brown Sugar*, New York, DaCapo, 1980.

Bowdle, D., "Holiness in the Highlands: A Profile of the Church of God," in B. Leonard (ed.), *Christianity in Appalachia: Profiles in Regional Pluralism*, Knoxville, University of Tennessee Press, 1999, pp. 243–56.

213

Bristow, J., "Being Gay: Politics, Identity, Pleasure," *New Formations*, Winter 1989, no. 9, pp. 61–82.

Britton, A., "For Interpretation: Notes Against Camp," *Gay Left*, 1978, no. 7, pp. 11–14.

Browne, A., *When Battered Women Kill*, New York, Free Press, 1987.

Browne, N., "The Undoing of the *Other* Woman: Madame Butterfly in the Discourse of American Orientalism," in D. Bernardi (ed.), *The Birth of Whiteness: Race and the Emergence of U.S. Cinema*, New Brunswick, Rutgers University Press, 1996, pp. 227–56.

Brunsdon, C., "A Subject for the Seventies," *Screen*, September–October 1982, vol. 23, nos. 3–4, pp. 20–9.

Buchanan, C., *Maiden*, New York, Milliam Morrow, 1999 (1972), p. 41.

Buscombe, E. (ed.), *Football on Television*, London, British Film Institute Television Monograph, 1974.

—— (ed.), *The BFI Companion to the Western*, London, British Film Institute, 1988.

Butler, C., "*The Color Purple* Controversy: Black Woman Spectatorship," *Wide Angle*, July–October 1993, vol. 13, nos. 3–4, pp. 62–9.

Butler, J., *Gender Trouble: Feminism and the Subversion of Identity*, New York, Routledge, 1990.

—— "Gender Theory, Feminist Theory, and Psychoanalytic Discourse," in L. Nicholson (ed.), *Feminism and Postmodernism*, New York, Routledge, 1990.

Capra, F., *The Name above the Title*, New York, Macmillan, 1971.

Charbonneau, C. and L. Winer, "Lesbians in 'Nice' Films," *Jump Cut*, March 1981, nos. 24–5, pp. 25–6.

Chomsky, N., "Power in the Global Arena," *New Left Review*, July–August 1998, no. 230, pp. 3–27.

Christian, B., *Black Feminist Criticism: Perspectives on Black Women Writers*, New York, Teachers College Press, 1993.

Clark, D., "Commodity Lesbianism," *Camera Obscura*, January–May 1991, nos. 25–6, pp. 144–79.

Clover, C., *Men, Women, and Chain Saws*, Princeton, Princeton University Press, 1992.

Cohn, N., *Women of Iron: The World of Female Bodybuilders*, Wideview Books, 1981.

Connolly, W., *Identity/Difference: Democratic Negotiations of Political Paradox*, Ithaca, Cornell University Press, 1991.

Correll, B., "Notes on the Primary Text: Woman's Body and Representation in *Pumping Iron: The Women* and 'Breast Giver'," *Genre*, Fall 1989, vol. 23, pp. 287–308.

Cortés, C., "Hollywood Interracial Love: Social Taboos as Screen Titillation," in P. Loukides and L. K. Fuller (eds), *Beyond the Stars II: Plot Conventions in American Popular Film*, Bowling Green, Bowling Green State University Press, 1991, pp. 21–35.

—— "Chicanas in Film: History of an Image," in C. Rodríguez (ed.), *Latin Looks: Images of Latinas and Latinos in the U.S. Media*, Boulder, Westview Press, 1997, pp. 121–41.

Crimp, D., "Portraits of People with AIDS," in D. Stanton (ed.), *Discourses of Sexuality: From Aristotle to AIDS*, Ann Arbor, University of Michigan Press, 1992, pp. 263–88.

Cumbow, R., *Order in the Universe: The Films of John Carpenter*, Metuchen, Scarecrow Press, 1990.

Custen, G., *Hollywood Bio/Pics: How Hollywood Constructed Public History*, New Brunswick, Rutgers University Press, 1992.

Daniels, R., *Coming to America: A History of Immigration and Ethnicity in American Life*, New York, Harper Collins, 1990.

Daugherty, M., "Serpent Handlers: When the Sacrament Comes Alive," in B. Leonard (ed.), *Christianity in Appalachia: Profiles in Regional Pluralism*, Knoxville, University of Tennessee Press, 1999, pp. 138–52.

de Beauvoir, S., *The Coming of Age*, New York, G. P. Putnam's Sons, 1972.

De Laria, L., "Whoopi Goldberg: Lesbian at Work," *The Advocate*, 7 February 1995, no. 674, pp. 46–52.

de Lauretis, T., "Sexual Indifference and Lesbian Representation," *Theatre Journal*, May 1988, vol. 40, no. 2, pp. 155–77.

Delli Carpini, M., "The Making of a Consensual Majority: Political Discourse and Electoral Politics in the 1980s," in M. Klein (ed.), *An American Half Century*, London, Pluto Press, 1994, pp. 232–73.

Desser, D., "The Martial Arts Film in the 1990s," in W. Dixon (ed.), *Film Genre 2000: New Critical Essays*, Albany, State University of New York Press, 2000, pp. 77–111.

de Silva, I., "Consumer Selection of Motion Pictures," in B. Litman, *The Motion Picture Mega-industry*, Boston, Allyn and Bacon, 1998, pp. 144–71.

Diawara, M., "Black Spectatorship: Problems of Identification and Resistance," *Screen*, Autumn 1988, vol. 29, no. 4, pp. 66–79.

Dinnerstein, L. *et al.*, *Natives and Strangers: A Multicultural History of Americans*, New York, Oxford University Press, 1996.

DiPiero, T., "White Men Aren't," *Camera Obscura*, May 1992, no. 30, pp. 113–37.

Dittmar, L., "Of Hags and Crones: Reclaiming Lesbian Desire for the Trouble Zone of Aging," in C. Holmlund and C. Fuchs (eds), *Between the Sheets, In the Streets: Queer, Lesbian, Gay Documentary*, Minneapolis, University of Minnesota Press, 1997, pp. 71–90.

Doty, A., *Making Things Perfectly Queer*, Minneapolis, University of Minnesota Press, 1993.

Dowell, P., "The Mythology of the Western: Hollywood Perspectives on Race and Gender in the 1990s," *Cineaste*, 1995, vol. 21, nos. 1–2, pp. 6–10.

Duggan, L. *et al.*, "False Promises: Feminist Antipornography Legislation in the U.S.," in V. Burstyn (ed.), *Women Against Censorship*, Vancouver, Douglas and McIntyre, 1985, pp. 130–51.

Dyer, R., "Don't Look Now," *Screen*, 1982, vol. 23, nos. 3–4, pp. 61–73.

—— "White," *Screen*, Autumn 1988, vol. 29, no. 4, pp. 44–65.

—— *White*, London, Routledge, 1997.

Edwards, A., "Why Whoopi: An Appreciation," *Essence*, January 1997, vol. 27, no. 9, pp. 57–8.

Ehrenstein, D., "Homophobia in Hollywood II," *The Advocate*, 7 April 1992, pp. 37–43.

Ellsworth, E., "Illicit Pleasures: Feminist Spectators and *Personal Best*," *Wide Angle*, 1985, vol. 8, no. 2, pp. 45–56.

Englehardt, T., *The End of Victory Culture: Cold War America and the Disillusioning of a Generation*, New York, Harper Collins, 1995.

Farley, R., *The New American Reality*, New York, Russell Sage Foundation, 1996.

Ferguson, A., "Patriarchy, Sexual Identity, and the Sexual Revolution," *Signs*, Autumn 1981, vol. 7, no. 1, pp. 158–72.

Fischer, L., *Shot/Countershot: Film Tradition and Women's Cinema*, Princeton, Princeton University Press, 1990.

Fiske, J., *Television Culture*, London, Methuen, 1987.

Flagg, F., *Fried Green Tomatoes at the Whistle Stop Cafe*, New York, McGraw-Hill, 1987.

Ford, G., "Mostly on *Rio Lobo*," in B. Nichols (ed.), *Movies and Methods*, Berkeley, University of California Press, 1976, pp. 344–53.

Foucault, M., "Body/Power," in *Power/Knowledge*, New York, Pantheon Books, 1980, pp. 55–62.

—— "The Confession of the Flesh," in *Power/Knowledge*, New York, Pantheon Books, 1980, pp. 194–228.

Fregoso, R., *The Bronze Screen: Chicana and Chicano Film Culture*, Minneapolis, University of Minnesota Press, 1993.

Freud, S., "The 'Uncanny'," in J. Strachey (ed.), *On Creativity and the Unconscious*, New York, Harper and Row, 1958, pp. 122–61.

—— "Fetishism," in J. Strachey (ed.), *Sexuality and the Psychology of Love*, New York, Macmillan, 1963, pp. 214–19.

—— "Anxiety and Instinctual Life," in J. Strachey (ed.), *New Introductory Lectures on Psychoanalysis*, New York, W. W. Norton, 1965, pp. 72–98.

Fuentes, V., "Chicano Cinema: A Dialectic between Voices and Images of the Autonomous Discourse Versus Those of the Dominant," in C. Noriega (ed.), *Chicanos and Film: Representation and Resistance*, Minneapolis, University of Minnesota Press, 1992, pp. 207–17.

Gabbard, K. and G., "Phallic Women in the Contemporary Cinema," *American Imago*, Winter 1993, vol. 50, no. 4, pp. 421–39.

Gadow, S., "Subjectivity: Literature, Imagination and Frailty," in T. Cole and S. Gadow (eds), *What Does It Mean to Grow Old?: Reflections from the Humanities*, Durham, Duke University Press, 1986, pp. 131–4.

Gaesser, G., *Big Fat Lies: The Truth about Your Weight and Your Health*, New York, Fawcett Columbine, 1996.

Gaines, C. and G. Butler, *Pumping Iron: The Art and Sport of Bodybuilding*, New York, Simon and Schuster, 1974; rev. ed., 1981.

—— *Pumping Iron II: The Unprecedented Woman*, New York, Simon and Schuster, 1984.

Gallafent, E., *Clint Eastwood: Filmmaker and Star*, New York, Continuum, 1994.

Gans, H., "Symbolic Ethnicity: The Future of Ethnic Groups and Cultures in America," *Ethnic and Racial Studies*, January 1979, no. 2, pp. 1–20.

Gever, M., "The Names We Give Ourselves," in R. Ferguson *et al.* (eds), *Out There: Marginalization and Contemporary Culture*, New York, New Museum of Contemporary Art, 1990, pp. 191–202.

Gilman, S., "Black Bodies, White Bodies," *Critical Inquiry*, Autumn 1985, vol. 12, no. 1, pp. 204–42.

—— *Creating Beauty to Cure the Soul: Race and Psychology in the Shaping of Aesthetic Surgery*, Durham, Duke University Press, 1998.

—— *Making the Body Beautiful: A Cultural History of Aesthetic Surgery*, Princeton, Princeton University Press, 1999.

Goetting, A., "Homicidal Wives," *Journal of Family Issues*, September 1987, vol. 8, no. 3, pp. 332–41.

Goldberg, J., "Recalling Totalities: The Mirrored Stages of Arnold Schwarzenegger," *differences*, 1992, vol. 4, no. 1, pp. 172–204.

Golden, C., "Diversity and Variability in Women's Sexual Identities," in Boston Lesbian Psychologies Collective, *Lesbian Psychologies*, Urbana, University of Illinois Press, 1987, pp. 21–2.

Gray, H., *Watching Race*, Minneapolis, University of Minnesota Press, 1995.

Gruman, G., "Cultural Origins of Present-day 'Age-ism': The Modernization of the Life Cycle," in S. Spicker *et al.* (eds), *Aging and the Elderly: Humanistic Perspectives in Gerontology*, Atlantic Highlands, Humanities Press, 1978, pp. 359–87.

Guerrero, E., *Framing Blackness*, Philadelphia, Temple University Press, 1993.

Gullette, M., "All Together Now: The New Sexual Politics of Midlife Bodies," *Michigan Quarterly Review*, Fall 1993, vol. 32, no. 4, pp. 669–95.

Haiken, E., *Venus Envy: A History of Cosmetic Surgery*, Baltimore, Johns Hopkins University Press, 1997.

Halberstam, J., *Female Masculinity*, Durham, Duke University Press, 1998.

Hall, S., "Notes on Deconstructing 'The Popular'," in R. Samuel (ed.), *People's History and Socialist Theory*, London, Routledge and Kegan Paul, 1981, pp. 227–41.

Hansen, M., *Babel and Babylon: Spectatorship in American Silent Film*, Cambridge, Harvard University Press, 1991.

Henderson, B., "*The Searchers*: An American Dilemma," *Film Quarterly*, 1980–1, vol. 32, no. 2, pp. 9–23.

Henwood, D., "Trash-o-nomics," in M. Wray and A. Newitz (eds), *White Trash: Race and Class in America*, New York, Routledge, 1997, pp. 177–92.

Herfray, C., *La Vieillesse: Une Interprétation psychanalytique*, Paris, Desclée de Brouwer, EPI, 1988.

Heywood, L., "Masculinity Vanishing: Bodybuilding and Contemporary Culture," in P. Moore (ed.), *Building Bodies*, New Brunswick, Rutgers University Press, 1997, pp. 165–83.

Higashi, S., "Ethnicity, Class, and Gender in Film: DeMille's *The Cheat*," in L. Friedman (ed.), *Unspeakable Images, Ethnicity and the American Cinema*, Urbana, University of Illinois Press, 1991, pp. 112–39.

Higgs, P., "Citizenship Theory and Old Age: From Social Rights to Surveillance," in Jamieson, A. *et al.* (eds), *Critical Approaches to Aging and Later Life*, Buckingham, Open University Press, 1997, pp. 118–31.

Higham, J., *Strangers in the Land: Patterns of American Nativism 1860–1925*, New Brunswick, Rutgers University Press, 1988.

Hillier, J., *The New Hollywood*, New York, Continuum, 1992.

Hollinger, K., *In the Company of Women*, Minneapolis, University of Minnesota Press, 1998, pp. 139–78.

Holmlund, C., "Sexuality and Power in Male Doppelgänger Cinema: The Case of Clint Eastwood's *Tightrope*," *Cinema Journal*, Fall 1986, vol. 26, no. 1, pp. 31–41.

—— "A Decade of Deadly Dolls," in H. Birch (ed.), *Moving Targets: Women, Murder and Representation*, London, Virago Press, 1992, pp. 127–51, reprinted Berkeley, University of California Press, 1994.

—— "Masculinity as Multiple Masquerade: The 'Mature' Stallone Loves the Stallone Clone," in S. Cohan and I. Hark (eds), *Screening the Male*, London, Routledge, 1993, pp. 213–29.

—— "Fractured Fairytales and Experimental Identities: Looking for Lesbians in and around the Films of Su Friedrich," *Discourse*, Fall 1994, vol. 17, no. 1, pp. 16–46.

hooks, b., *Yearning, Race, Gender, and Cultural Politics*, Boston, South End Press, 1990.

Horney, K., "The Dread of Woman," in *Feminine Psychology*, New York, W. W. Norton, 1967, pp. 133–46.

—— "The Neurotic Need for Love," in *Feminine Psychology*, New York, W. W. Norton, 1967, pp. 245–58.

—— "The Overvaluation of Love," in *Feminine Psychology*, New York, W. W. Norton, 1967, pp. 182–213.

Idowu, O., "Black Like Me," *Vibe*, February 1997, vol. 5, no. 1, pp. 80–2.

Irigaray, L., *Speculum of the Other Woman*, G. Gill (trans.), Ithaca, Cornell University Press, 1985.

Jaehne, K., "CEO and Cinderella: An Interview with Dolly Parton," *Cineaste*, 1990, vol. 17, no. 4, pp. 16–20.

Jarvie, I., "Stars and Ethnicity: Hollywood and the U.S., 1932–51," in L. Friedman (ed.), *Unspeakable Images*, Urbana, University of Illinois Press, 1991, pp. 82–111.

Jeffords, S., *Hard Bodies: Hollywood Masculinity in the Reagan Era*, New Brunswick, Rutgers University Press, 1994.

Jewell, K., *From Mammy to Miss America and Beyond: Cultural Images and the Shaping of U.S. Social Policy*, London, Routledge, 1993.

Johnson, A., "Moods Indigo: A Long View, Part 2," *Film Quarterly*, Spring 1991, vol. 44, no. 3, pp. 15–29.

Johnson, V., "Polyphony and Cultural Expression: Interpreting Musical Traditions in *Do the Right Thing*," *Film Quarterly*, Winter 1993–4, vol. 47, no. 2, pp. 18–29.

Johnstone, I., *The Man with No Name: The Biography of Clint Eastwood*, New York, Morrow Quill, 1981.

Jones, L., "Mountain Religion: An Overview," in B. Leonard (ed.), *Christianity in Appalachia: Profiles in Regional Pluralism*, Knoxville, University of Tennessee Press, 1999, pp. 91–102.

Joseph, G., "The Media and Blacks – Selling It Like It Isn't," in G. Joseph and J. Lewis (eds), *Common Differences: Conflicts in Black and White Feminist Perspectives*, Garden City, Doubleday, 1981, pp. 51–65.

Julien, I. and K. Mercer, "Introduction: De Margin and De Centre," *Screen*, Autumn 1988, vol. 29, no. 4, pp. 2–11.

Kabir, S., *Daughters of Desire: Lesbian Representations in Film*, London, Cassell, 1998.

Kaplan, E., "Trauma and Aging: Marlene Dietrich, Melanie Klein, and Marguerite Duras," in K. Woodward (ed.), *Figuring Age: Women, Bodies, Generations*, Bloomington, Indiana University Press, 1999, pp. 171–94.

Kearney, J., "Whoopi Goldberg: Color Her Anything," *American Film*, December 1985, vol. 11, no. 3, pp. 24–8.

Kell, C. and L. Camp, *In the Name of the Father: The Rhetoric of the New Southern Baptist Convention*, Carbondale, Southern Illinois University Press, 1999.

Kellner, D., "Aesthetics, Ethics, and Politics in the Films of Spike Lee," in M. Reid (ed.), *Spike Lee's "Do the Right Thing,"* Cambridge, Cambridge University Press, pp. 92–105.

Kipnis, L., *Bound and Gagged: Pornography and the Politics of Fantasy in America*, New York, Grove Press, 1996.

Kitses, J., "An Exemplary Post-modern Western: *The Ballad of Little Jo*," in J. Kitses and G. Rickmann (eds), *The Western Reader*, New York, Proscenium Publishers, 1998, pp. 367–80.

—— "Introduction: Post-modernism and the Western," in J. Kitses and G. Rickmann (eds), *The Western Reader*, New York, Proscenium Publishers, 1998, pp. 15–31.

Klare, M., "Permanent Preeminence: U.S. Strategic Policy for the Twenty-first Century," *NACLA*, November–December 2000, vol. 34, no. 3, pp. 8–15.

Kleinhans, C., "Siempre Selena!," *Jump Cut*, December 1998, no. 42, pp. 28–31, 121.

Kuhn, A., *The Power of the Image*, London, Routledge and Kegan Paul, 1985.

—— "The Body and Cinema: Some Problems for Feminism," in S. Sheridan (ed.), *Grafts*, London, Verso, 1988, pp. 11–24.

Lehman, P., " 'Don't Blame This on a Girl': Female Rape-revenge Films," in S. Cohan and I. Hark (eds), *Screening the Male*, London, Routledge, 1993, pp. 103–17.

—— *Running Scared: Masculinity and the Representation of the Male Body*, Philadelphia, Temple University Press, 1993.

—— "In an Imperfect World, Men with Small Penises Are Unforgiven: The Representation of the Penis/Phallus in American Films of the 1990s," *Men and Masculinities*, October 1998, vol. 1, no. 2, pp. 123–37.

Leonard, B., "Introduction: The Faith and the Faiths," in B. Leonard (ed.), *Christianity in Appalachia: Profiles in Regional Pluralism*, Knoxville, University of Tennessee Press, 1999, pp. xv–xxxii.

Levitt, T., *The Marketing Imagination*, London, Collier-Macmillan, 1983.

Limerick, P., *The Legacy of Conquest*, New York, W. W. Norton, 1987.

List, C., *Chicano Images: Refiguring Ethnicity in Mainstream Film*, New York, Garland Publishing, 1996.

Litman, B., *The Motion Picture Mega-industry*, Boston, Allyn and Bacon, 1998.

Litwak, M., *Reel Power: The Struggle for Influence and Success in the New Hollywood*, New York, New American Library, 1987, pp. 21–31.

Ljungmark, L., *Swedish Exodus*, K. B. Westerberg (trans.), Carbondale, Southern Illinois University Press, 1979.

Lorde, A., *Sister Outsider*, New York, Crossing Press, 1984.

Lott, E., *Love and Theft*, New York, Oxford University Press, 1993.

Lurie, S., "The Construction of the 'Castrated Woman' in Psychoanalysis and Cinema," *Discourse,* Winter 1981–2, no. 4, pp. 52–74.

McSherry, J., "Preserving Hegemony: National Security Doctrine in the Post-Cold War Era," *NACLA*, November–December 2000, vol. 34, no. 3, pp. 26–7.

McWhiney, G., *Cracker Culture: Celtic Ways in the Old South*, Tuscaloosa, University of Alabama Press, 1988.

Maland, C., *Frank Capra*, Boston, Twayne, 1980.

Marchetti, G., *Romance and the "Yellow Peril": Race, Sex, and Discursive Strategies in Hollywood Fiction*, Berkeley, University of California Press, 1993.

Martin, K., "Diversity Orientations: Culture, Ethnicity, and Race," in L. Naylor (ed.), *Cultural Diversity in the United States*, Westport, Bergin and Garvey, 1997, pp. 75–90.

Mattelart, A. *et al.*, *International Image Markets*, London, Comedia, 1984.

May, W., "The Virtues and Vices of the Elderly," in T. Cole and S. Gadow (eds), *What Does It Mean to Grow Old?: Reflections from the Humanities*, Durham, Duke University Press, 1986, pp. 43–61.

Mayne, J., "Walking the *Tightrope* of Feminism and Male Desire," in A. Jardine and P. Smith (eds), *Men in Feminism*, New York, Methuen, 1987, pp. 62–70.

—— *Cinema and Spectatorship*, London, Routledge, 1993.

—— *Framed: Lesbians, Feminists, and Media Culture*, Minneapolis, University of Minnesota Press, 2000.

Mellancamp, P., "From Anxiety to Equanimity: Crisis and Generational Continuity on TV, at the Movies, in Life, in Death," in K. Woodward (ed.), *Figuring Age: Women, Bodies, Generations*, Bloomington, Indiana University Press, 1999, pp. 310–28.

Mellon, J., *Women and Their Sexuality in the New Film*, New York, Horizon Press, 1973.

Merck, M., "*Lianna* and the Lesbians of Art Cinema," in C. Brunsdon (ed.), *Films for Women*, London, British Film Institute, 1986, pp. 166–75.

—— "Dessert Heart," in M. Gever *et al.* (eds), *Queer Looks*, New York, Routledge, 1993, pp. 377–82.

Merigeau, P., "Eastwood in His Carmel," in R. Kapsis and K. Coblentz (eds), *Clint Eastwood Interviews*, Jackson, University Press of Mississippi, 1999, pp. 233–8.

Millett, K., *Sexual Politics*, Garden City, N.Y., Doubleday, 1970.

Morley, D. and K. Robins, *Spaces of Identity: Global Media, Electronic Landscapes and Cultural Boundaries*, London, Routledge, 1995.

Naremore, J., *Acting in the Cinema*, Berkeley, University of California Press, 1988.

Neale, S., "Masculinity as Spectacle," *Screen*, 1983, vol. 24, no. 6, pp. 2–16.

—— *Genre*, London, British Film Institute, 1983.

—— and M. Smith (eds), *Contemporary Hollywood Cinema*, London, Routledge, 1998.

Negrón-Muntañer, F., "Jennifer's Butt," *Aztlán: A Journal of Chicano Studies*, Fall 1997, vol. 22, no. 2, pp. 189–94.

Nestle, J., "The Fem Question," in C. Vance (ed.), *Pleasure and Danger: Exploring Female Sexuality*, London, Routledge and Kegan Paul, 1984, pp. 232–41.

—— *A Restricted Country*, New York, Firebrand Books, 1987.

Newman, K., "Latino Sacrifice in the Discourse of Citizenship: Acting against the 'Mainstream,' 1985–1988," in C. Noriega (ed.), *Chicanos and Film: Representation and Resistance*, Minneapolis, University of Minnesota Press, 1992, pp. 59–73.

Newton, E., *Mother Camp: Female Impersonators in America*, Englewood Cliffs, Prentice Hall, 1972.

—— "The Mythic Mannish Lesbian," *Signs*, Summer 1984, vol. 9, no. 4, pp. 557–75.

Noe, P., "Who Is Whoopi Goldberg and What Is She Doing on Broadway???," *Ebony*, March 1985, vol. 40, pp. 27–34.

Noriega, C., " 'Waas Sappening?': Narrative Structure and Iconography in *Born in East L.A.*," *Studies in Latin American Popular Culture*, 1995, vol. 14, pp. 1–22.

Norment, L., "*The Color Purple*: Controversial Book Becomes an Equally Controversial Movie," *Ebony*, February 1986, vol. 41, no. 4, pp. 146, 148, 150, 155.

Nugent, W., "Frontiers and Empires in the Late Nineteenth Century," in P. Limerick *et al.* (eds), *Trails: Toward a New Western History*, Lawrence, University Press of Kansas, pp. 161–81.

Oehling, R., "The Yellow Menace: Asian Images in American Film," in R. Miller (ed.), *The Kaleidoscopic Lens: How Hollywood Views Ethnic Groups*, Jerome S. Ozer, 1980, pp. 182–206.

Omi, J. and H. Winant, *Racial Formation in the United States from the 1960s to the 1990s*, New York, Routledge, 1994.

Pally, M., "Women of 'Iron'," *Film Comment*, July–August 1985, vol. 21, no. 4, pp. 60–4.

Partington, A., "Feminist Art and Avant-gardism," in H. Robinson (ed.), *Visibly Female: Feminism and Art Today*, 1988, New York, Universe Books, pp. 228–49.

Parton, D., *Dolly: My Life and Other Unfinished Business*, New York, Harper Collins, 1994.

Peters, R., *Television Coverage of Sport*, Birmingham, Centre for Contemporary Cultural Studies, 1976.

Prince, S., *Visions of Empire: Political Imagery in Contemporary American Film*, New York, Praeger, 1992, pp. 81–115.

Randolph, L., "The Whoopi Goldberg Nobody Knows," *Ebony*, March 1991, vol. 46, no. 5, pp. 110–16.

Reid, M., *Redefining Black Film*, Berkeley, University of California Press, 1993.

Rich, A., "Compulsory Heterosexuality and Lesbian Existence," *Signs*, 1980, vol. 5, no. 4, pp. 177–203.

Rickman, G., "The Western under Erasure: *Dead Man*," in J. Kitses and G. Rickman (eds), *The Western Reader*, New York, Proscenium Publishers, 1998, pp. 381–404.

Ridgeway, J., *Blood in the Face: The Ku Klux Klan, Aryan Nations, Nazi Skinheads, and the Rise of a New White Culture*, New York, Thunder's Mouth Press, 1995.

Riviere, J., "Womanliness as a Masquerade," in V. Burgin (ed.), *Formations of Fantasy*, London, Routledge and Kegan Paul, 1986, pp. 35–44.

Rodríguez, N., "The Real 'New World Order': The Globalization of Racial and Ethnic Relations in the Late Twentieth Century," in M. Smith and J. Feagin (eds), *The Bubbling Cauldron: Race, Ethnicity and the Urban Crisis*, Minneapolis, University of Minnesota Press, 1995, pp. 211–25.

Rodríguez, R., *Rebel without a Crew*, New York, Penguin, 1995.

Rosen, D., *Off-Hollywood: The Making and Marketing of Independent Films*, New York, Grove Weidenfeld, 1987.

—— "Crossover: Hispanic Specialty Films in the U.S. Movie Marketplace," in C. Noriega, *Chicanos and Film: Representation and Resistance*, Minneapolis, University of Minnesota Press, 1992, pp. 241–60.

Rubin, G., "Thinking Sex: Notes for a Radical Theory of the Politics of Sexuality," in C. Vance (ed.), *Pleasure and Danger: Exploring Female Sexuality*, London, Routledge and Kegan Paul, 1984, pp. 267–319.

Russo, V., *The Celluloid Closet*, New York, Harper and Row, 1987.

Ryan, D. and D. Kellner (eds), *Camera Politica: The Politics and Ideology of Contemporary Hollywood Film*, Bloomington, Indiana University Press, 1998.

Ryder, J., *Clint Eastwood*, New York, Dell, 1987.

Said, E., *Orientalism*, New York, Vintage, 1979.

Schickel, R., *Clint Eastwood*, New York, Alfred A. Knopf, 1996.

Schulze, L., "Getting Physical: Text/Context/Reading and the Made-for-TV Movie," *Cinema Journal*, 1986, vol. 25, no. 2, pp. 35–50.

—— "On the Muscle," in J. Gaines and C. Herzog (eds), *Fabrications: Costume and the Female Body*, New York, Routledge, 1990, pp. 59–78; reprinted in P. Moore, *Building Bodies*, New Brunswick, Rutgers University Press, 1997, pp. 9–30.

Scott, J., "Deconstructing Equality-versus-Difference: Or, the Uses of Post-structuralist Theory for Feminism," *Feminist Studies*, Spring 1988, vol. 14, no. 1, pp. 33–50.

Seid, R., *Never Too Thin: Why Women Are at War with Their Bodies*, New York, Prentice Hall, 1989.

Sheldon, C., "Lesbians and Film: Some Thoughts," in R. Dyer (ed.), *Gays and Film*, New York, Zoetrope, 1984, pp. 5–26.

Shohat, E., "Ethnicities in Relation: Toward a Multicultural Reading of American Cinema," in L. Friedman (ed.), *Unspeakable Images: Ethnicity and the American Cinema*, Urbana, University of Illinois Press, 1991, pp. 215–50.

Silverman, K., *Male Subjectivity at the Margins*, New York, Routledge, 1992.

Slotkin, R., *Gunfighter Nation: The Myth of the Frontier in Twentieth-century America*, New York, Harper Collins, 1992.

Smith, P., *Clint Eastwood: A Cultural Production*, Minneapolis, University of Minnesota Press, 1993.

Snitow, A., "Retrenchment versus Transformation: The Politics of the Antiporn-ography Movement," in V. Burstyn (ed.), *Women Against Censorship*, Vancouver, Douglas and McIntyre, 1985, pp. 107–20.

—— et al., "Introduction," in A. Snitow et al., *Powers of Desire: The Politics of Sexuality*, London, Routledge and Kegan Paul, 1983, pp. 9–50.

Sobchak, V., "Scary Women: Cinema, Surgery, and Special Effects," in K. Woodward (ed.), *Figuring Age: Women, Bodies, Generations*, Bloomington, Indiana University Press, 1999, pp. 200–11.

Sollors, W., *Beyond Ethnicity: Consent and Descent in American Culture*, New York, Oxford University Press, 1986.

Stacey, J., "'If You Don't Play, You Can't Win': *Desert Hearts* and the Lesbian Romance Film," in T. Wilton (ed.), *Immortal Invisible: Lesbians and the Moving Image*, London, Routledge, 1995, pp. 92–114.

Steinem, G., "Coming Up: The Unprecedented Woman," *Ms.*, July 1985, vol. 14, no. 1, pp. 84–6.

Straayer, C., "*Personal Best*: Lesbian/Feminist Audience," *Jump Cut*, February 1984, no. 29, pp. 40–4.

—— "The Hypothetical Lesbian Heroine," *Jump Cut*, April 1990, no. 35, pp. 50–8.

—— *Deviant Eyes, Deviant Bodies: Sexual Re-orientation in Film and Video*, New York, Columbia University Press, 1996.

Stuart, A., "*The Color Purple*: In Defense of Happy Endings," in L. Gamman and M. Marshment (eds), *The Female Gaze*, Seattle, The Real Comet Press, 1989, pp. 60–75.

—— "Making Whoopi," *Sight and Sound*, February 1993, vol. 3, no. 2, pp. 12–13.

Tasker, Y., *Spectacular Bodies: Gender, Genre and the Action Cinema*, London, Routledge, 1993.

—— *Working Girls: Gender and Sexuality in Popular Cinema*, London, Routledge, 1998.

Thompson, A., "Beyond the Pale Riders," *Film Comment*, July–August 1992, vol. 28, no. 4, pp. 52–4.

Tibbetts, J., "Clint Eastwood and the Machinery of Violence," *Literature/Film Quarterly*, January 1993, vol. 21, no. 1, pp. 10–17.

Tompkins, J., *West of Everything: The Inner Life of Westerns*, New York, Oxford University Press, 1992.

Troyansky, D., "Historical Research into Aging, Old Age and Older People," in A. Jamieson *et al.* (eds), *Critical Approaches to Aging and Later Life*, Buckingham, Open University Press, 1997, pp. 49–61.

Tucker, S., "Sex, Death, and Free Speech: The Fight to Stop Friedkin's *Cruising*," in E. Jackson and S. Persky (eds), *Flaunting It*, Vancouver, New Star Press and Toronto, Pink Triangle Press, 1982, pp. 197–206.

Vance, C., "Pleasure and Danger: Toward a Politics of Sexuality," in C. Vance (ed.), *Pleasure and Danger: Exploring Female Sexuality*, London, Routledge and Kegan Paul, 1984, pp. 1–28.

Vickers, L., "Excuse Me, Did We See the Same Movie?," *Jump Cut*, 1994, no. 39, pp. 25–30.

Waldman, D., "Film Theory and the Gendered Spectator: The Female or the Feminist Reader?," *Camera Obscura*, September 1988, no. 18, pp. 80–94.

Wallace, M., "Negative Images: Towards a Black Feminist Cultural Criticism," in L. Grossberg *et al.* (eds), *Cultural Studies*, New York, Routledge, 1992, pp. 654–63.

Ward, C., "The Southern Landscape in Contemporary Films," in P. Loukides and L. Fuller (eds), *Beyond the Stars: Studies in American Popular Film*, vol. 4, Bowling Green, Bowling Green University Popular Press, 1993, pp. 103–17.

Wasko, J., *Hollywood in the Information Age: Beyond the Silver Screen*, Cambridge, Polity Press, 1994.

Waugh, T., "The Third Body," in M. Gever *et al.* (eds), *Queer Looks*, New York, Routledge, 1993, pp. 141–61.

Weisheit, R., "Female Homicide Offenders: Trends over Time in an Institutionalized Population," *Justice Quarterly*, 1984, vol. 1, no. 4, pp. 471–89.

Weiss, A., *Vampires and Violets*, New York, Penguin Books, 1992.

Welch, J., "Uneven Ground: Cultural Values, Moral Standards, and Religiosity in the Heart of Appalachia," in B. Leonard (ed.), *Christianity in Appalachia: Profiles in Regional Pluralism*, Knoxville, University of Tennessee Press, 1999, pp. 52–93.

Wenner, J., "This Sister's Act," *Us*, 7 April 1985, no. 195, pp. 58–74, 88.

West, C., "The New Cultural Politics of Difference," in R. Ferguson *et al.* (eds), *Out There: Marginalization and Contemporary Cultures*, New York, New Museum of Contemporary Art, 1990, pp. 18–38.

West, D., "Filming the Chicano Family Saga," *Cineaste*, 1995, vol. 21, no. 4, pp. 26–9.

Weston, K., *Families We Choose*, New York, Columbia University Press, 1991.

Wexman, V., *Creating the Couple: Love, Marriage and Hollywood Performance*, Princeton, Princeton University Press, 1993.

Whannel, G., "Fields in Vision: Sport and Representation," *Screen*, 1984, vol. 25, no. 3, pp. 99–107.

White, P., "*Madame X of the China Seas*," *Screen*, Autumn 1987, vol. 28, no. 4, pp. 80–95.

Wiegman, R., *American Anatomies: Theorizing Race and Gender*, Durham, Duke University Press, 1995.

—— "Whiteness Studies and the Paradox of Particularity," *boundary 2*, Fall 1999, vol. 26, no. 3, pp. 115–50.

Wiley, R., *Dark Witness: When Black People Should Be Sacrificed (Again)*, New York, One World, Ballantine Books, 1996.

Willemen, P., "Anthony Mann: Looking at the Male," *Framework*, 1981, nos. 15–17, pp. 16–20.

Williams, L., "*Personal Best*: Women in Love," *Jump Cut*, July 1982, no. 27, p. 1.

—— *Hard Core: Power, Pleasure, and the "Frenzy of the Visible"*, Berkeley, University of California Press, 1989.

Williamson, J., *Hillbillyland: What the Movies Did to the Mountains and What the Mountains Did to the Movies*, Chapel Hill, University of North Carolina Press, 1995.

Willis, E., "Feminism, Moralism, and Pornography," in A. Snitow *et al.*, *Powers of Desire: The Politics of Sexuality*, London, Routledge and Kegan Paul, 1983, pp. 460–7.

Willis, S., *High Contrast: Race and Gender in Contemporary Hollywood Film*, Durham, Duke University Press, 1997.

Wilson, P., "Mountains of Contradictions: Gender, Class, and Region in the Star Image of Dolly Parton," *South Atlantic Quarterly*, Winter 1995, vol. 94, no. 1, pp. 109–34.

Winant, H., *Racial Conditions: Politics, Theory, Comparisons*, Minneapolis, University of Minnesota Press, 1994.

—— "Dictatorship, Democracy, and Difference: The Historical Construction of Racial Identity," in M. Smith and J. Feagin (eds), *The Bubbling Cauldron: Race, Ethnicity, and the Urban Crisis*, Minneapolis, University of Minnesota Press, 1995, pp. 31–49.

—— "Behind Blue Eyes: Whiteness and Contemporary U.S. Racial Politics," *New Left Review*, September–October 1997, no. 225, pp. 73–88.

Wolff, E., *Top Heavy: The Increasing Inequality of Wealth in America and What Can Be Done about It*, New York, New Press, 1995.

Woodward, K., *Aging and Its Discontents*, Bloomington, Indiana University Press, 1991.

—— "Introduction" in K. Woodward (ed.), *Figuring Age: Women, Bodies, Generations*, Bloomington, Indiana University Press, 1999, pp. ix–xxii.

Wright, W., *Sixguns and Society: A Structural Study of the Western*, Berkeley, University of California Press, 1975.

Wyatt, J., *High Concept: Movies and Marketing in Hollywood*, Austin, University of Texas Press, 1994.

Zilberg, J., "Yes It's True: Zimbabweans Love Dolly Parton," *Journal of Popular Culture*, Summer 1995, vol. 29, no. 1, pp. 111–14.

Zimmerman, B., "Lesbian Vampires," *Jump Cut*, March 1981, nos. 24–5, pp. 23–5.

Zita, J., "Historical Amnesia and the Lesbian Continuum," *Signs*, Autumn 1981, vol. 7, no. 1, pp. 172–87.

Zmijewsky, B. and L. Pfeiffer, *The Films of Clint Eastwood*, New York, Citadel Press, 1994.

INDEX